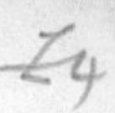

GEMSTONES
of the British Isles

OTHER WORKS BY V. A. FIRSOFF

The crust of the Earth
The Cairngorms on foot and ski
Arran with camera and sketchbook
In the hills of Breadalbane
On foot in the Cairngorms
On ski in the Cairngorms
Strange world of the Moon
Surface of the Moon
Life beyond the Earth
Exploring the planets
Facing the universe
Life, mind and galaxies
The interior planets
The world of Mars
The old Moon and the new
The universe of living uncertainty
  (*in preparation*)

V. AXEL FIRSOFF
M.A., F.R.A.S.

GEMSTONES
of the British Isles

OLIVER & BOYD

EDINBURGH

Oliver & Boyd
Tweeddale Court
Edinburgh EH1 1YL
A Division of Longman Group Limited

First published 1971

ISBN 0 05 002162 1 — Hardback
      0 05 002472 8 — Paperback

Printed in Great Britain by
R. & R. Clark Ltd., Edinburgh

Preface

No comprehensive mineralogy of the British Isles has been published since 1858, and, although this work by R. P. Greg and W. G. Lettsom is of considerable merit and may still be consulted with profit, it is out of date in many respects. When it comes to gemstones, however, we have to fall back on regional guidebooks of variable excellence and occasional information scattered in technical geological memoirs and mining surveys. Yet the growing popular interest in the collecting of native gemstones has made a work dealing comprehensively with the British Isles from the gem-seeker's point of view a pressing need.

I first thought of writing *Gemstones of the British Isles* some twenty years ago and had assembled a good deal of material for it at the time. But publishers showed little enthusiasm for this idea, so that it had to be put into cold storage and could not be successfully revived until 1968, by when the climate of opinion and the condition of the book market had undergone considerable changes.

The book is as non-technical as is consistent with scientific accuracy and is addressed primarily to the amateur, although it contains a good deal of information that is at least partly new or not readily available, so that it may be of interest to a more technical reader as well. The task of preparing a work of this kind is truly never-ending: it is always possible to discover something new, to amplify or correct the published information, and nobody knows all the answers. This necessitates a constant interplay of field work and library research for which one lifetime is not enough. On the other hand, economic necessity must limit the time available for research, nor can the publisher be expected to wait indefinitely for completion. The book has to be concise as well as exhaustive and readable. The result must be a compromise between these incompatible requirements, which, I suppose, is true of any human effort.

In any case I cannot help feeling some surprise at my having brought this project to conclusion, which would not have been possible without the generous and valuable help received from the following:

G. W. T. Barnett, Director of Lea Cross Geophysical Co. Ltd., Shrewsbury; C. M. Bristow, Exploration Manager, English Clays Lovering Pochin & Co. Ltd.; M. A. Cunningham, of the Geological Survey of Ireland; W. F. Davidson, of Penrith; J. N. M. Firth; L. S. Garrad, Assistant Keeper, the Manx Museum; R. K. Harrison, of the

Institute of Geological Sciences, Leeds; Miss M. C. Hill, County Archivist, Salop County Council; P. G. Hines; Robert Hogg, Curator of the Carlisle Museum; R. G. Hughes, Deputy Curator of Derby Museum and Art Gallery; Ron James, Curator, Shrewsbury Museum; D. O. Jones, County Librarian, Anglesey; K. A. Jones, of Queen's University, Belfast; R. A. Kennedy, Curator, Pembroke County Museum; E. G. Langholme, Secretary of The Shap Granite Co. Ltd.; R. D. Penhallurick, Assistant Curator, County Museum, Truro; B. J. Pyrah, Curator of Geology, the Yorkshire Museum; D. A. Robson, University of Newcastle-upon-Tyne; D. Rushton, Assistant Keeper of Geology, the Manchester Museum; C. D. Sandison, of Baltasound, Shetland; T. M. Thomas, Principal Scientific Officer, Welsh Office; G. R. Tresise, Keeper of Geology, City of Liverpool Museums; A. E. Truckell, Curator of the Dumfries Burgh Museum; F. S. Wallis, Honorary Curator, Wells Museum, Wells, Somerset; F. E. L. Weaver, Manager, Meldon Quarry, Okehampton, Devon. This help is gratefully acknowledged. Some further acknowledgments will be found in the text and references.

In addition I am particularly indebted to P. S. Doughty, Keeper of Geology at Ulster Museum, Belfast; J. S. Jackson, Keeper of the Natural History Division, National Museum of Ireland, Dublin; E. A. Jobbins, of the Institute of Geological Sciences, London; H. S. Macpherson, Curator of Minerals at the Royal Scottish Museum, Edinburgh; and Miss P. M. Statham, of the Institute of Geological Sciences, London, who have kindly read and commented on parts of the manuscript. It will be understood, however, that my advisers are in no way responsible for any errors of fact or judgment that the book may contain.

The colour plates within the book, and that used on the cover, are the property of the Institute of Geological Sciences, London, and are reproduced by permission of the Director, apart from the photographs of amber, and jasper and agates, which are reproduced by permission of Mr E. A. Jobbins. The crystal forms of quartz, topaz and fluorite are given after R. P. Greg and W. G. Lettsom[31], the small crystal drawings at the section headings have come from Rudolf Börner's book *Minerals, rocks and gemstones*[4], and the permission to use these by the author and the publisher is gratefully acknowledged. The geological maps were drawn from material originally perpared by G. I. Firsoff, and the line drawings at the end of chapters are my own.

V. A. FIRSOFF

Contents

1 An invitation

'Romance' is one of those shopworn words that make you wince. Yet it has a meaning; and there is romance: a sense of mystery, expectancy, sudden thrill, as well as disappointment, discomfort, plain hard work, perhaps danger—in the search for gemstones.

It puts me in mind of diffuse sunlight seeping through the mist, the travelled boulders on a bleak moor, the bleating of sheep and the skirls of curlews, aye, and the feel of wet feet . . . or of following a pegmatite vein into difficult rocks, where an as-yet-unrifled druse lurks concealed. Precariously perched on a narrow ledge, I deliver carefully dosed blows with a geological hammer, to remove an awkward piece of stone obstructing a cavity filled with decayed rock and sticky mud. The stone cracks and yields. As I plunge my fingers into the unappetizing mess within, they touch a sharp point, then a smooth surface. A loose crystal! What will it be when the clammy clay is rubbed off—the dark gleam of smoky quartz, or perhaps the blue-green of a beryl?

I remember sliding a hand under a rock awning, but instead of the expected harsh mineral facets, it encountered warm little things— chicks in a wren's nest. The hand withdrew with gentle surprise. It was on the day the sun went blue with the smoke from the forest fires in Canada. . . . On other days there were mountains and the sea and cloud vistas.

As the crested breakers recede from the cliffs among the insistent mewing of gulls and the petulant piping of oyster-catchers, you may seek out clearways through the slippery wrack to the pebble-strewn sand. That little stone glowing red in a tidal pool is jasper. The pitted pebble of unexciting appearance may or may not be an agate, but there is peace at the edge of the water and the iodine tang of seaweed. With some knowledge, experience and that great imponderable—luck, you will come upon some little treasure.

Another thrill awaits you when you see it cut and polished by a lapidary, or even better—by yourself!

You need not take any interest in jewellery and may never wear any, but an experience of this kind will make you see the stones in the jeweller's window with a different eye.

They may have been raised from deep down below by sweated labour in a remote tropical mine and passed through the well-oiled wheels of a large industrial combine, or else washed out of a river-bed by a lone prospector and smuggled over a dozen frontiers. Yet, whichever may be the case, they are flowers of rock.

Nowadays gem crystals can be nursed artificially in a laboratory furnace or tank—a scientifically exciting achievement. An artificially grown crystal of emerald or ruby is chemically identical with its natural counterpart, often flawless and nowise inferior to it in beauty. Yet such synthetic productions fetch only a fraction of the price paid for flawed natural gems. What they lack, I suppose, is romance; they have not been born of the Earth's secret alchemy. And, of course, there is nothing to compare in value to a find of your own!

No human pursuit, no pastime can escape fashion. Some two or three generations back there was a great craze for collecting semi-precious stones, crystals and fossils for the 'cabinet'. Geology and mineralogy still wore a cloak of novelty and were very much the thing. An army of lapidaries ministered to the needs of the collectors and found in them a livelihood. Today they are gone, partly swept away by the ebb and flow of fashion, the cheap stones from Germany and Brazil, and the objectively beautiful 'paste'* imitations of costume jewellery, partly ousted by the large, more economic and efficient firms, which execute the same jobs with greater expedition and skill. No doubt, Hatton Garden represents an altogether different standard of stone-cutting from the old-fashioned shops of the seaside with their display of choanites, ventriculites, agates and jaspers. Yet this old world had a charm lost to our computer-wise space age.

On a dusty library shelf you may chance upon a slender volume by J. G. Francis entitled *Beach Rambles in Search of Seaside Pebbles and Crystals*.[28] Its mineralogy may be questionable by modern standards, but here and there you may glean some information that has weathered the storms of progress, and you will certainly be able to savour the taste of that glorious pioneering past, for the year of publication is 1861.

On page 47 the author imparts the following instruction:

> 'If he (the pebble-collector) is going far, and it is as well to count upon eight to ten miles from home, let him carry a flask of any liquid he likes best to imbibe; together with a hunch of bread and cheese.... Lastly a few mild cigars, not omitting the usual implements for striking a light *sub dio*.'

This, we are assured, 'will bring to mind Sir Walter Raleigh, who was a great man'. Should a fair lady wish to conjure up a picture of Sir Walter she need but follow the same prescription *mutatis mutandis* (no cigars), 'only, in addition, ladies should engage some stalwart arm to lean upon; and should on no account venture themselves among slippery rocks. As for those knights and esquires who accompany the

---

* Jeweller's glass.

gentle dames on such a quest, they must look for themselves. I cannot now stop to warn them of their peculiar peril. . . .'

We live in a tidal world, and history has its cycles. The wheel appears to have turned full circle, and gem collecting is once more in fashion and increasing in popularity by leaps and bounds. Professional stone cutting is expensive—I have recently paid over four pounds to have two small cairngorms dressed, and so the modern accent is on do-it-yourself kits, with low-gear electric motors humming gently in a garden shed as they turn over and over tumbling drums filled with Scotch pebbles, water with a pinch of detergent and carborundum grit. At the moment, however, there exists no adequate guide to the gemstones of the British Isles, though some small books dealing with this or that area may be found useful and are listed at the end of this one, whose object it is to fill this gap.

I am a scientist by training, and scientific accuracy is important, but in the present case my approach is rather that of an artist and sportsman. While I hope that this work will not be without interest to a scientific mineralogist, please take it first and foremost as an invitation to a treasure hunt. I cannot take you outside the British Isles, but inasmuch as geology and mineralogy are universal, and the mode of occurrence of any particular mineral is much the same the world over, the basic information and the practical hints know no frontiers. Even in Britain and Ireland the situation is much less thoroughly explored than you might expect and there is still room for surprises. I have made a conscientious effort to visit most of the important gem-bearing localities myself and so am able to speak from personal experience, but in other cases I have had to rely on second-hand information, whether written or unwritten, published or unpublished. Every effort, however, has been made to ascertain its accuracy and reliability.

Do not expect too much. But it is still good fun.

2 *Rules and tools of the game*

So on a treasure hunt we are bent. In fairy tales treasures are well hidden in deep caverns or in inaccessible cliffs, guarded by dragons, griffins, trolls or demons, in addition to the rage of the elements under the command of a witch or a wizard, not to mention the mere hardships of travel in devious places, beset with traps of all kinds. Success requires a stout heart, a firm will, a keen mind, as well, of course, as sheer physical prowess. A hoard of buccaneer doubloons may dispense with dragons, bar an occasional crocodile, a few mambas, or a band of hungry cannibals who keep their cauldrons expectantly boiling, but it would not be there if it were easy to reach and find. In either case the clues must be scrupulously followed and the eyes kept skinned for signs and portents.

The same rules of the game apply in our case, as J. G. Francis might have said, *mutatis mutandis*. In the British Isles at least the dragons may be no more formidable than an irate farmer on whose land we have ventured without permission, or some local prohibitions regarding the collecting of minerals. For instance, in the Isle of Man we may be had up for collecting on what is vaguely termed 'a commercial scale'; St. Michael's Mount in Cornwall is out of bounds to all gem-hunters; in Wales it is an offence to climb over stone dykes, and so on.

Such dragons may not be deadly and can at times be propitiated with success. The magical incantation 'Please, may I?' opens many doors. But a few judicious enquiries on the spot will help. In visiting mines and quarries it is wise to be on good terms with the dwarfs, especially Grumpy, who is apt to assume the transparent disguise of the works manager or secretary. In disused establishments of this kind it is highly dangerous to enter underground workings without adequate knowledge and experience. Moreover, generally speaking the old galleries will be wholly barren. It is easier, safer and more profitable to excavate the dumps or explore the surrounding country for industrially unprofitable mineral lodes and veins, which have been left unworked.

As for the elements, they are not open to propitiation, but neither are they controlled by witches and wizards, not even of the Met. Office kind. Still, attention to weather forecasts may save a few tears, while tide tables are essential on the seashore. The fairy tales are right about inaccessible places. With some exceptions, gem treasures lie concealed on distant lonely beaches and in roadless mountain recesses, at times in deep caverns and inaccessible cliffs, and guarded, if not by demons, at least by weary miles, high wind, rain, cold and mist, which may make the going difficult and dangerous. If for no other reason, this is so by the process of elimination, the easily accessible localities being exhausted first. Fairytales are reality seen through the logic of dreams.

'Mild cigars' you may carry if you wish, and 'implements for striking a light *sub dio*' in the form of a box of matches may come in handy, if dry. If, however, you 'like best to imbibe' intoxicating liquids you are well advised to desist, especially in the mountains. On the other hand, on a long or difficult expedition, where bad weather may supervene or a mishap occur, energizing foods, such as dried fruit, chocolate, or lump sugar, as well as glucose tablets, are to be recommended. Appropriate clothing and footwear are vital. So, too, are a map, advantageously supplemented with a geological one, and a compass, neither of which is much good unless you know how to use it.

The special gem-hunting equipment includes a geological, or at least chipping, hammer. This is usually worn hung round the neck on a double loop of strap or cord, so that one loop can be slipped off for easy handling when the hammer is used without it being necessary to take it off. A winding of surgical dressing or other suitable cover on the handle will protect the hand from shock: wielding a hammer is quite hard work, as well as an art, which it takes time to acquire. Carefully-placed light blows are usually more effective than big whacks. Small chips of stone are ejected in the process with considerable force, and it is often advisable to wear goggles for shielding the eyes against these. One or two mason's chisels will be useful for delicate rock work, possibly a small digging tool, such as a gardening trowel, and for extracting crystals from narrow decayed cavities in the rocks a long blunt knife and a spoon with a long handle. Horn is a good material for the latter, as metal can easily damage the fine edges and points of crystals.

If you travel by car and confine your attention to old mines and quarries there is nothing to stop your carrying a pick-axe, a spade and a sledge-hammer for splitting large boulders. From personal experience, however, I would say that a sledge-hammer makes surprisingly little impression on a obdurate rock face. The use of gelignite may be frowned upon. For visiting active quarries permission should be obtained and due care must be taken if blasting is in progress. Quarry walls have often been loosened by blast and rock falls may be expected, which also applies to some sea-cliffs. Warning notices are usually posted in the more frequented places; elsewhere you must rely on your own judgment. In any event a crash helmet may be recommended.

Field glasses will be found useful for spying out likely rock formations. It all depends, however, on the scope of your operations, the type of terrain and what minerals you are looking for, which may make some or most of the listed items superfluous. If you are simply searching for ornamental beach pebbles you may dispense with the ironmongery altogether: a pair of sharp eyes will suffice, though a trowel may still come in handy. If the expected finds are few and small and can be accommodated in your pockets you need nothing more. Generally speaking, though, you will require a rucksack or at least a shoulder bag for your equipment, food, extra clothing and finds. Sturdy polythene bags will do nicely for the latter, but fragile crystals are best carried in a tin or plastic box and wrapped in lint or foam-rubber sheeting, failing which newspaper will do, for protection.

The job of identifying a find may be tricky and will be considered in more detail in a further chapter. A magnifying glass may sometimes be useful and is often recommended, but I do not consider it essential. It is advisable not to over-work a piece of rock which contains interesting minerals, as these may easily be shattered by too much hammering. It is much better to take it home and chip off the redundant parts at leisure. Moreover, the minerals, even if of a gem species, may not be of gem quality—misty, flawed with inclusions or internal fractures, clouded with carbon dioxide bubbles or simply too small for cutting; in this case it may be better to leave them in their parent rock. While they are still there the whole makes an instructive mineralogical specimen; but, once broken up, it will not amount to much.

A find will often be grimy. If taken out of the sea, it may be coated with organic matter, giving it colourings that bear no relation to the hard mineral underneath. An application of hot water and detergent, perhaps aided with a brush (not Brillo!), should be adequate to clean up the specimen. This is true also of most stones found on dry land. Frequently, however, the true colour and even shape of crystals is disguised by a reddish or brown coating of haematite or limonite, which is identical in appearance and composition with household rust, and can be removed with oxalic acid, obtainable from a chemist. This though is a nasty corrosive substance, to which the nettle owes its sting, and must be treated with great respect. Being a poison, it generally requires a permit to buy.

Incidentally, colour shows best when the specimen is wet, and for this reason a rainy day may prove more profitable in exploring gravels, screes, pebble banks or similar surface deposits than dry sunny weather when minerals lose their lustre and escape detection under a thin coat of dust.

3 *Signs and portents*

This is all about geology and mineralogy, and, even if not scientifically minded, we cannot get very far without a working knowledge of their language, which provides clues to those 'signs and portents' that lead to our treasure. This language departs somewhat from the everyday usage. Thus to a geologist anything that goes to make the body of Mother Earth is rock: sand, clay, mud, even water, as is also, of course, granite or limestone. Limestone is organic, being formed from the shells and skeletons of marine animals, accumulated to a depth of thousands of feet at the bottom of vanished seas and compacted into hard stone. It may additionally have been subjected to the internal heat of the Earth and turned to marble, which is almost pure carbonate of lime, and so—a mineral. Granite, however, has usually begun its life as molten rock, or *magma*, which becomes *lava* if poured out on the surface *sub dio*. The magma contained various substances, and as it cooled slowly under a thick cover of overlying rock strata these substances crystallized out of the originally molten mass. Thus granite and other similar rocks, described as *igneous* or fire-born, are mixtures of crystals.

3.1 ROCKS AND MINERALS

This brief description already provides an answer to how a rock differs from a mineral. A large mass of a mineral makes a rock, but a small piece of a rock does not necessarily make a mineral. Minor impurities apart, a mineral is a chemical compound of fixed composition, which remains the same, be it a ton or a grain. A rock, on the other hand, is commonly a mixture of various minerals, so that one small piece of it may have as much in common with another as the proverbial chalk and cheese. A chip of granite may be pure felspar or quartz.

Quartz is a common example of a mineral. It is a crystalline form of silica, or oxide of silicon, every invisibly small molecule of which contains one atom of silicon and two atoms of oxygen. This is briefly expressed thus: SiO_2 (one Silicon $+ 2$ Oxygens). Other minerals have more complicated compositions and chemical formulae, but the principle is the same.

The chemical properties of a substance are defined by its composition, but its appearance and other physical properties may vary with the 'accident of birth'. For instance, there exists a rare form of silica produced by violent impact and known as *coesite*, which differs from ordinary quartz;[29] while silica deposited from solution usually assumes a massive form called chalcedony.

The arrangement of the atoms in the molecule is fixed, though there may be left- and right-handed variants. Thus every molecule of a mineral has a well-defined shape. Imagine having a large number of tiny blocks, all of the same shape and size, say, cubes or tetrahedra. They can be fitted together face to face only in a limited number of ways, which betrays itself in the resulting structure. Molecules are such blocks. If dispersed in a solution or melt (magma) they tend to flock together like birds of a feather, and in combining observe strictly defined rules, the result being a geometrical solid which we call a crystal. Few crystals found in nature are as simple as the idealized drawings in a textbook; they become intergrown, smaller crystals develop on the sides of a large one, some faces are much bigger than others, and the outcome may be nothing like what we are led to expect. Yet, however extravagantly complicated the natural form may be, the rules founded in the shape of the molecule cannot be violated: the angles between the neighbouring faces and the basic symmetries of structure are preserved.

The physical properties of the mineral go with its crystalline form, or *habit*, and this in turn may be affected by the temperature and pressure. We may have two minerals with different physical properties, such as hardness, specific weight, and, of course, crystalline habit, yet of identical chemical composition; of this diamond and graphite form a striking example. As we have already seen, silica may be massive, as well as crystalline. The massive form, however, usually shares structural properties with the crystalline variant, but either the crystals have been unable to develop, for instance, owing to the original molten rock cooling too quickly, or they are so small as to be invisible with the naked eye. Thus it is still the same mineral of the same crystalline habit. In some cases the mineral may be incoherent, or *earthy*, and obviously enough such a mineral cannot be a gem.

This may seem confusing, but it is how things are in nature. No two leaves on a tree are exactly alike; yet we would not mistake an oak leaf for a pine needle. So, too, with minerals. When the crystal shape defeats us, we can fall back on hardness, streak, specific weight and sometimes colour, which, although conspicuous, is often deceptive. Some minerals have a fixed colour, appropriate to them: most garnets, for instance, are red. Very often, however, the colouring is due to a minute impurity. Thus not only are the red ruby and the blue sapphire one and the same mineral, corundum, which is the crystalline form of aluminium oxide, or alumina, Al_2O_3 (2 atoms of aluminium + 3 of oxygen), but there are violet, yellow, green and colourless sapphires as well.

3.2 GEMSTONES

All that has been said so far applies to any mineral. A gem, however, is a mineral distinguishable by beautiful appearance, durability and rarity, although there are a few gems of organic origin, as are, of course, some rocks, to mention only limestone and mineral coal.

The not-so-rare gems are often described as 'semi-precious' (mineralogists strongly disapprove of this term) and the really rare ones as precious. This classification, however, is at least partly a matter of supply and demand, the latter of which is affected by fashion. Sometimes an originally plentiful source of some stone or other may become exhausted, as has happened, for example, to the Derbyshire 'Blue John', used for ornamental purposes though not as a gem; or, conversely, there may be a sudden glut of a hitherto rare variety. In consequence a gemstone may be promoted from the second to the first division, or the other way round. Thus prices fluctuate, although where large financial interests are at stake, as in diamond production, the supply will be so manipulated as to keep the price screwed up. It may, indeed, be doubted if diamond is all that rare, even if its occurence in gem-worthy specimens in the British Isles is questionable.

All this, however, has nothing to do with the intrinsic beauty of a mineral, which may be of many kinds.

The opaque stones have only their colour or attractive design to offer. In translucent stones this is supplemented by a play of light, which may include *chatoyancy*, or a kind of misty sheen due to internal reflection, *dichroism* where the colour changes with the angle of viewing or lighting, or a rainbow effect, due to the interference of light, as in precious opal or labradorite.

These attractions are not wholly foreign to transparent stones either. There is rainbow quartz, where internal fractures cause iridescent reflections, cat's-eye, tiger-eye and star sapphire owe their fame to chatoyant bands of light, due to fibrous inclusions. Yet the distinctive feature of transparent minerals is their 'crystal clearness', which, married to an attractive coloration and a high refractive index, yields the beautiful sparkle of a perfect jewel. The refractive index measures the angle by which the light is bent in entering or leaving the stone and goes with sharp differences in the brightness of facets, seen on and through the cut gem or crystal, and usually with high *dispersion*, of the property of splitting white light into rainbow colours. The two combine to the so-called 'fire'.

The natural colouring of diamond is almost as variable as that of sapphire, if generally less pronounced, but characteristically diamond is colourless, like window glass. If it had the same refractive index it would look equally 'dead', however skillfully fashioned; in 'paste' jewellery the low refractive index is often made up for by a backing of tinfoil. A diamond needs no such artifice; the high refractive index and strong dispersion give it a natural 'fire'. The green or yellow sphene surpasses diamond in this respect, but is comparatively soft, so that it is easily scratched and loses its lustre when worn as a personal ornament; whereas diamond is the hardest of all natural substances and correspondingly durable. In fact, adequate hardness is necessary for a mineral to graduate as a gem, and many attractive species are disqualified on this account.

Crystalline minerals are beautiful: they are like flowers. Part of the beauty lies in the shape itself, but this is not taken into consideration when a mineral is judged as a gem, for the latter is admired in the cut and polished state. In a collection, however, the fine crystal shape resumes its rightful place, for like all good things it is rare. So I would plead with you to leave it as formed by the hand of nature.

Yet the natural appearance of an intrinsically beautiful gem may be anything but attractive. Crystals may be thickly encrusted with lime, haematite or limonite. I have seen big, clear cairngorms—a brown variety of quartz—completely encased in opaque felspar. More often than not the crystal is turbid, full of internal fractures and inclusions, only a small part being suitable for cutting. You may kick a water-worn pebble of diamond without a suspicion of its true value or what it would look like when dressed.

Water-worn crystals are often difficult to distinguish from similarly rounded bits of bottle glass, which all adds to the uncertainties of the quest. In one respect, however, such specimens score over undamaged crystals. Only the sound, flawless stones stand a chance of surviving the hurly-burly, although some stones, including amethyst and topaz, tend to fade on prolonged exposure to sunlight. So the stream-beds in a gem-bearing locality are well worth attention. Indeed, this is where many of the 'Oriental gems' of India, Burma and Ceylon come from. In a richly vegetated land, where the bedrock lies hidden beneath a thick mantle of soil and plant growth, the streams and the sea-shore are the only places of natural exposure of the bones of the Earth. And these bones are being constantly gnawed at by the fret of moving water, which continually uncovers fresh layers, however slowly. Artificial exposure occurs in railway and road cuttings, or any kind of constructional excavation, as well as in pits and quarries. All of these, if publicly accessible, deserve a visit, always with the proviso that the rocks are of the right kind.

We have seen that gems are mainly crystals, though a few are massive. Occasionally both types may be formed from solutions percolating through the rocks without an intervention of heat, but most gems are born of heat and pressure.

3.3 DIFFERENT ROCK TYPES

Rocks are divided into two main categories. The primary rocks are igneous; they are frozen magma. The secondary rocks are derived from their decay, with or without the action of plants and animals. The igneous rocks weather to scree, grit, sand, clay, mud and ooze, which are washed out to sea and bed on its floor deeper and deeper, are compressed by their own weight, as well as by that of the water above them, and so in the course of millions of years harden to stone that can be quarried and built into mansions and cathedrals. Limestone and coal consist of organic remains.

It is clear that these *sedimentary rocks* are unlikely to harbour gems, except for the *alluvials*, such as river gravels, or deposits where larger undigested fragments of the pre-existent surface, igneous or otherwise, are cemented by sand, limestone or other matrix into a sort of rock pudding, which is even known as *puddingstone*. More technically it is called *conglomerate* if it contains rounded water-worn pebbles, and *breccia* (brecha) if the fragments are angular. These fragments, however, may also be of volcanic origin and the rock is then known as *agglomerate* (see p. 13).

As sediments pile up stratum upon stratum, they sink farther into the bowels of the Earth, where the temperature rises steadily. Great movements of the Earth's crust, which fold solid rock like Plasticene and raise it into mighty mountain ridges, also generate great heat and pressure and under their influence the mineral constituents begin to crystallize out. This process is called *metamorphism* and the resulting rocks *metamorphic*. Many metamorphic rocks are *schists*; they are foliated, somewhat like pages in a squashed book, through the terrible pressing and sliding when mountains are being built. Slate and the silvery mica-schist are examples of such rocks; they both were mud once upon a time.

The degree of metamorphism may vary, but when sufficiently advanced some gem minerals will appear in the rocks, principally garnet, but also tourmaline, kyanite, perhaps emerald. It all depends on the initial chemical composition of the rocks, as well as on how much heat and pressure has been applied to them, and for how long. The end product is a kind of banded granite, called *gneiss* (nice). It may contain kyanite, garnet, cordierite and zircon.

The cycle is substantially from granite to granite and may span up to 2000 million years, which is worth sparing a thought for.

What has just been described is known in geology as *regional metamorphism*; it involves wholesale alteration of large areas of the Earth's crust, underneath which there is great heat and pockets of molten rock, or magma, which is powerfully compressed by the weight of miles of rocks above it, and if only a little chink of a crevice opens in them will be squeezed up towards the surface, possibly reach it and start a volcano. This will puff and roar for some thousands of years or more, sending up towering cauliflower clouds, heavy with corrosive gases and volcanic ash, pour out scorching streams of lava down its sides, then go to sleep, waking up now and again to destructive fury, until its sources of magma run dry and it is slowly razed by the patient rub of erosion. Only a stump of igneous rock is left, or a feed-pipe clogged with debris. It is in such ancient volcanic pipes, filled with 'blue ground', that diamonds are found in South Africa; and the pyrope garnets, misleadingly named 'Elie rubies', are also scattered through a volcanic pipe filling on Elie Ness, in Fife, Scotland.

Yet even if the rising magma fails to reach the surface it will bake and alter the rocks with which it comes in contact. Such *contact metamorphism* may also give rise to interesting and precious minerals. The hot fluid-rich magma may bring with it valuable ores and form a *lode*. A lode is bordered by *gangue minerals*, among which are quartz, fluorite, topaz and tourmaline, and often contains chain-cavities, known in Cornwall as *vuggs* or *vughs*, where fine crystals may develop. From the miner's point of view the gangue minerals are of little use—he is after the ore, and so they find their way to the mine dumps together with other barren rock rubble. The miner is no fool and will know the value of a gemstone that catches his eye, but he is busy and cannot find the time to examine every bit of rock with the diligence of a true rock-hound, so that old mine dumps are well worth turning over, except that so many geologists and mineralogists have had the same idea. If the mine is still working the chances of a good find are much improved, but miners and managements are not keen on having strangers pottering about, so that permission must be sought beforehand. It may or may not be granted.

However, anything that secondary rocks contain must originally have been in the primary igneous ones from which they are derived, so that igneous rocks are the main source of gemstones.

Gem minerals, if generally not of gem quality, may occur as essential or accessory rock minerals. Thus quartz, felspar and mica are essential minerals of granite, but the accessory minerals of this rock include tourmaline, garnet, topaz, beryl, zircon, sapphire, even diamond. These need not be all present at the same time, or present at all, in fact.

The complete classification of igneous rocks is something of a teaser, full of 'supercalifragilistic' names, but it is simple in principle: the rocks are divided vertically into acid, intermediate, basic and ultrabasic according to the percentage of silica in their chemical make-up; and horizontally according to the size of crystal grain. The acid rocks contain over 65 per cent of silica, over 10 per cent being in the form of quartz; in basic rocks there is usually no quartz at all and the percentage of silica drops below 55. The acid rocks are lighter both in colour, in which greyish and reddish tints predominate, and in specific gravity, than the basic rocks, which tend to be black, greenish or bluish.

The size of crystal grain depends on the rate of cooling of the original magma, and this in turn on the size of the intrusion and the depth below the surface where it solidified before being exposed on the surface by erosion. In deep-seated, or *abyssal*, intrusions the component crystals are large. At the medium *hypabyssal* level they become small, with sometimes larger crystals scattered through the fine-grained mass, such structure being described as *porphyritic*. But when the consolidation has occurred at the surface the texture becomes micro-crystalline or glassy. In the *acid group*, or *clan*, the typical coarse-grained rock is granite, followed by microgranite, or aplite, and porphyry, with rhyolite and glassy obsidian at the tail end. In the *intermediate clan* the sequence is: diorite, micro-diorite and diorite-porphyry, andesite; in the *basic*: gabbro, micro-gabbro, basalt. *Ultrabasic* rocks, such as dunite and eclogite, with less than 45 per cent of silica, are very rare on the surface of the Earth and contain olivine, which decays to serpentine.[4]

All these rocks have started off solid, so to speak, but there are also *clastic* volcanics, consisting of small fragments, described as *ash*, though this has nothing in common with ordinary ash from a fireplace, and *lapilli* when larger. These form deposits and are eventually turned to hard rock, known as tuff and agglomerate respectively.

Since we are looking for crystals, our chief interest will be in the coarse-grained rocks.

Generally speaking, in dense 'live' rock crystals have little chance to develop fully, are much flawed and intergrown. Molten magma, however, contains various gases, more particularly steam, in solution, and these escape from it as it cools. These escaping gases form bubbles over which the rock is unable to close, and large crystals grow out of the walls of the resulting cavity, called a *druse*. Druses may occur in medium-and small-grained varieties as well, and are often associated with veins of quartz, aplite or other igneous intrusions, which give the rock a maggoty look. But the type of rock especially to be sought after is *pegmatite*, which is of giant grain, sometimes to be measured in inches and even feet! Pegmatites, too, occur as veins or larger masses within the main body of the rock and have their complement of vuggs and druses. They often contain rare minerals.

It is not easy to extract a crystal from massive rock, nor even from a druse, unless this has been weakened by decay, but it will often pay to trace a pegmatite vein into the scree, where some digging will yield material derived from the weathering of the vein.

The lavas are not quite so exciting, but they contain almond-shaped hollows, called *amygdales*, in which agates and crystals may develop, and then weather out, perhaps to be recemented in puddingstone.

The general lesson is clear. Look for the mountains and hills, especially where the Earth has bled red on the geological map, preferably the bright red of acid rocks.

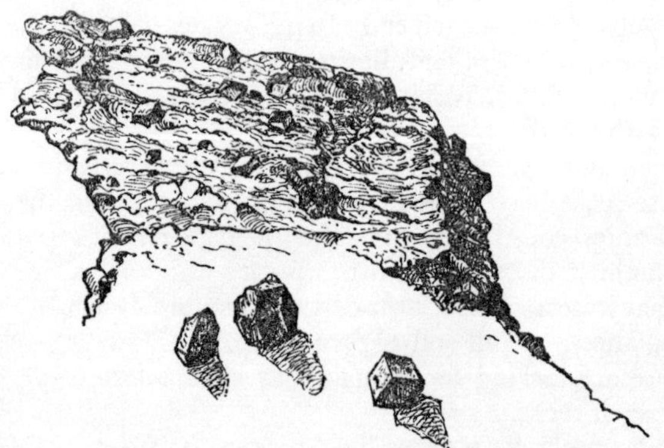

Almandine garnets, the Braes o' Balquhidder

4 Round the British Isles
Part 1, England and Wales

It is a frequent practice among those bent on breaking walking records to start off from Land's End and work their way through progressively fouler weather up to John o' Groats, and we may vicariously follow in their footsteps. Not being committed, however, to any particular mode of locomotion, we are free to range east and west, over sea and land, with that supreme disregard for natural and unnatural obstacles, such as road jams and British Railways, which is the prerogative of paper travel.

4.1 SOUTHERN ENGLAND

We are in the south-west of England, and a very useful part of Great Britain this is, richly blotched on the geological map with the bright red of granite. The Scilly Isles are solid granite, as are the lone Lundy with its razorbills and puffins, and the Channel Isles. A large outcrop of granite spans the Cornish peninsula from Land's End to St. Ives and Penzance. The windswept moors of Carnmenellis, St. Austell, Bodmin, and farther east, in Devon, Dartmoor, the largest of them all, with its tors, ponies, H.M. Prison and artillery ranges, sit on the same igneous rock (*see* Map), containing tourmaline, though mainly black, and locally beryl, topaz, amethyst, apatite and fluorite.

The granite 'bosses' extend over a distance of 125 miles from WSW to ENE, the line that marks the ancient Armorican or Hercynian Mountains. The earth movements which elevated these vanished ranges have determined the lie of the land in south Wales and the south of Ireland as well, and made their impact felt as far afield as Poland. This was a great convulsion of the Earth's crust at the end of the Carboniferous and the beginning of the Permian period, over 200 million years ago, when our venerable ancestors, the first reptiles, took to dry land. The granite was injected into the roots of the mountain folds as a glowing molten mass, whose heat had baked and hardened the surrounding sedimentary formations, known locally as *killas*, in a *metamorphic aureole*, one to two miles wide.

In time the granite magma cooled and crystallized into its present porphyritic condition, characterized by large imperfect crystals of white plagioclase felspar and 'etched' with the Indian ink of *schorl* (black tourmaline). But the rocks had not come to rest yet; they cracked and splintered as further molten material, both acid and basic, pressed in from below, laden with corrosive fluids and metallic ingredients, and squeezed into the gaps in dykes and veins or overflowed in volcanic eruptions. Thus came into being the metalliferous lodes with their companion, or gangue, minerals: quartz, tourmaline, fluorite (or fluorspar), chlorite, barite, calcite and sometimes topaz.[13]

The hot fluids affected the granite, as well as the surrounding sediments. Where boron vapours predominated the mica and felspar of the granite were turned to tourmaline; with chlorine as the main reagent the result was less interestingly chlorite, a soft green mineral often with a silky or pearly sheen, but perhaps also chlor-apatite; fluorine yielded topaz, apatite and fluorite. The crumbly fluorinated granite, called *greisen*, is not uncommon in these parts. Kaolinization, where felspar is converted to china clay, or *kaolin*, is due mainly to the action of superheated steam. Such has been the genesis of the clay pits of St. Austell Moor with their pyramidal dumps, which give the country about Belowda its Egyptian look. Kaolinization has released the harder crystalline constituents of granite, such as quartz and tourmaline, which can thus be obtained in good crystals without much trouble. Some of the best Cornish amethysts have come from the area of St. Austell, which also has to offer a variety of turquoise, called *rashleighite*. The effects of such *pneumatolysis* on the killas have been not unsimilar, and where basic rocks or limestones were encountered garnet, axinite, epidote, apatite and fluorite may be expected.[8, 13, 22]

The heat declined away from the intrusions, and the resulting minerals are correspondingly zoned. Tourmaline comes first in the order of decreasing metamorphism, then fluorite, while quartz occurs throughout the aureole.

All this happened deep underground and was not exposed on the surface until erosion had ground the proud Armorican peaks down to mere stumps. It must be borne in mind, though, that even now only the tops of the granite intrusions are laid bare, so that in considering the mineral zoning the distance must be reckoned not just from the surface outcrop, but also from its buried continuation.

Tin, lead, zinc, arsenic, copper, tungsten, uranium, gold and silver— the whole mineral wealth of the two south-western counties has come from this source. It has been worked since pre-Roman times and largely exhausted, at any rate in the more accessible upper reaches, very few mines being still in operation. However, a good deal of Cornwall, some of Devon and a little of south Somerset is honeycombed with old workings, like a rabbit's warren,[13] and it is in the old mine dumps, often overgrown with clumpy grass, brambles, nettles and all manner of rank weed, that interesting minerals are mainly sought and occasionally found. Although they may also be looked for in the parent rocks, containing pegmatite and other veins of insufficient commercial interest to have been dug up, in coastal cliffs and on the beaches at their foot.

The gem minerals of Cornwall and Devon are very numerous and so are the localities where they have been or may be found, so that it is rather difficult to give the subject full justice in the present compass. Moreover, gem-seekers and mineralogists have been on the prowl for decades, if not centuries, so that in most cases the best and most accessible specimens have been removed. For instance, the beach at Marazion opposite St. Michael's Mount was once known as the 'Crystal Beach', where amethyst and citrine could be picked up without much trouble, but you will be lucky if you come across any of these now. Many museum specimens have come from mines, deep underground, where operations were discontinued many years ago. However, there is no need to despair; good finds can still be made.

Some amethyst has been found quite recently in the Scillies. Jersey and Guernsey are known for good crystals of epidote, which occur uncharacteristically in granite.[31] Lundy has topaz, rock crystal and tourmaline.[8, 31]

Black tourmaline is no gem and is of widespread occurrence throughout Cornwall and Devon; so, too, is quartz, of course, and only their gem varieties deserve mention. Amethyst is not particularly rare, although good clear crystals are not so easy to come by. It may be looked for in Nanjizal and Sennen Coves near Land's End and farther north on the mine dumps about St. Just. Here the rocks are faulted between Cape Cornwall and Pendeen Watch and a basic intrusion along the coast has contributed a whole crop of gem minerals. These include blue beryl, blue, yellow and colourless (achroite) tourmaline (Geevor mine—in operation, but permission to explore dumps granted on request), yellow-green apatite, fluorite, grossular and almandine garnet, epidote, axinite, actinolite, fire opal, amethyst, chalcedony, jasper, haematite and malachite (Wheal Levant), as well as the zeolites: prehnite and natrolite, recorded between Botallack and Wheal Cock.[8, 13, 31, 45, 46] 'Wheal', by the way, is the Cornish for mine. R. F. Penhallurick[45] has told me that 'good deep-red jasper' may be had at the Ding-Dong Mine deeper inland, which is remarkable inasmuch as most Cornish jaspers are variegated, brownish and somewhat lacking in colour.

As we move south-east, we come across some more axinite (plum-coloured), epidote and topaz near St. Burian and Lamorna Cove. St. Michael's Mount off Penzance, out of bounds to collectors, is something of a treasure house, its granite rocks being traversed by numerous vuggy pegmatite veins, containing beryl (blue), topaz (likewise), almandine garnet, 'diamond tin' (cassiterite), apatite, fluorite, rose quartz, citrine

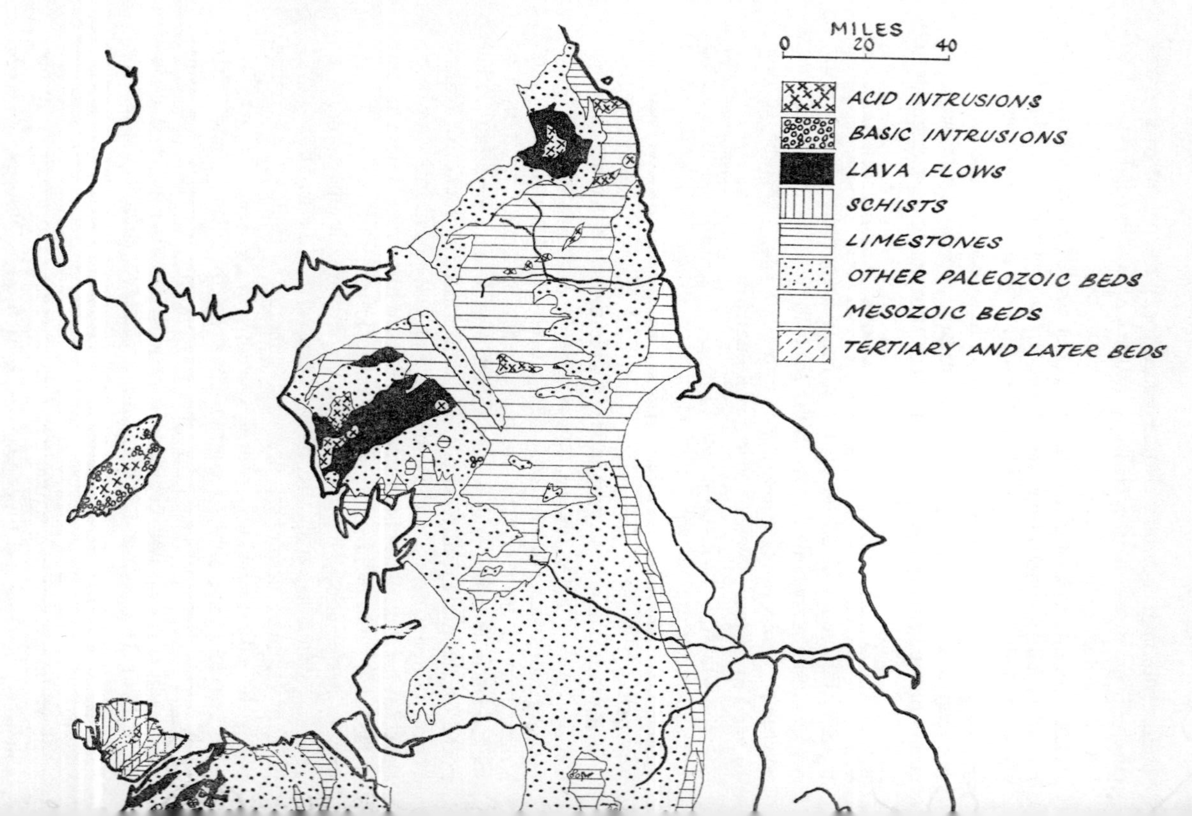

MILES
0   20   40
ACID INTRUSIONS
BASIC INTRUSIONS
LAVA FLOWS
SCHISTS
LIMESTONES
OTHER PALEOZOIC BEDS
MESOZOIC BEDS
TERTIARY AND LATER BEDS

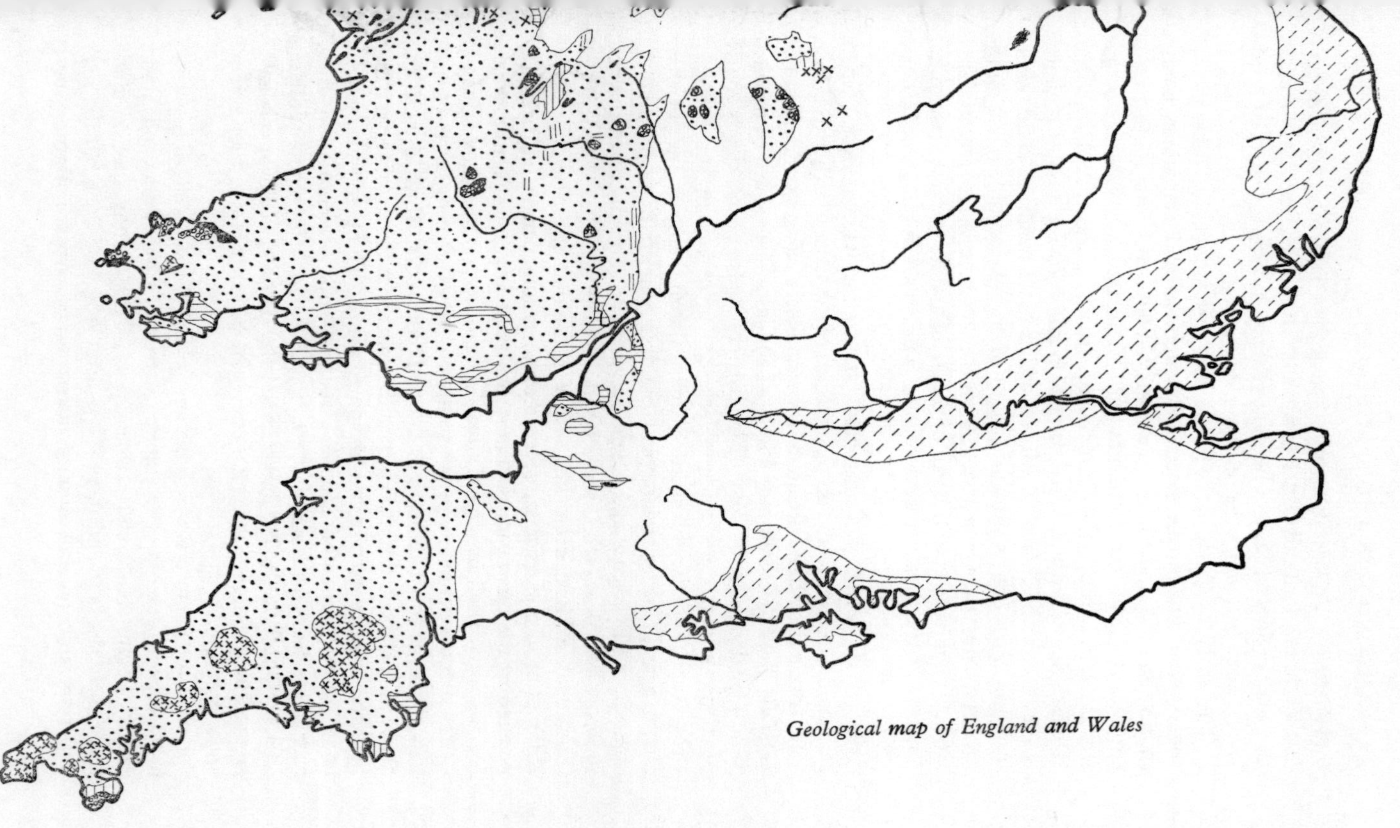

Geological map of England and Wales

and amethyst. At least in theory some of these minerals, as well as agate (rather flinty), sard and carnelian wash up on the beaches near Marazion, and may be looked for in Magilligar Rocks, half-a mile short of Porthleven, eastwards along the seashore.[52]

The St. Ives district in the north is less productive, but it has yielded some green and purple fluorite, ferruginous and cairngorm quartz, morion and topaz, the latter in a quarry about half a mile south-west of Cornish Arms on the east highway. There are some basic dykes and sills between here and the Carnmenellis granite, south of the Camborne-Redruth district, which is rich in old tin and copper mines. Camborne is the seat of the School of Mines, which has a beautiful collection of local minerals, but its proximity has had an unfavourable effect on the local mine dumps, which have been worked more or less bare by students. However, north-east and north of the main granite there are two minor outcrops: Carn Brea and Carn Marth. The druses in the former contain green-blue fluorite, though brown and purple crystals, too, have come from the Gwennap-Redruth area, known for its amethyst. Green tourmaline may be found on the margins of the Carn Marth intrusion as well. Prase used to be obtained from the North Roskear mine, but this is fatally close to Camborne. Fire opal and jasper have been recorded at Wheal Gorland near St. Day. The district has also been a steady source of copper minerals, including malachite, azurite and chrysocolla.

For topaz, apatite, phenakite,[52] more fluorite and, if you put these among gems, cassiterite and sphalerite, it is better to move north to the coast, about St. Agnes and Cligga Head. It is, indeed, one of the best localities for topaz, which here occurs in slate at Wheal Kind, Wheal Trevaunance, Seal Hole and other tin mines. A rare beryllium-aluminium silicate, euclase, which resembles aquamarine, has been discovered in the quartz-tourmaline-topaz veins at Cligga Head,[46] where Sir Arthur Russell has found topaz crystals up to eight inches long.[54]

The Lizard peninsula in the south is a very different kettle of geological fish, as very old metamorphic and basic rocks, which also outcrop above Bolt Head and Prawl Point at the southernmost tip of Devon, take here the place of granite and Devonian killas. The peninsula sports a large body of serpentinite (crude serpentine rock), much used for small ornaments, as well as some gabbro. There is a doubtful report of olivine crystals found on the beaches.[52] Bronzite, datolite, zeolites, cordierite and jadeite are other Lizard minerals. St. Keverne is listed for epidote and zeolites.[31, 46]

Across the Helford River to the north small blue crystals of beryl and topaz occur sparsely in the granite quarries of Constantine and Mabe. Agates, potato-stones and various types of chalcedony may be found along the coast here and there (Kynance Cove, Loe Bar), but the next important mineral and mining district is St. Austell Moor. South

Terras is a uranium mine in the metamorphic aureole of the granite near St. Stephen, and J. Phemister has found prismatic actinolite here, with purplish axinite and yellow garnet.[13] The granite itself is extensively kaolinized and quarried for claystone. Its accessory minerals include fluorite, topaz, apatite (mainly cloudy), beryl and tourmaline, which is usually brown, sometimes zoned in blue, but may also be blue-green[22] (see p. 107). Amethyst and turquoise have already been mentioned in this connection (p. 16), but associated with kaolin is also milk opal, and the County Museum at Truro has some fine opal, showing iridescence, from the Slip China Stone Quarry.[45] There is serpentine near Duporth on the coast, south-east of St. Austell.[8]

Northwards, on the way to Bodmin, mines cluster about Luxulyan, Lanlivery and Lostwithiel. The first of these has produced the blue and green apatite crystals to be found in many museums. The Lanlivery and Maudlin mines have yielded scheelite, garnet, chalcedony, jasper, opal and fluorite.[21]

The northern and central parts of Bodmin Moor are less extensively mineralized and mined, except for china clay in the west, so that one does not hear much about its gemstones. This, though, may be a very good reason for trying one's luck there, as the granite is much the same as in St. Austell Moor.

On the north coast Tintagel, enshrined in Arthurian legend, is a well-known beauty spot and mineralogically remarkable for the fine clusters of rock crystal, found embedded in sticky clay in slate.

As for the Bodmin granite itself, most of the mines and minerals appear to be concentrated on and near its southern and eastern margins, about Liskeard and Callington. Wheal Mary Ann, north of Menheniot, is a favourite collector's port of call. Apart from the ores, such as galena, sphalerite and pyrite, it has quartz crystals and chalcedony, as well as fluorite, mainly of a honey-yellow hue, but occasionally purple, green or blue. North of Liskeard cairngorm and amethyst, 'finely crystallized in prisms', may be looked for in the area of St. Cleer and St. Ewe. Malachite, azurite, chrysocolla and more fluorite (South and West Caradon) occur at many places from here on to Callington and Gunnislake in the Tamar Valley, on the Devonshire border.

There is serpentine at Clickor Tor near Liskeard, and more at Pollyphant, about four miles west of Launceston in the north.

The Tamar Valley is known for green fluorite, e.g. from East Tamar Mine near Tavistock and Bere Alston.[21] The 'killas' between Bodmin Moor and Dartmoor has been penetrated and overlaid by volcanic rocks, both intrusive and extrusive (lavas), basic and acid, and we find a similar situation in the south, about Plymouth, and in the east, towards Torquay. Expectedly, this has given rise to contact metamorphism and mineralization, although most of the mines are out of action.

According to Dines and Phemister,[13] the dumps of the Bedford United (not a football club!) conceal 'considerable amounts of green, reddish-yellow and white fluorite'. Rhodonite is to be found at Milton Abbot to the north-west, and northwards, along the edge of Dartmoor, axinite, jasper and garnet at Brent Tor. There is also jasper at Ivybridge, south of the granite, and a pale-red variety may be picked up at Heldon near Teignmouth. Budleigh Salterton appears to be the source of best West Country agates.[45] Agates, sards and carnelians, as well as potato-stones, containing geodes lined with rock crystal or amethyst, occur, however, on many beaches to the east of this point: near Sidmouth and Seaton, in Devon; Chesil Bank, Charnmouth and Portland, in Dorset; and as far east as Sandown Bay and Undercliffe, on the Isle of Wight. The latter locality it also known for 'Isle of Wight diamonds', which are only rock crystal on our reckoning.[31]

However, to return to Devon, as we proceed north along the west edge of Dartmoor, we come to Okehampton and the Meldon Quarries, where garnet, axinite, andalusite, rhodonite, jasper, opal, cairngorm and rock crystal are to be found. Amethyst, axinite and garnet have been recorded in the nearby Copper Hill, while the Aplite Quarry has yielded cairngorm, blue beryl and gem-quality tourmaline, red, blue and green. In quarries new layers of rock are constantly exposed and removed, playing hide-and-seek with mineral veins and druses, so that no particular account can be up to date. It is, however, fair to assume that the same minerals occur at other points on the margins of the Dartmoor granite, which is, indeed, known to contain green beryl and garnet. The mineral resources of the high moors themselves are comparatively modest,[13] nor are they readily accessible, so that they have never been extensively worked, and all mining operations have now been abandoned.

The land is in the nature of a plateau, exceeding 2000 feet above sea level in Yes Tor and High Willhays (2038 feet) and somewhat lower elsewhere, little broken by streams, except in the east and south. The plateau is crossed by roads at Two Bridges, and it is possible to reach high levels on wheel at several points. Nevertheless, ten miles of rough moorland can be a long way in bad weather, so that perhaps it is not too surprising that finds are reported chiefly from the periphery of Dartmoor. My own search of the interior has not been too productive, but I did find some rock crystal, faintly tinged with violet, and a few prisms of citrine.

East of Okehampton, garnet, axinite and actinolite may be expected about Sticklepath and Ramsley. In eastern Dartmoor beryl, garnet and opal have been recorded at Lustleigh; agate, chalcedony, garnet and opal at Haytor nearby; fluorite and marcasite at Buckland; and in the metamorphic aureole apatite at Chudleigh, Bovey Heathfield and Bovey

Tracey, the latter of which has also produced large, well-formed crystals of black tourmaline. The apatite appears to be cream-coloured. and its supply is said to have been exhausted at Bovey Tracey. There is also some malachite at Hemor near Chudley and at Buckfastleigh farther south.[8, 13, 31, 45, 46, 52]

In the north of the county, on the Somerset border near Wellington, agate, jasper and wood opal may be found on the Blackdown Hills; and, finally, the Combemartin mines near Ilfracombe contain marcasite and malachite.

If we draw a line approximately from the middle of Lyme Bay to the mouth of the Humber, the country to the south-east of it is composed of geologically recent sediments, which do not contain much to interest a gem-hunter, save for marcasite in the grey chalky marls at Beachy Head in Sussex, near Folkstone, Dover and on the Isle of Sheppey in Kent, and near Devizes in Wiltshire. The agates and other forms of chalcedony on the Channel coast have already been referred to, as have also been the 'Isle of Wight diamonds', but some amber is washed up on the beaches of Isle of Wight, Sussex, Kent, East Anglia and northwards. A *Manual of Mineralogy*[31] published in 1858 speaks hopefully of amber being found 'in sand at Kensington *near* London'—*sic transit* . . .

Thus the most populous part of England is also the least interesting from our point of view, which is perhaps just as well.

To return to our interrupted journey, as we leave Devon, we come across some pink and white alabaster in the sea-cliffs near Watchet, Old Clive being another Somerset locality for this soft ornamental stone. Old books speak of malachite and azurite from the Doddington and Buckingham mines near Bridgwater. Andesitic lavas of Old Red Sandstone (Devonian) age peep up thinly in the Mendips, north-west of Shepton Mallet, and in Gloucestershire, south of the Severn. The conglomerates, fringing the base of the Carboniferous Limestones of these hills and largely derived from the old volcanics, have produced some fine jasper agates, a little rose quartz and potato-stones lined with rock crystal and occasionally amethyst, notably at Clifton, near Cheddar and some Gloucestershire localities, where a 'fine ribbon jasper' and chalcedony are to be found at Dressing Green, near Tortworth, also agates in a 'trap' (basic) dyke at Mickleton. There is a questioned report of prehnite from Woodford Bridge in the same county.[31]

The Mendip limestone is mineralised, and galena used to be mined there by the Romans and up to the present century. The Wells Museum contains attractive specimens of fluorite, apparently associated with it. Fluorite occasionally crops up in the Mendip quarries and large crystals were once obtained from the Providence mine at Clifton. If you fancy the steel-grey sheen of polished haematite you may find some suitable material near Bristol.

Somerset and Gloucestershire are geologically west of our Lyme Bay Humber line, where the soils are generally poorer, the rocks harder, older, and the fire-wrought bones of the Earth begin to stick out through the 'sedimentary flesh'.

There is a body of very ancient pre-Cambrian rocks in Charnwood Forest, in Leicestershire, and in the Malvern Hills, which, gentle on the Worcestershire side, drop in a steep escarpment towards the Hereford plain, a scenic pattern that repeats itself throughout the Pennines farther north. Similar formations appear once more on the Welsh border— sparsely, and more massively in the far west of Wales, in Pembrokeshire, the Lleyn Peninsula and Anglesey.

'Pre-Cambrian' is to the geologist what 'Here be lions' used to be to the mediaeval cartographer: it serves to cover up multitudinous ignorance, in this case of the 4000 million years before the Cambrian period, which ushered in the Age of Old Life, or Palaeozoic Era, some 600 million years ago. Yet Charnwood Forest has yielded fossils of fairly advanced marine life which are twice as old, although nothing to excite a gem-searcher so far as I have been able to ascertain, unless you count the red porphyry used locally for small ornamental objects. There is some epidote on the east side of the Malverns,[31] but otherwise they seem to be similarly barren, as also does the minor Ordovician volcanic complex near Hereford. It may, however, well be that a thorough investigation on the spot will reveal some minerals overlooked in the general surveys.

4.2 WALES

South Wales, although mountainous, is predominantly sedimentary, its chief wealth being coal, and correspondingly a little unpromising from our point of view. Carboniferous or Mountain Limestone, coeval with that of the Mendips and Gloucestershire hills, is exposed in Monmouthshire, Glamorganshire and Brecknockshire, and some jasper, agate and potato-stones may be found in it and in the Triassic strata, notably at Kenfig Point and near Llantrinsant in Glamorgan. Rutile, if we put it among the gems, and rock crystal in doubly terminated prisms occur in the cavities of argillaceous (= clayey) ironstone near Aberdare and Merthyr Tydfil. The quartz crystals from Taff's Well and the Mwyndy Mine, Llantrinsant, are often tinted yellow, amber, red and occasionally violet.[31, 43, 49, 62]

In the south and east the Armorican lie of the land predominates, but gives way northwards and westwards to the north-east and south-west trends typifying the still earlier Caledonian foldings. Initiated between 400 and 350 million years ago, in the Silurian, and long since destroyed, the Caledonian ranges were once comparable to the Himalayas, and their upraised and dismembered stumps continue to dominate the scenery of much of Wales, Ireland, parts of England, and most of Scotland and Scandinavia.

Mineral lodes of Caledonian provenance thread their way through the bedrock of Carmarthenshire, notably about Llandovery. Gold is scattered in the quartz veins, and the Romans used to mine it at Ogofan near Llanpumsaint. T. H. Thomas has found some smoky quartz on the dumps of the Rhandirmwyn lead mines, while amethyst occurs in druses and 'small vuggy veins' in the former haematite mines of Mwyndy and Garth Ward, farther west.[62] There is a substantial Ordovician volcanic complex between Builth Wells and Llandrindod, in Radnorshire, exposed to advantage in the Llanellwedd quarries. The greenish lavas contain mineralized hollows (amygdales) up to six inches and more in diameter, but mostly small. The filling is chiefly soft green chlorite, felspar, finely divided sphene, with minor quantities of other minerals, which may be wholly or partly replaced by calcite and turbid or water-clear quartz. Some of the latter is banded (G. D. Nicholls), but whether it can be classed as agate, I am unable to say.

Igneous rocks of pre-Cambrian and Ordovician age, including basic and small acid intrusions and lavas, diversify the Pembrokeshire landscape. Near Llanhowel an outcrop of greenish diorite at the Hollybush quarry contains hornblende crystals up to three-quarters of an inch long. Hornblende is usually opaque and not a gem, but may be of interest. Another diorite mass, near Knaveston, is even more remarkable: it is a mixture of hornblende, white felspar, some augite, much sphene with ilmenite and apatite as accessory minerals.[49] These minerals will generally be opaque and intergrown, but if there are any veins with vuggs or pegmatite bodies, which may be expected on the periphery of the intrusions, clear crystals ought to have developed in these—and at least sphene and apatite are gemstones.

Paul G. Hines,[34] who is an authority on the geology of Pembrokeshire, mentions, however, only 'jasper dykes' associated with volcanic rocks near Strumble Head on the Cardigan Bay and occasional crystals of haematite in quartz veins as worthy of a gem-hunter's attention.

The Cambrian Mountains forming the eastern backbone of Cardiganshire swell up into bleak undifferentiated moors, and their Silurian rocks are correspondingly monotonous. On the beaches ferruginous (flesh-pink) and colourless quartz pebbles, as well as red and green jaspers, eroded from the pre-Cambrian rocks of the Lleyn Peninsula, may be picked up northwards of Aberystwyth. J. G. Francis[28] mentions aquamarine among the sea offerings at the latter, where various rock debris have been dumped by the glaciers of the Ice Age, but I have been unable to confirm this information.

As we continue north to Cader Idris and beyond, the mountains grow higher, more rugged, with massive outcrops of basic and acid igneous formations, to achieve their full glory in the *llyns* and peaks of Snowdonia, carved out of Ordovician volcanics, in Caernarvonshire. For the most part, however, these rocks are tuffs, or hardened volcanic ash, shading into clinky porcellanite, as in the ridge of Crib Goch, and as such contain little of mineralogical interest. Ores and gems congregate along faults and fractures, which have given access to mineralizing solutions rising from the depths; and in north Wales these features are aligned with the Caledonian and Armorican movements.[12]

There are veins of copper pyrite and galena (lead sulphide) near Dolgelley in Merionethshire and in the Snowdon massif and they often carry some malachite and azurite. These two colourful copper ores are recorded in the Gammalt Mine, near Ffestiniog, Merionethshire, and on Great Ormes Head, near Llandudno in Caernarvonshire.[31]

Clear quartz, or rock crystal, is a fairly common mineral, and, although most of the north Welsh quartz veins are tight and vugg-less, some fine crystals have come from Snowdon, where they are accompanied by adularia, a glassy variety of felspar. Half-inch 'pyramidal crystals', recalling the 'Buxton diamonds' of Derbyshire, have been extracted from the Bettws-y-coed and Bryn-eisteddfod mines, near Llanrwst, in Denbighshire, and I have heard tell of a cluster of amethysts found at an unspecified 'engineering site' in north Wales by Professor J. G. C. Anderson of Cardiff University.[25] Epidote occurs with calcite in the acid (elvan) dykes about Dolgelley and with pale-green cat's-eye quartz in the Pass of Llanberis. 'Magnificent crystals' of brookite, as well as anatase, varieties of titanium oxide which are chemically identical with rutile but differ from it and each other in crystalline habit (see p. 131), and small crystals of sphene have been found in a 'white quartz rock' at Fronolen near Tremadoc.[31] The Manchester Museum has crystals of axinite from Caernarvonshire, but the exact locality is not specified.[53]

Those quartz veins may be well worth looking at anyway, for they often contain gold, which though too scattered for commercial exploitation does occur in nuggets!

Of the massive forms of silica you may come across hornstone along the Menai Strait, jasper, chalcedony and agate on the north coast of the Lleyn Peninsula and in Anglesey, which also has glaucophane in the mica-schists and serpentine at the Parys copper mine and Bullock's quarry, while carnelian occurs on the coast of Flintshire.[31] The land in this county and the neighbouring Denbighshire is much faulted across the Caledonian trend and the Carboniferous Limestone forms westward scarps extending south into Shropshire across the border. These rocks contain lead and zinc lodes with colourless and purple fluorite as a gangue mineral, especially at the west end of the veins, near Minera, Halkyn Mountain, Pen-y-bryn and Coed Cymric.[21] The same ores, however, extend also as 'thin ribs' along joints and faults through Ordovician and Silurian rocks and lead used to be mined in the Llangynog district of Montgomeryshire, so that this list of localities need not be exhaustive. Lavas, basic dykes and acid stocks of this age are exposed in southern Denbighshire's Berwyn Mountains, and have their Carboniferous counterpart near Oswestry, in Salop, where malachite is found in Llanymynich Hill.

4.3 SALOP AND THE MIDLANDS

Salop, extending from the Teme to the Dee, is a geological, as well as ethnic, borderland. Its scenery is as varied as are its rocks. In the south, east and north of Ludlow, there is an inlier of Carboniferous Limestone and several basic intrusions of the same age in the Brown Clee Hills. To the north the undulating lowland of Church Stretton is hemmed in between the Longmynd escarpment of pre-Cambrian slates and the equally ancient volcanics of the Caer Caradoc ridge, whose Caledonian trend is continued towards Wellington by the hogbacks of Lawley and the Wrekin. There is a substantial outcrop of gneiss here, which, though, seems to be innocent of garnets or other gems. A striking scenic feature is the Wenlock Edge, a scarp of Silurian limestone laid straight like a ruler in alignment with the other ridges and cut by the spectacular Severn Gorge. Of more interest to us, however, is the Shelve district to the west of the Longmynd. It is much fractured, penetrated by igneous dykes and extensively mineralized. Its mines, initiated by the Romans, have yielded great amounts of lead and, later, some zinc, but have been largely abandoned in the present century.

The old dumps may well be worth exploring and the veins following into the hills beyond the diggings. The main offerings are rock crystal (e.g. at Snailbeach), chalcedony and malachite, the latter to be found at several mines.[42, 57] There is also some fluorite as a gangue mineral, although apparently not 'highly coloured'. Crystalline quartz is to be had in some of the igneous-rock quarries as well. There is no mention of amethyst or cairngorm in the mining records, but then nobody seems to know very much about the gem minerals of Shropshire, which leaves some room for modest surprises.

East of Shropshire lie Warwickshire and Staffordshire, a hive of industry in the shadow of its waste. Basic igneous rocks of Carboniferous age show up at the edges of the Coal Measures near Kidderminster and in the built-up areas of Birmingham and Wolverhampton—and so out of bounds, even if they contained anything of interest, which they do not. Yet much of Staffordshire has escaped overcrowding. The gravels about Lichfield in the east have yielded agates.[31] Northwards we move to Cannock Chase, a pleasant hilly and wooded land, mainly of Sandstone and marl, but along the Dove, beyond, our old friend, the Carboniferous Limestone comes over from Derbyshire in picturesque brown cliffs. Some fluorite may be expected here. It does, in fact, occur in the thin veins of galena that thread their way into Cheshire, farther west, where malachite and azurite may also be found in sandstone near Alderley Edge. I have, however, no record of fluorite in Staffordshire. On the other hand, Greg and Lettsom list azurite near Breaston, prehnite in the concretions of Ponck Hill and natrolite in the decomposed basalt dykes. Amethyst is known from the Calton Hill quarry and D. Rushton has seen small but distinct crystals of olivine in basalt there.[53]

The Cheshire plain of red marl has nothing much to offer, but north Staffordshire is a prelude to Derbyshire, remarkable for scenery and geology alike. The country round Derby itself does not differ from the adjacent areas of Staffordshire and Leicestershire, but beyond Ashbourne the Carboniferous Limestone, enveloped in the obdurate Millstone Grit, piles up into the dales and heights of the Peak District, attaining 2088 feet in Kinder Scout. The latter is carved out of grit, which tends to produce subdued heathery uplands and waterlogged bleak moors, perhaps not devoid of lonely beauty, but not as exciting as the bright limestone crags rising over the deep valleys with their complement of caves between Matlock and Buxton. Here, as elsewhere in the Pennines, the land dips gently to the east and breaks off in abrupt scarps on the west side, a tendency already noted in Flintshire.[64]

The Derbyshire limestone has been heavily injected with Carboniferous volcanics and mineralized. This is bluejohn country. Bluejohn is a massive, banded variety of purple, though sometimes yellow, fluorite, much used for ornamental objects, such as vases. It may have been known to the Romans. Indeed, some bluejohn articles have been found in Pompeii, but their origin is uncertain[6] and there appears to be no record of Roman mines in this part of England. Fluorite, or fluorspar, has, however, been mined in Derbyshire for ornamental purposes since 1775 or so, and great quantities of bluejohn have been extracted from the Blue John Mine near Castleton. This has been largely exhausted and become a tourist attraction, with its chains of caves and occasional pockets of fluorite, both of which extend to deeper levels, as yet untouched. The bluejohn industry, though, is not extinct and souvenirs and other articles of this material continue to be made locally on a small scale.[21]

Fluorite occurs in veins and larger bodies, mainly on the east side of the limestones, and, though typically purple, red, yellow, colourless and black varieties are also known from this county in high-temperature veins and in association with haematite. Rock crystal, fancifully described as 'Buxton diamond', has developed at contact with and within the 'toadstones'—which is a North Country name for the speckled lavas, predominently greyish-green in colour—near Buxton, Matlock and elsewhere. Good amethyst and smoky quartz (cairngorm and morion) have been found at Calton Hill, Waterswallows and some other localities. Chalcedony, agate and jasper fill the amygdaloidal cavities in the toadstones, notably in Cavedale and Monsal Dale, while opal occurs at the Glebe Mine near Eyam and in small pockets in the Bakewell Chert. The igneous rocks contain olivine, zircon, labradorite and serpentine. Malachite and azurite have been recorded at Matlock, Middleton, the Hassop Station Quarry and a few other places, with haematite and marcasite to complete the list.[28, 31]

4.4 NORTHERN ENGLAND

As we proceed farther north, the Millstone Grit and Coal Measures progressively yield to the carboniferous Limestone, which, with its caves, 'scaurs' and 'grikes', forms the bulk of the Pennines beyond Skipton, in Yorkshire. Although the Pennine chain runs roughly north and south, it originates primarily in the Armorican earth movements and consists of east-west segments, chopped up by faults ranged along and across this trend, as well as at right angles to the Caledonian foldings. Such fractures arise from the relief of stress when the main folding pressure subsides. A ragged strip of fault-bounded magnesian limestone of Permian age extends from Nottingham to Sunderland.

Igneous activity and mineralization increase northwards, where basic magmas have risen in dykes along the rock fractures or spread out horizontally between the strata as sills, the main complex of which is referred to as the Great Whin Sill, outcropping in the counties of Durham and Northumberland, and providing in the latter the steep escarpments on which Hadrian's Wall and Bamburgh Castle are perched. There are two volcanic complexes. In the Ordovician what is now the English Lake District was a very hot spot, where great floods of ash and lava, later reinforced by injections of granite in the Devonian, laid down the foundations of the Cumbrian Mountains, with their sharp pikes and gleaming 'meres' and 'waters'. In the north-east the Cheviot boss of pink granite, ringed by andesitic lavas, tuffs and dykes, marks the site of Devonian or pre-Devonian volcanoes and composes billowy panoramas scattered with occasional tors and cut by deep river gorges.[51] The Cheviot hills themseves fall in with the Caledonian lie of the land, prevalent throughout Scotland, save for east Berwickshire, which is geologically one with Northumberland.

Southwards along the coast the land is clothed in progressively younger strata. The Cleveland Hills and Yorkshire Moors are Jurassic limestone, geologically if not scenically comparable to that of the Cotswolds, and some way beyond Scarborough Cretaceous sediments take over. If we now jump over into the Irish Sea, Isle of Man is different again. It may be said to belong to Wales and recalls Merionethshire in structure; segmental acid dykes ranged along the Caledonian trend and some basic ones at right angles to it form a kind of grid, interspersed with minor outcrops of granite, in the high interior (Snaefell, 2034 feet), which is composed of Cambrian strata. But the northern tip is Triassic sandstone, and the Carboniferous Limestone shows up between Rue Point and Ramsey Bay and again near Castletown in the extreme south.

Such in rough outline is the geology of northern England.

Gemwise there is some amber along the North Sea coast, jasper and chalcedony pebbles on the beaches near Scarborough and Whitby, jasper being also found inland about York. Whitby, however, is best known for its jet, a soot-black compact kind of lignite which does not soil the hand and will take a dull polish. Being easy to fashion, jet beads were the favourite ornament of ancient Britons, and as mourning jewellery jet experienced a brief revival in the reign of Queen Victoria after the death of Prince Albert. On the whole, however, neither its colour nor texture commends it to the modern taste. Strafford and Roseberry are other Yorkshire jet localities, and yellow fluorite is present as a gangue mineral in lead veins and where limestone has been permeated by emanations from granite magmas as yet unrevealed by erosion in the north-west of the county.

Beautiful crystals of vari-coloured fluorite from the northern English mines grace the mineralogical collections of the world's museums, and, nearer home, of the British Museum at South Kensington and the City Museum in Carlisle.

Fluorite has industrial uses as a flux in steel manufacturing, as a source of hydrofluoric acid, in plating processes, and in the preparation of certain plastics and insecticides. It is also used in lenses to correct optical aberrations, which requires flawless crystalline material. Accordingly, it is mined on a large scale and the bulk of industrial fluorite comes from northern Derbyshire and Weardale in west Durham. The mineral, however, occurs in considerable amounts on both sides of the northern Pennines and more sparsely in the Magnesian limestone of east Durham, notably in the Chilton Quarry. It has also been mined near Ulverston, in Lancashire; Allenheads, in Northumberland; and Alston, in east Cumberland. In the two latter localities the prevailing colouring is purple, and a magnificent mass of purple fluorite with quartz from Alston can be seen at the Carlisle museum, which also has some beautiful sky-blue crystals from west Cumberland. The west Cumbrian fluorite may be green, yellow and pale or dark purple as well; it is associated with haematite and is found in sandstone. Veins of amber-coloured fluorite, up to two feet wide, have been encountered at the Force Crag and Brandlehow mines in the Lake District, but fluorite occurs in smaller quantities at many other localities, not only as a secondary metamorphic mineral in sedimentary, but also as an accessory constituent of acid igneous rocks.[21]

The rocks adjoining the dykes and sills have been more or less extensively metamorphosed, and various minerals have crystallized out in them and in the associated thermal veins. The latter often contain quartz, chalcedony, rutile, anatase and sphene. The Great Whin Sill is the most massive of these igneous bodies, and its metamorphic aureole is correspondingly wide, although nowhere over 100 feet. The sill may embody 'rafts' of country rock. Quartz, andalusite, diopside, idocrase, rutile and garnet are the usual aureole minerals, and in particular pale-yellow to near colourless grossular garnets have been recorded at Falcon Clints.[20] Greg and Lettsom refer to the sporadic occurrence of garnet in County Durham without qualification.[31]

Pale brown, blue and grey, 'delicately banded' chalcedony is present in the veins at the Groverake and Shildon mines. Quartz is massive or sugary for the most part, but clear rock crystal is not uncommon towards the middle of the fluorite zone, between Alston and Allenheads, at the latter in the form of double pyramids. Malachite and azurite are widespread in small amounts, and appear more massively in the copper veins of Tynehead and Crossgill. Marcasite may be found with pyrite in the Weardale fluorite veins.[20, 31]

It will be appreciated that most of this information comes from the mining records, concerned with industrial deposits rather than with collector's pieces, which are not necessarily to be found in one and the same place. If, however, any particular mineral is mentioned this means that it is there in considerable quantity, if not necessarily of gem quality. The area discussed here is extensive and sparsely populated, so that, while the spots of outstanding scenic beauty may attract a steady flow of visitors and are correspondingly well known, there is no shortage of bleak moors, left to winds and sheep, where interesting mineralogical finds may be made.

This would seem to apply more particularly to the Cheviot massif, whose heather moors are shunned for the more exciting sights. The granite here is traversed by siliceous dykes, 'consisting almost exclusively of crystals of quartz'.[51] Being harder than the country rock, the dykes often stand up above it like low walls, whence indeed the name 'dyke', so that they are easy to spot and follow. The best examples are to be found at Raker Crag above Carshope in the Upper Coquet valley. Such names as the Diamond Burn bear witness to the relative abundance of rock crystal. On D. A. Robson's authority, however, the coloured varieties of quartz and the accessory gems of granite (see Chapter 11) appear to be absent. On the other hand, I have seen at Dumfries a beautiful cluster of amethysts from the 'English border', and am inclined to suspect that a diligent search would reveal something beyond plain rock crystals. Indeed, I have heard of 'fine blue topaz' from Northumberland, although I have not been able to substantiate this information. At any rate it is difficult to imagine that the cavities in all those lavas, covering together with the main granite mass a total area of 400 square miles, partly in Scotland, contain no chalcedony, layered or unlayered, the more so as agates are to be found at Jedburgh in the corresponding rocks on the Scottish side of the complex.

4.5 LAKE DISTRICT AND ISLE OF MAN

The Lake District is at the opposite end of the scale. Almost everybody' including myself, has been there, and its mineralogical attractions are well catalogued. Even so the District sprawls over three counties: Cumberland, Westmorland and Lancashire, and some pikes and dales are 'more equal than others'. It so happens that the most interesting mineral localities are tucked well away from the beaten track. These are Shap Fell in Westmorland, and Cleator Moor and the Caldbeck Fells in Cumberland.[56]

The finest scenery is accounted for by the Borrowdale volcanic series of tuffs and lavas and the granite and granophyre intrusions of Eskdale and Ennerdale. The speckled lavas (toadstones) contain lilac grains of almandine garnet, which may attain pea size at the head of Wastwater and to the west and north-west of the Haweswater Reservoir. Various minerals, including beryl and epidote, have been recorded in the crags rising east of Derwentwater, where agates and carnelians have developed in the lava amygdales. Postlethwaite[44] mentions jasper in Castlerigg Fell near Keswick. All this is, no doubt, true, but I for one have not found anything very exciting there and such specimens found by others as I have seen did not amount to very much either. Still, it is lovely mountain country and makes a delightful excursion on a fine summer's day.

The Eskdale granites do not appear to have produced anything of note, but Cleator Moor at the west end of the Ennerdale intrusion is known for its smoky quartz (cairngorm). The main igneous mass is supposed to contain zircon and sphene, but I have neither seen nor heard of any sizable clear crystals of these. There are many other minor intrusive igneous bodies and dykes in this part of the mountain, but the most important of them is the boss of pink porphyritic granite in Shap Fell at the south-east end of the Borrowdale series. The Shap granite contains occasional areas of pegmatite with druses, where fine crystals of cairngorm, garnet and fluorspar may develop. Brown and green garnets (grossularite and andradite) reach a diameter of over two inches in the metamorphic aureole of the Shap Granite, but are mostly turbid.

In the northern area Skiddaw Slates and associated rocks have like-wise been penetrated by acid and basic magmas and mineralized. The map is dotted with disused mines. Quartz, colourless, ferruginous and yellow, may be picked up on many dumps. There is some malachite in Glenderaterra. Greg and Lettsom[31] mention brown garnets in the Skiddaw Slates of Saddleback (Blencathra) and near Keswick, tourma-line near Force Crag again on Saddleback, and ferruginous quartz on Skiddaw itself. Andalusite and chiastolite are to be found in the meta-morphic aureole of the Skiddaw granite.[56]

Farther north, the igneous complex and its associated veins in the Caldbeck Fells never fail to attract geologists and mineralogists. For-tunately perhaps, these hills are not too easy to reach without appro-priate private transport. The Wolfram or Carrock Mine is chiefly known for its scheelite, but it contains colourless, ferruginous and citrine quartz, tourmaline, green apatite, even blue corundum, though not of gem quality, and, of course, gold! as well. Across the hill towards Caldbeck, Roughtengill at the foot of Iron Crag is a weirdly fascinating place, where the volcanic wrath of long-ago has left a legacy of many-tinted crystals among the sad lonely hills. Malachite, sometimes of good compact kind, and chrysocolla are fairly common here and in other Caldbeck mines, even though the times when the Caldbeck Fells were 'worth all England's else' belong to story.[48]

A band of sandstone runs along the coast of the Irish sea, and, as already mentioned, haematite and fluorite of several hues may be found here. Quartz is fairly ubiquitous, and I am informed by Mrs Edith Constable[9] of Frizington that the amethyst variety occurs on St. Bees Head and in Fleswick Bay between St. Bees and Whitehaven. Pebbles of chalcedony, agate, carnelian, red, purple and yellow jasper are washed up on the shore from the glacial drift, and malachite may be picked up, too, although it is becoming scarce. Local lapidaries have used silicified banded volcanic ash, miscalled 'jasper', for brooches and ornamental objects. It takes a good polish, but the colour is rather dingy. Since, however, the ash bands between the layers of silica are highly absorbent, this stone may look very attractive if steeped in chemical dyes, as is often done with agates.

The riches of the Isle of Man are comparatively modest. Agate, carnelian, red and green jasper of glacial provenance is found on the northern beaches. At one time agate used to be obtained from the North Bradda Mine, but this source seems to have run dry. There is a pocket of conglomerate near Peel on the west coast, and the adjacent Peel Bay is well known for its carnelians.[30, 31]

So ends the story of southern Britain, although further particulars will be found in later chapters, dealing with individual gemstones.

5 Round the British Isles
Part 2, Scotland

If Caesar's British campaign had taken him as far north as Scotland he might have perceived that, like Gaul, she was divided into three parts— geologically. This might have been apparent to him, despite the fact that natural sciences had generally been neglected in classical antiquity and scientific geology was non-existent in his time. Rome was all civic, military, administrative and literary, washed wondrously with human tears and inscribed in resounding hexameters on marble tombs ... SENATVS POPVLVSQVE ROMANVS ...

It was left to the legions of Agricola and Vespasian to take the Imperial Eagles to Mons Graupius (the Grampians?) and beyond, to Moray Firth—and they built. The layout of the city of Perth is that of a Roman camp, with a *via praetoria* and a *via decumana*. But they built of wood and never quarried or mined beyond Hadrian's Wall. The chained slaves never scraped the ore with wooden shovels from dim galleries, lit by thick tapers with hempen wicks, as they did in Shropshire.

5.1 BIRD'S-EYE VIEW OF SCOTTISH GEOLOGY

So Caesar might have raised his stylus to write, *Caledonia est omnis divisa in partes tres*, and paused, not knowing what to say next, for, although this division is impressed on the scenery, the science of geology, as adumbrated, was only born less than 200 years ago, and largely in Britain, in which the granite 'Athens of the North' has played no mean part—shades of Murchison and Hutton.... There are the Southern Uplands, the Midland Valley and the Highlands, bounded by faults, along which the Earth's crust has shifted—up, down and side- ways, exposing different strata to the grind of erosion. The main faults all run south-west to north-east, as the winds blow, which, having tramped, climbed and skied over the 'Hielan' bens and glens for twelve years, I can feel in my bones. This, of course, is the trend of the great Caledonian folds (p. 24), and so the basic structure of the land was laid down in the Silurian, perhaps as far back as 400 million years. Seashores shifted, magma rose towards the surface and volcanoes burst out all over the place, blanketing hundreds and thousands of square miles with ash, lapilli and lava. This continued into the Devonian, or Old Red Sandstone, age, when vast masses of molten granite were intruded contemporaneously with those of the English Lake District and the Cheviot, under the overlying strata in the west of the Southern Uplands and in the Highlands. Formation of dykes and mineral veins followed. Hot alkalized solutions percolating through the porous lavas deposited in their cavities various minerals, but chiefly silica, either in the crystalline form of quartz or as massive chalcedony, often in concentric bands, forming agates or 'Scotch pebbles'. Mountains grew down, deserts came and went, leaving behind thicknesses of red sandstone and associated conglomerate, studded with the hard cavity-fillings eroded from the lavas.

Sometime towards the end of the Carboniferous and the beginning of the Permian the Armorican mountain-building spasm disturbed the old Caledonian fractures. Earthquakes shook the ground and the Midland Valley to-be sank into a trough, separating the Southern Uplands from the Highland block. These movements brought fissure eruptions and outpourings of basalt in Renfrewshire and Stirlingshire, as well as a rash of new volcanoes, especially in the south-east, where the friable mantles were stripped off the congealed magma of the feed pipes by the weather of ages, leaving them to stand up as 'volcanic necks' that often form those steep conical hills known as 'laws' in this part of the country. There was further intrusion, contact metamorphism and mineralization by hot fluids.

Giant horsetails and clubmosses flourished in the tropical jungles of the Clyde, the dinosaurs came to rule the world, then 'like an insubstantial pageant' faded into the boneyards of coal, marl and limestone. So ended the Era of Middle Life in the Cretaceous. Flowering plants, mammals and birds took over, and in the Miocene, about thirty million years from our times, new convulsions gripped the bowels of the Earth, raising from the deep sea-troughs thousands of feet of metamorphosed sediments into the Alpine ranges that now girdle the globe. The foldings did not extend to Britain, but the slumbering giants of Pluto's underground kingdom sprang to life once more.

The ground cracked open, releasing floods of basalt in Northern Ireland and the Western Isles. The volcanoes of Skye, Mull and Arran roared defiance to the skies, and swarms of dykes spread out of them into the Highlands and as far as the north of England, eventually to be revealed by erosion. This did not happen in a day; new species developed and died out; the same volcanic activity is still going on in Iceland. The poles shifted position, the climate grew colder, and about a million years ago the great Pleistocene Ice Age turned Britain into what Greenland is today. Inland glaciers, thousands of feet thick, sliced off the mountain-tops, deepened and broadened the valleys, dredged the beds of future lochs, and spread out the rubble of their

MILES
0   20   40
ACID INTRUSIONS
BASIC INTRUSIONS
LAVA FLOWS
SCHISTS
LIMESTONES
MAJOR FAULTS AND THRUSTS

Geological map of Scotland

progress in thick layers of glacial drift. It is not more than 5000 years since the last of the ice relinquished the Highland glens, after having gouged the corrie cauldrons, and left as its visiting card gleaming sheets of water among the undulating kames and drumlins, popularly called 'fairie knowes'. And in its wake came Man. But it is well to remember that there have been warm interglacial periods longer than the whole of his recorded history, all of it but a single breath in the long life of Mother Earth.

5.2   THE SOUTHERN UPLANDS

The Cheviot Hills divide the Southern Uplands from England, and in the north the Southern Upland Fault makes a clear geological boundary. South-eastward thereof a belt of Ordovician strata, up to twenty miles in width, leads to Silurian formations, which have much in common with those of Cardiganshire in Wales, except for the large granite bosses, reminiscent of Cornwall, in Kirkcudbrightshire and east Ayrshire, pockets of Permian desert sandstone and an abundance of minor igneous bodies. For the most part it is a gaunt, stern upland, split by the fertile river valleys into segmental hills, attaining 2764 feet in Merrick and 2754 feet in Broad Law. The valley of the Tweed in the east has a more variegated geology, mainly of Devonian and Carboniferous provenance, scattered with volcanic necks and patches of lava.

MacCallien in *Scottish Gem Stones*[37] has little to say about the Southern Uplands, and it may well be that other parts of Scotland are more pleasing to the eye and mineralogically more rewarding. In fact, he lists only zircon in the granite boulders of the Burn of Palnure, west of Cairnsmuir, and also at the edge of the Shaw Hill granite boss, which is about the size of Bodmin Moor and whence these boulders have presumably been derived; tourmaline in Knocknairling Hill, near New Galloway, on the other side of the same granite mass; and amethyst near Needle's Eye. All of these places are in Kirkcudbrightshire. Yet the geology of this and other Upland counties clearly shows that this account could not possibly be exhaustive. Indeed, Greg and Lettsom[31] mention malachite at Castle Douglas and sphene 'in distinct crystals' with allanite in the felspathic granite of the Criffel Hills near New Abbey. This is an even larger granite intrusion in the south of the same county, and presumably the occurrence of sphene is not limited to this one spot. One must also expect at least rock crystal. The Museum at Dumfries has good amethyst from Glen Burn near New Abbey, as well as some massive amethystine quartz from Southwick, Kipford and Brittle. There is also cairngorm from Kinharvie, jasper and agate from the same locality, and from Sowie's Pot, at Langholm in eastern Dumfries-shire.

Haematite from Achincairn, at the south-west end of the Criffel granite, may also deserve mention.

The Wanlockhead-Leadhills district on the border of Dumfries-shire and Lanarkshire, where gold was once mined, is among the fluorite localities listed in the Geological Survey memoir on *Fluorspar*.[21] The fluorite from this area in the Dumfries Museum is hardly a patch on the magnificent material from north England, but shows that it is there. So, too, is malachite and azurite, often well crystallized, and blue and yellow hemimorphite, which though not usually considered a gemstone, is a grade harder than fluorite and quite attractive, as may be seen from the specimens at the Royal Scottish Museum in Edinburgh. Recently rhodonite has been found in the Leadhills.

The eastern counties contain, as expected, some agate, recorded at Jedburgh, Roxburghshire, and at Carlops in north Peebleshire, which though is already within the Midland Valley, also chalcedony at Allan Bank in east Berwickshire.

5.3 THE MIDLAND VALLEY

The Southern Uplands are chopped off quite sharply by the Southern Upland Fault, running almost straight from the northern tip of the Galloway peninsula to Dunbar on the North Sea, through the counties of Ayr, Lanark, Peebles, Midlothian and East Lothian. Beyond it we enter the Midland Valley, which, though a geological valley, is no plain and includes a good deal of high heathery or grassy ground, attaining its uppermost point of 2335 feet, in Tinto Hill near Lanark, just across the Fault. There are also several chains of individualized hills: the Pentlands near Edinburgh, the Campsie Fells north of Glasgow, the Ochils between Stirling and Perth, and the Sidlaws north-east of the latter. Yet their stature falls well short of Archibald Geikie's 'High Plateau', from which the Highlands have been carved. Indeed, viewed from the Lowlands about Stirling, the land beyond the Highland Boundary Fault stands on the horizon like a blue castellated wall.

The Highland Boundary Fault is a clear-cut geological line, drawn from near Helensburgh in Dunbartonshire to Stonehaven in Kincardine-shire and cutting in half the islands of Bute and Arran in the Firth of Clyde. The Tertiary granites of Arran look to the Mountains of Mourne in Ulster for their nearest geological counterpart, but the rest of the island is one with the Midland uplands. The division crosses the counties of Bute, Dunbarton, Stirling, Perth, Angus and Kincardine.

On a geological map the Midland Valley is as colourful as a clan plaid, which is a sure sign of mineral riches. Ordovician strata encroach on southern Ayrshire and there is a block of Silurian rocks in mid Lanarkshire and thereabouts. For the rest, however, the surface of the land is substantially Carboniferous with Old Red Sandstone lavas, sandstones and conglomerates round the edges, and especially in the north and north-west.

Scotland has been described as the 'geological epitome of the world', and we can find almost any kind of rock within the Midland Valley. We have here the Carboniferous (Mountain) Limestone, Millstone Grit and Coal Measures as in the north of England, but in penny packets and intercalated with large stretches of Carboniferous basalt and all manner of tuff and lava, as well as injected much more thickly, if not more massively, with igneous intrusions. These are almost exclusively basic, some rare ultrabasic formations peeping out in south-western Ayrshire. In fact, Arran apart, there is only one bit of granite of any size, near Darvel, on the eastern border of Ayrshire.

Thus the general situation is very promising, but many areas are densely populated, built up or cultivated, which somewhat cramps the gem-hunter's style. There is no law of trespass in Scotland, and such notices 'Trespassers will be Prosecuted' as may occasionally be encountered are meaningless, accordingly. Yet the right of entry as such does not include the right to remove minerals, which may raise a legal point, and in any case it is both prudent and courteous to ask for permission to enter privately owned land, though access to heaths, hills and the seashore is generally free to all. Quarries and other excavations often reveal otherwise inaccessible rocks, which may also appear in section in gorges or riverbanks.

Wherever the Old Red Sandstone lavas or conglomerates outcrop you may confidently expect agates and other forms of chalcedony, perhaps opal and crystalline quartz, coloured or uncoloured, in geodes. The sea cliffs and beaches anywhere south of Stonehaven, and about Montrose in particular, the Firth of Tay and parts of the inland Perthshire, the Sidlaws and the Ochils, which are largely Old Red Sandstone lava, afford a good hunting ground for 'Scotch pebbles'. Heddle[33] mentions those from the Agate Knowe near Inchture as outstandingly beautiful. The same rocks, however, reappear in Ayrshire, for instance, at Burn Anne near Galston, and on the Dunure beaches, in Arran, in the Pentlands and farther south-west along the Southern Upland border. The Carboniferous lavas are not barren either, and there are agates near Kinross in Fife, at Dunbar and Dunglass in East Lothian, on the Kilsyth and Campsie Fells near Glasgow and on the Renfrewshire uplands.[31, 37] The agate localities are too numerous to be listed, and the best plan is to follow the geological map in the light of local enquiries, judiciously made (they may sometimes be misleading).

Also associated with Carboniferous lavas are two minerals of the zeolite family: natrolite and prehnite, which have been recorded at Bishopstown and on Hartfield Moss in Renfrewshire, and prehnite near

Beith in the adjacent part of north Ayrshire. These rocks may also contain garnet, as they do in the southern part of the Isle of Bute, which boasts some prase in quartz veins and a little jet as well. Ayrshire limestones about Beith, Lugton and Dunlop have some fluorite to offer, and amethyst occurs at Catburn, Largs, on the west side of Kaim Hill and near Galston, the already mentioned agate locality, which also has milk opal further south. Some minute diamonds have formed by contact metamorphism in a coal seam near New Cumnock, and the ultrabasic rocks at the south end of the county have been partly altered to serpentine.

Arran is something of a scenic and geological gem,[23, 69] containing within its miniature compass almost every rock and type of structure Scotland has to offer and attracting geological parties from universities all over Great Britain. The String Road between Brodick and Machrie may be taken as the boundary of the southern 'Lowland' part of the island, which is largely a high heathery or boggy plateau, chivvied by seaward glens and flanked by raised beaches. The rocks are chiefly Carboniferous and Permian sandstones and lavas with basic intrusions, and a Tertiary volcanic ring of granite and gabbro just below The String. Amethyst and rock crystal have formed in sandstone at contact with the magma in Glen Cloy, near Lamlash and Drumadoon, but I have also come across an amethyst vein in the northern granite. The Old Red Sandstone and Carboniferous conglomerates contain agates, carnelian, milk opal and red jasper in both parts of the island. Above the String, however, a Tertiary granite has pierced Dalradian schists and been carved into craggy mountains of great scenic beauty (Goatfell, 2866 feet). The granite is vuggy and contains a good deal of cairngorm or smoky quartz, often markedly dichroic with a violet tone in transmitted light, some blue and blue-green beryl (aquamarine), as well as colourless or honey-tinted topaz. Almandine garnet has likewise been recorded. I have, however, found neither topaz nor garnet, and only very few and small, though flawless, beryls. Greg and Lettsom mention epidote.[31] Small crystals of sapphire have been discovered in the hornfels formed in Glen Rosa, near Brodick, at the contact of the Dalradian rocks with the granite, but are generally full of flaws and inclusions and unsuitable for jewellery.

Moving up the Firth of Clyde we come to Gourock at the northernmost tip of Renfrewshire, where a porphyry quarry deserves attention. It has yielded cairngorm and amethyst, as well as fluorite in purple, emerald-green, honey-yellow, pink and 'rarely' colourless cubes and octahedra. Amethyst has also been found near Lochwinnoch, in the Linthills and on the Lairdside. In the neighbouring Dunbartonshire fluorite occurs at Dumbarton as purple and deep-green cubes with calcite in greenstone cavities. There is also natrolite and prehnite, the former at Bowling and on Dumbarton Moor; the latter at Cochayn,

Duntocher and Old Kilpatrick. The Campsie Fells of Stirlingshire are again Carboniferous basalt and contain natrolite, while amethyst has been recorded between these hills and Flinty and near Cathcart Castle.[21, 31, 33, 37]

As we pass eastwards into the Lothians there are more records of amethyst quartz—from Corstorphine Hill, Craiglockhart Quarry, Blackford Hill Quarry, Southferry and opposite Bass Rock at North Berwick, most of which are within easy reach of Edinburgh and must have been extensively searched. Olivine is present in the rocks of Arthur's Seat and natrolite in the Braid Hills.[31] Azurite from the Torduff Reservoir in the Pentlands may be seen at the Royal Scottish Museum in Edinburgh.

Across the Firth of Forth, the 'Kingdom of Fife' is famed for 'Elie rubies', which are fine red pyrope garnets from a Carboniferous volcanic filling at Elie Ness, also containing zircon. Newburgh, Pettycur and Burntisland in the same county are listed for amethyst and the Royal Scottish Museum has a fine dark specimen from Heather Hill, near Luthrie. At Burntisland natrolite may be found in a basic tuff known locally as 'Blin'. Glenfarg is another natrolite locality, which has yielded some fine crystals of a flesh-pink colour, as well as some fluorite.[31] In fact, according to A. Geikie's *Geology of Central and Western Fife and Kinross*,[71] fluorite occurs in nests and veins in the volcanic rocks.

The Lowland Perthshire is known chiefly for its agates, chalcedonies and jaspers; milk opal may be found in Peeble Knowe, Ballindean. In Angus tourmaline is found near Loch Bandy and White Catterhun near Brechin. Cairngorm and amethyst occur with agates in the Lunnan Bay and the Craig Quarry south of Montrose, where girasol opal may also be looked for. In Kincardineshire amethyst has been recorded at Long Gallery and tourmaline at Torry and the Stoney Hill of Bigg, and so we reach the Highland line beyond Stonehaven Bay, where epidote occurs in long crystals in puddingstone.

5.4   BEYOND THE HIGHLAND BOUNDARY FAULT

The geological Highlands are not all high ground. All round the coast from Stonehaven to the Moray Firth there is a wide belt of lowland, which historically and scenically belongs with the Midland Valley, and even farther north, about Wick and Thurso, to say nothing of the broad glacial straths (flat valleys) along the main rivers, the bens recede into the background. Yet, high or low, the country rock is typically metamorphic, Dalradian and Moinian schists with their associated limestones, intruded by large masses of granite and some diorite in the Grampian Mountains,[50] which sprawl somewhat amorphously between the Highland Boundary Fault and the Great Glen. Indeed, these mountains are so-called *monadnocks*, or segmentary heights isolated from a high plateau by the streams and glaciers of the Ice Age. The plateau has been differentially affected by erosion and lofts up highest in the resistant igneous bosses, but is clearly recognizable in distant panoramas, where all the peaks approximate to the same level. Characteristically they are flat-topped, though steep on the sides and precipitous within the corrie cauldrons, which often cradle a lochan (tarn) or two.

These features are best illustrated by the Cairngorms, which straddle the counties of Inverness, Aberdeen and Banff and comprise the largest compact area of high ground in the British Isles (200 square miles over 2000 feet above sea level), although their highest point, Ben Macdhui, at 4300 feet falls somewhat short of the lonelier volcanic peak of Ben Nevis (4406 feet) at the west end of the Great Glen (Glen Mor).[68, 70, 72]

The Atlantic winds range freely over these subarctic heights, and the breath of the Ice Age still hangs over the gleaming waters and the lonely vastness of Rannoch Moor or Loch Ericht. In fine weather one can roam footloose as far as the eye and the legs will carry, but a high-top trek may become a grim survival test in bad weather, so keep your map and compass handy.

The Grampian granites are generally classed as Devonian (Old Red Sandstone) and volcanic activity of this age has left its mark on the Western Highlands about Loch Etive, the cauldron subsidence of Glen Coe, held to be an eroded remnant of a quasi-lunar crater, and Ben Nevis. A large area of andesitic tuff and lava recalls the Midland Valley, and the whole is seamed by intersecting Permian and Tertiary dykes.

The latter stem from the Alpine volcanic 'episode' in Arran, Mull, Morven, Ardnamurchan, Skye and the intervening lesser isles, which together with north-west Ireland belong to the Thulean Province, including Iceland and Greenland and characterized by enormous flows of basalt and igneous intrusions. This disturbance occurred within a very ancient land mass, largely engulfed by the ocean and represented in the North-West Highlands and the Outer Hebrides. The country rocks of Lewis, Uist and the coastal strip of the North-West Highlands from the Sound of Sleat to Cape Wrath are pre-Cambrian gneisses and foliated granites radioactively dated at some 2000 million years and assigned vaguely to a 'Lewisian period'. They compose barren hummocky landscapes, interspersed with sheets of water, thinly lined with alluvium and padded with glacial drift, over which on the mainland the later red and grey Torridonian sandstones rise into precipitous stacks, crowned by gleaming white quartzite, up to well over 3000 feet. Swarms of basic and ultrabasic dykes, which have sprung from some volcanoes lost in the hoary mist of geological antiquity and been turned to hornblende-

schist, strike west-north-west and east-south-east across the gneiss base-
ment. Landwards the 'province' is bounded by Cambrian limestones
with igneous intrusions.

There are more granite bosses in Ross and Cromarty, Sutherland and
Caithness, whose unpopulous interiors still await, as does that of northern
Inverness-shire, a detailed geological survey. The age of these intrusions is probably Old Red, and corresponding sediments, including thin
slivers or Jurassic and Triassic rocks, make up most of the northern and
parts of the southern shorelands of the Moray Firth, as well as the
Orkneys and Fair Isle. Farther north the Shetlands resemble Banffshire
in their geological liquorice-all-sorts.

5.5   BELOW THE GREAT GLEN

The Grampian Highlands[24, 50] provide a classic example of regional
metamorphism, which intensifies away from the Highland Boundary
Fault, but the situation is complicated by the metamorphic aureoles
(p. 15) of the numerous igneous masses and by overthrusts where rock
strata have been pushed over one another, often over distances of many
miles. The matter of metamorphic minerals is considered in more
detail in Chapter 12, but these are typically almandine garnet, staurolite,
sillimanite and kyanite, and locally tourmaline, diopside and idocrase.
Quartz is ubiquitous in veins and minor bodies, mainly coarse and
opaque, but sometimes crystalline and coloured.

It is, of course, also present in the granites, usually in the smoky
variety as cairngorm or morion. In fact, the name *cairngorm* comes from
the Cairngorm Mountains, where single crystals exceeding fifty pounds
in weight have been found. The granites contain their share of accessory
minerals, such as topaz, beryl, spodumene and tourmaline (see Chapter
11). The volcanics have their expected complement of chalcedony,
agate, jasper and opal, as well as crystalline quartz and a few rarer
minerals, while contact metamorphism has given rise to further gemstones. Serpentine is formed by the alteration of basic rocks rich in
magnesia, but also in limestones, where it hobnobs with marble, and
in schists. Fluorite occurs at many places, in good quality and colour, but
generally in quantities unsuitable for commercial exploitation,[21] which
from our point of view is just as well.

County-wise we will follow our usual plan and start in the south-west
with Argyll, where our first call is at the long peninsula of Kintyre,
which in the days 'when Lochlin ploughed the billowy way' the wily
King Harold Barefoot, having had his galley trundled on wheeled
trestles over the isthmus of Tarbert, claimed as an island. It thus became part of the Hebrides.

Agate and chalcedony are to be found on many beaches, and Greg and

Lettsom single out the Mull of Kintyre for fine rock crystal in lava cavities. Farther north some desirable stones appear to be crowded in the area of Machrihanish and Campbeltown, including yellow topaz in boulders near the former and amethyst, cairngorm and girasol opal, red in transmitted light, in drusy cavities near the latter. Crystalline quartz is, of course, quite widespread, but that from the mica-schist at the head of Holy Loch deserves special notice for its unusual form. It occurs in pseudo-cubes (main faces stand to each other at an angle of 94° 15′—see p. 90), either plain or with minor facets at the tips.[31] Some twenty years ago I was privileged to see the collection of the late Archibald Cook at Corrygills near Brodrick, in the Isle of Arran, shortly before his death. The collection included a cluster of lilac 'cubes', which I mistook for fluorite, but was told were amethysts. I cannot be sure where they had come from, but it may have been the same locality.

Garnets are scattered generously through the hornblende schists and mica-schists of Argyll and Perthshire, but vary greatly in size, quality and composition, which shades from the red almandine into brown andradite, from place to place. Most of the largest stones have been fractured by land movements and resealed with silica,[24] but apparently there are some good ones near Pitlochry, and after the rain sand-grain-sized almandines shine like rubies in the wet rocks of the Braes of Balquhidder. I have had one or two pea-size Perthshire garnets cut. In Argyll good almandine is to be had at the summit of Ben Resipol above Loch Sunart,[31] whither we shall have occasion to return shortly. A jeweller in Oban showed me a boxful of clear waterworn garnets, blood-red to purple in colour, and I have a couple of these, but cannot pin-point their place of origin.

Oban is the gateway to the Isle of Mull, noteworthy not only for the Tobermory wrecks, but also for its geology and mineralogy. The town is a port of call for American cruise ships, in honour of which Shipton's of Birmingham have on the waterfront an impressive gem shop, resplendent with every colour known and unknown to the rainbow, but I would reserve judgment with regard to the authenticity of some local specimens on display. However, the winged Isle of Mull was a hot place in the Tertiary. The hinterland of Oban itself is andesitic tuff and lava, and these reappear patchily on the island, most of which is basalt, as is the nearer part of Morven across the Sound of Mull. Staffa with Fingal's Cave is not far behind. Ben More (3169 feet) marks the highest point of the volcanic complex of Mull, with its assortment of quasi-lunar ring-dykes, acid, intermediate and basic intrusions.

In the Ross of Mull you can look for agates, tourmaline, acicular (i.e. needle-shaped) epidote with prehnite and other zeolites in lava amygdales (cavities), and for blue crystals of kyanite up to three inches long.[37] But perhaps the greatest attraction of Mull, Morven and Ardnamurchan farther north is sapphire, which has crystallized in thin hexagonal plates in the rocks invaded and enveloped by basic magma (of which more in Chapter 9).

Iona, St. Columba's holy island, and Tiree farther out to sea have serpentine marbles, and zircon has been located on the latter. It is also known from Strontian, which has given the name to the element strontium, by Loch Sunart on the mainland. It lies within a large granite mass which extends southwards to Loch Linnhe and contains fluorite as an accessory mineral and in lode gangues. There is more granite around Loch Etive, the lower Glen Coe and A'Chruach, spilling over into Rannoch Moor in Perthshire and to Loch Laggan beyond the Inverness border, but all this area seems to be blanketed with silence in mineralogical records, except for some vague references to cairngorms. Greg and Lettsom[31] mention rosettes of tiny crystals of brilliantly red transparent epidote of the variety known as withamite, present also in massive form, in Glen Coe, but this is all I have been able to discover.

Tourmaline is recorded in Glen Finart and on the south-west slopes of Ben a'Chabair, as well as in Glen Falloch and the south-east corrie of Beinn a'Chaisteil, a Perthshire sentinel height looking towards Glen Coe across Rannoch Moor. There is also some tourmaline near Dunkeld, just within the Highland line in the east of the county. I have passed through Glen Falloch and over Ben a'Chabair, but in too much of a hurry for more than a perfunctory look at their rocks. Just west of the glen, in Argyll, the granite stock of Garrabal Hill is said to contain zircon, but of what quality or size I have no idea. Large garnets, up to and over an inch across, may be found on Cruach Ardrain above Crianlarich, but all seem to be badly flawed.

Idocrase occurs in the Loch Tay limestones, which also contain garnets, and I suspect diopside, but I have no record of this.

Broad quartz veins thread their white way across the schists of Creag na Caillich above Killin, and according to the local guidebook are 'famed for their beautiful cairngorms'. The source of this statement is, no doubt, to be sought in the activities of Henry Horwood, a native of Somerset and a skilled lapidary, who held the Killin Post Office Stores between 1883 and 1930 and always had a few brooches mounted with his finds on display.[24] In any event I have had no luck with cairngorms on Creag na Caillich, and am inclined to think that Rannoch Moor, especially in its western part, would make a happier hunting ground for these and possibly for beryl and topaz. In fact, beryl without qualification has been recorded at Kinloch Rannoch. On the other hand, on Creag na Caillich I have come across Venus' hairstone, a wiry form of rutile which looks like reddish blond hair slightly touched with the frost of age (I used to think goddesses never aged, but one cannot believe anything these days), and some *flèches d'amour* of the same material piercing glass-clear quartz of the colour of heavily baptized burgundy. Apparently yellow sphene is there, too—decomposed.

Speaking of Kinloch Rannoch, MacCallien[37] mentions finding 'beautiful blue kyanite in the schists between Kinloch Rannoch and Trinafour (on the road to Struan) where it has been segregated out of the schists themselves into quartz-veins'. Continuing east, we reach Glen Tilt and the fault of that ilk, along which limestone outcrops and near Marble Lodge contains inclusions of serpentine, while farther up, on the east side, by Beinn a'Ghlo, fluorite may be found in red cubes. At the summit of this mountain kyanite occurs in quartz veins. So 'we'll pass Glen Tilt afore the nicht' and enter Royal Deeside under the aegis of Aberdeen.

Here it is mainly granite country, with a chain of large and some smaller 'bosses', extending from Speyside in the county of Inverness, through southern Banffshire to as far east as Aberdeen and to the northern fringes of Perthshire and into Kincardineshire. The intervening rocks are chiefly quartzose schists with some quartzite, limestone, diorite and 'greenstone' (i.e. schistose rocks derived by metamorphism from old basic formations) thrown in for good measure. The granites form the backbone of the Grampians and are responsible for the rugged mountain features of Lochnagar and the Cairngorms (p. 35).[50] Citrine, cairngorm and morion are widespread throughout these granites. The localities are too numerous to list, and the Peterhead granite, which is credited with spodumene,* in north-east Aberdeenshire must be included in the count.

In the reign of Queen Victoria, during the so-called 'Balmoral period', cairngorm stones became very fashionable, and promising veins and boulder-screes in the mountains of this name were regularly mined for these. According to the Rev. J. Stewart as much as ten hundred-weights of cairngorm were once extracted from a single cavity.[31] An equally rich find would be difficult today, as the more obvious spots have been worked bare, but floods, the movement of screes and land-slides, to say nothing of quarrying, continuously expose new layers of rock, and in any case the area is so large that nobody could have possibly examined it all at any time. Oddly enough, sardonyx is said to occur on the south-west side of Cairngorm and on the summit of Braeriach, although I cannot say I have ever seen any there. On the other hand, I have come across some khaki-coloured banded silica in quartz veins in the eastern Cairngorms. Beryl, usually green and sometimes in the form of emerald, but occasionally multicoloured, is found sparsely in the Cairngorm Mountains, as is topaz, which is characteristically sky-blue, but may also be 'wine-yellow', colourless, green or reddish-brown.

* The Royal Scottish Museum in Edinburgh has been unable to confirm this report.

Once more different colours may be present in the same crystal, though I have never seen any such myself. Single crystals exceeding a foot in length are not unknown.[33, 37]

The Rubislaw quarry (Aberdeenshire) has yielded some large yellow beryls, as well as garnet and tourmaline, which also occur in the Cairngorms (green-black and red). The Pass of Ballater on Deeside is likewise quoted for yellow beryl, and in Inverness-shire yellow-green beryl, usually turbid, zircon, tourmaline and almandine garnet may be found near Struy Bridge, though the original site Heddle[33] records is very difficult to locate.

Tourmaline, as a rule in the black non-gem form of schorl, is not uncommon in this area, but Clashnarae Hill in Glen Clova may be singled out in this context, for it contains garnet and, according to Heddle,[33] minute crystals, about one-thirtieth of an inch long, of sapphire as well.

The Royal Scottish Museum has some idocrase from Aberdeenshire, most probably from Glen Cairn, where it occurs together with calcium-aluminium garnet that may assume either the guise of honey-yellow cinammon-stone or of pale olive-green grossular (see p. 109). The Dalnabo quarry in Glen Gairn is referred to in this connection. The Crathie quarry, Creag Mhor and Lean Gorm near Balmoral on Deeside, Ord Bàn above Loch an Eilein near Aviemore and the Achnagonalin quarry east of Grantown on Speyside, are listed as garnet localities. Greg and Lettsom[31] speak of sphene at Aviemore, which they place, rather disconcertingly, together with Freeburn in Morayshire (Elgin). Apatite is said to occur in Glen Dee, which is almost equally vague, but then it is a frequent accessory of granite; also in the parish of Kildrummy, where it is found in porphyry.

Northwards, in Banffshire and Aberdeenshire, cinnamon-stone is replaced by a heather-coloured almandine in mica-schists. Geometrically well-shaped (euhedral) crystals over an inch across are not unusual, but for the most part this is an empty show and they are like sand inside. Knock Hill, however, about halfway between Keith and Portsoy, is said to have produced some good almandines. Greg and Lettsom[31] mention several places about Huntly for both types of garnet, including garnets of a 'dark red colour and translucent' in conglomerate at Huntly (Aberdeenshire) itself.

Fluorite is another gemstone found in the local limestones, notably in the quarry at Crathie and in the Muir quarry, near Ballater House, at Abergairn and near Aboyne along the Dee, as well as in Glen Muick (blue). As we move north, we find some more of it in a fault-breccia between Inchrory and Tomintoul, at the Ardonato quarry (purple) near Ardonald, Maisley quarry near Keith and the Burn of Boharm, which also sports grossular, in Banffshire. In Morayshire, blue and green fluorite crystals are known from Inverugie and yellow and red ones from the Findlassie sandstone quarry. The Triassic rocks about Elgin contain a high proportion of this mineral as a replacement. There is, further, a report of 'fine blue crystals' at the Murdoch Head granite quarry, four miles south of Peterhead.[21] Returning to Banffshire, there is tourmaline east of Whitehills and near Portsoy, where it hobnobs with cinammon-stone. The coast near Portsoy is regularly invaded in the search for serpentinite and hornstone, but the same rocks thread their way inland towards Knock Hill and continue outcropping intermittently between Huntly and Bridgend and as far south as the neighbourhood of Strathdon, with minor bodies near Grantown-on-Spey and on the sides of The Buck Hill in Aberdeenshire.

To be found in the latter area is also rose quartz, otherwise rare in the British Isles. The Royal Scottish Museum has some in crystal form from Black Middens near Rhynie. Kildrummy, Auchindoir and Glenbuchat in the area of greenstone rocks are the other promising places.[31]

Amethyst is not plentiful. In fact, there is a kind of antipathy between it and cairngorm, and they seldom go together. But it occurs on the south side of Brindy Hill, in Aberdeenshire, and in the Cairngorms. The next amethyst locality is way in the west, by Loch Morar, the deepest of the freshwater lochs of Scotland, where the crystals have a 'delicate pink tint', described by Heddle as 'surpassingly beautiful'.

5.6 WEST AND NORTH OF THE GREAT GLEN

Sphene occurs on the south side of Loch Ness and at Culloden of the grim battle fame, as well as on Ben Nevis in the 'lofty Lochaber'. There is beryl in Knoydart (p. 97) and epidote and spinel (p. 115) at Glenelg and in the Isle of Skye across the water.[41] *Sky-öya*, Isle of Cloud, is ruled from Inverness and starts off with Torridonian sandstone and Lewisian gneiss, but the bulk of it is Tertiary volcanics with two large intrusive bodies, of gabbro with some dunite in the 'Black Cuillin' and of granite in the 'Red Cuillin'. The subdued skylines of the Red Cuillins can hardly compete with 'the dark Cuillins', which with their sharp ridges, bold precipices and peaks attaining 3167 feet in Sgùrr nan Gillean have 'cast their love' on the climbing fraternity; but they have cairngorms to offer, also found in the north of Rona (the largely granite Raasay is not included, which may be an oversight). There is granite along the north-west coast of Skye as well. The Black Cuillin, on the other hand, has only some prehnite, which usually goes with natrolite (not recorded), somewhat dubious spinel and good crystals of green augite, which is not reckoned a gemstone.

In the Skye lavas there are agates, jasp opal south of the Stack of Tallisker in the west, some epidote, serpentine and onyx,[37] which is simply agate horizontally banded in black and white. The variety where the bands are red, brown and white, called sardonyx, is to be found on Sgùrr Mòr on the Isle of Rum, which is centred on a sizable outcrop of ultrabasic rock (olivine?). There is nothing on Eigg, it seems, which is a rum do, for its geology resembles that of northern Skye, but Scalpay is credited with zircon. Idocrase is found between Broadford and Kilbride in the east of Skye.

If we set sail for Lewis we will come about halfway up, on the little island of Shiant, which is chiefly diorite and holds some rose quartz. The southernmost part of Lewis goes by the name of Harris, is known for its tweeds and belongs to Inverness. Gemmologically it has some olivine and zircon, encountered in gneiss druses, and all Lewisian gneisses contain garnet and cordierite. Brann a'Bharra, half a mile north of Ballalan on Loch Erisort in Lewis, is recommended for zircon. Greg and Lettsom[31] refer to topaz 'in fine crystals' in the Harris druses, which MacCallien does not mention, though he lists 'white beryl' on Chapavall.

Having found or not some worthwhile zircons, we may now cross the North Minch to the mainland, and so for the lonely beauty of the North-Western Highlands, where the late sunset glows crimson on the battlements of Torridonian sandstone as white horses ride over the deep-blue sea. The *Geological Map of Great Britain, Sheet 1*, leaves significant gaps in Western Inverness-shire and the adjacent parts of Ross and Cromarty, which have not been surveyed in detail; but even in the areas farther north which have so been dykes appear in tiny snippets that are somewhat suspect, and minor detail is noticeably thicker near the coasts and roads than deeper inland. Reports of minerals tend to show a similar preference, so here we have miles and miles of rough heath and mountain land, which, if not exactly virgin, still has a few secrets to yield to the enquiring and the dogged.

However, the divide is the Great Glen between Loch Linnhe and Loch Ness, leading to the Moray Firth, where the two parts of the Highland block have slid past each other along a fault that occasionally still wakes up to a minor earthquake. North-west of the line near Milton in Glen Urquhart there is some serpentine and zircon, kyanite in 'bladed blue crystals, nearly half an inch in length' at Gortally, and andalusite in clear crystals on An Cruachan.[44] These are joined by fluorite by Loch Bhrucheach farther north,[21] thenceforth—silence, broken by the voice of Greg and Lettsom[31] announcing the presence of grass-green apatite in quartz in Ross-shire. The proverbial needle in a haystack can't compare! Serpentine is also listed without localities, and may possibly be looked for in the Cambrian limestones bordering on the Torridonian.

Far in the west, where the Five Sisters of Kintail rear their conical heads, zircon may be found on Mam Ratagan by Loch Duich. It is also present deep inland, in Glensgaich near Achnasheen and in granite boulders at the head of Allt Graad by Kiltearn on Loch Glass in the east of the county. There is tourmaline as well on the south side of Loch Luichart in Glensgaich, where crystals may reach half an inch. By Loch Hourn and in Strathfarran, across the border in Inverness-shire, however, they are twice as big, to reach five inches in the Loch Fannich district of mid-Ross, where we can also look for amethyst on the south slopes of Meallan Rairigidh.[31, 33, 37]

Garnets may be expected in the mica-schists and gneisses, and according to Greg and Lettsom[31] are 'common in Ross-shire granites'. Cinnamon-stone is mentioned near Kincardine in the north-east, while almandine occurs in granite (not shown on the map) near Strathpeffer, not far from Dingwall in the south-east, and westwards, where according to Heddle a five-inch crystal was found in a railway cutting at Glensgaich.[33] A quarry half a mile north of Achnasheen and the hills north and south of Clunie Inn are also listed. This is not far south of Loch Fannich as the crow flies, and the rocks are mica-schist.

From there it is not a long way to Kinlochewe to the north, where blue fluorite occurs in veins in Lewisian gneiss in Glen Logan and thereabouts. It has also been reported from the area between Jeantown and Kishorn on Loch Carron and the Abriachan granite quarry. It occurs 'as a rare accessory mineral in biotite-granite augen gneiss' on the east side of Carn Chuinneag.[21]

The overall geology and topography of Sutherland is closely comparable to that of Ross and Cromarty, but there is rather more acid igneous rock in the east along the Caithness border, and Norse place-names begin to oust the Gaelic. In the west the Assynt district is geologically exciting. It contains all kinds of rock, from acid to ultrabasic, gneiss, quartzite, Cambrian and Ordovician limestone, and is heavily faulted. This looks promising, and the general references to olivine and serpentine, as well as to fluorite found in gneiss are pertinent. D. S. Freir[77] lists beryl, spinel, tourmaline and kyanite 'in huge crystals'. Garnet and cordierite may likewise be expected in gneiss. On the other hand, cairngorm is pinpointed as present near the summit of Quinag, on the east side.

Most of the reports of Sutherland gem minerals, however, come from the two peaks in the north, Ben Hope and Ben Loyal. Possibly they are the most visited. Ben Loyal is credited with zircon, tourmaline (near Culrain inn) and cairngorm in the north cliff, the first of which occurs on Ben Hope as well. There is a doubtful report of a full-size diamond having been found there, and more definitely, Heddle 'suspected' small diamonds to occur about three miles north-east of the mountain.[33]

Otherwise there is some fluorite in syenite near Laird and in Helmsdale granite in the east, which extends into Caithness, where small crystals and veins of deep purple fluorite have been reported at the Ord of Caithness, the Burn of Ousdale, and Scholl near Noss Head.[21]

The rocks of Caithness and the Orkneys are comparatively undifferentiated Old Red Sandstone, with a few small igneous bodies in dykes and intrusions. To the best of my knowledge nothing much is to be found here.

So we have passed John o'Groats and must to the Shetlands. Fair Isle on the way has some malachite, but our eventual destination is highly rewarding. The Islands occupy a large area, about a degree of latitude south to north and as much in longitude, which is crammed with all manner of metamorphic and igneous rocks, rich in mineral species.

Taking Mainland first, there is fluorite on the west shore of Sandwick Bay and a body of serpentine about two miles north of Sandwick. At Swinaness it is said to occur in beds four feet thick, but I am not quite sure if this is the same locality.[21] Amethyst is found at Northmaven, The Cannon and Esha Ness in the northwest. A remarkable locality in this part of the island is Hillswick, which has not only tourmaline, almandine and grossular garnet, but also blue kyanite and pale-green fluorite in mica-schist, while violet fluorite occurs with epidote in calcite veins in diorite on the Hillswick promontory. Tourmaline is widespread and may also be found around the Colla Firth, and kyanite north of Vanleep.[31, 37]

Pale violet and dark blue fluorite occurs at Kirksands on the little island of Papa Stour with chalcedony, quartz, calcite and barytes in druses in clay-slate, greenstone and basalt. Another small island, Burra, has sphene in gneiss, while fluorite may be found with amethyst at Kirkavoe, on the north-east shore of Yell. Malachite has come from Sandlodge and Dunrossness in Unst, also known for tourmaline and radiating clusters of transparent blue kyanite with quartz. In addition to ordinary garnet, however, Unst and the neighbouring island of Fetlar are the only British localities for uvarovite, a green calcium-chromium garnet, found sparsely in the deposits of chromite once worked at Baltasound and on Fetlar.

It is usually described as being of an emerald hue, but the Unst garnets in the Heddle Collection in Edinburgh are of a bright vernal green, while the imperfectly crystallized garnets in my possession resemble aquamarine. Some specimens have been good enough for cutting.

There is more sphene about Loch Tresta on Fetlar, whereafter the ocean rolls grey under a lowering sky and we have to turn south, past Cape Wrath and through the Minches to Ireland.

6 *Round the British Isles*
Part 3, Ireland

The wind is keen in the glassy air, with sleet-squalls blowing, and the sun leaping out behind them, as spindrift waltzes away over the wave-crests and clouds like angry swans race down-sky. The sea is ink-blue, foam-fringed, curling-in and gurgling in the wake, as we sail from Unst on the old Viking trail to Ireland, where the evening light from the vast ocean circle lingers long on the green green grass, furrowed with shadow, and the grey headlands, bardic strings singing strife, love and sorrow from the past unforgotten and passions yet unborn. But ours is the quest for a billion manless days frozen into rough-grained granite, ceramical basalt, clinky quartzite and scaly, twisted schist.

The geology of Ireland has a personality all its own, but it has something of Scotland in it, and of England, and of Wales, so that such wisdom as we have gleaned on the way will stand us in good stead.

6.1 THE SOUTHERN COUNTIES

The bulk of the land conforms to the Caledonian pattern, save for the southernmost counties of Kerry, Cork and Waterford, where the Armorican trend prevails, as in the south of Wales and the south-west of England. Here the rocks are Devonian and Carboniferous: sandstones, slates and marls, edged with limestone on the lowest ground, and in northern Kerry and Limerick—the Millstone Grit, which spreads out wider and rises higher in Clare. The Lower Carboniferous volcanics occur at Knocknanuss Hill near Kanturk in county Cork and more massively in Limerick near Limerick city, south of the Shannon, and at Knockbrack, north of the city, as well as near Tulla, in county Clare. There are a few patches of rhyolite in the Derrynasaggart Mountains near Killarney, but Carrantoohil, at 3414 feet Ireland's highest point in MacGillycuddy's Reeks, is sandstone. Lavas and pyroclastic rocks show up again at Ballinleeny and Knockferine in north-west Cork. The general situation, however, does not change until we reach the easternmost part of Waterford, where the lie of the land turns Caledonian and the rocks are Ordovician volcanics, as in the English Lake District.

The mineralization is limited, but lead, zinc and copper lodes appear, mainly in limestone, in the counties of Kerry and Cork, and the corresponding mines have produced some malachite and azurite. Thus botryoidal malachite and azurite may be found at Muckross near Killarney, county Kerry, and at the Audley, Classadaugh and Cappagh mines near Four Mile Water, county Cork; but the best malachite seems to come from the Coosheen mine near Skull, in the south-west of the latter county. There are several old copper mines where malachite is present in the igneous formations of Waterford, notably at Bunmahon on the coast.

The Old Red Sandstone of Kerry and Cork is traversed by quartz veins, which contain crystals, both colourless and tinted. These occur singly and of a yellow colour (citrine) near Killarney, at Mullock Veil. Cahia-com-Righ in the Slieve Mish Mountains, north of Castlemaine, is also known for its fine rock crystal.

The south-western coastline is deeply dented with picturesque submerged valleys (rias), the skerries continuing the line of the headlands, and here the rock strata and veins are exposed to advantage along the sea-shore. Rock crystal may be profitably looked for on Blasket Island, amethyst at Dingle and Kerry Head, and Ballyheige in particular. The Royal Scottish Museum in Edinburgh has some beautiful lilac amethyst crystals, which measure up to five inches across, from county Cork. Greg and Lettsom[31] mention a quarry near Cork town, on the right bank of the Lee, as particularly promising. Skull and the western headlands also deserve a visit.

6.2   THE LEINSTER GRANITE

To the north and east of Waterford, in the counties of Kilkenny, Wexford, Carlow, Wicklow and the eastern part of Kildare, all the way to Dublin, the land is largely igneous, except in the wings, and has correspondingly more to offer to a rock-hound. The Leinster Granite of Caledonian age, the largest mass of this rock exposed in the British Isles, occupies an area of some 625 square miles and extends for sixty-eight miles from a point about four miles north of New Ross in Wexford to Dun Laoghaire on Dublin Bay. It forms the backbone of the Blackstairs and Wicklow Mountains, the latter of which attain 3039 feet, in a peak bearing the lovely name of Lugnaquillia. The granite dips steeply westwards, where in Carlow it lies in contact with the much-later Carboniferous Limestone. In the east and south, however, it sinks gently beneath Ordovician strata, bobbing out through these now and again in isolated outcrops. Acid and basic dykes and lavas seam the country rock along the Caledonian trend farther south-east, in the counties of Wexford and Wicklow, while the extreme south-east recalls north-west Wales, with Pre-Cambrian gneisses, Cambrian and Eo-

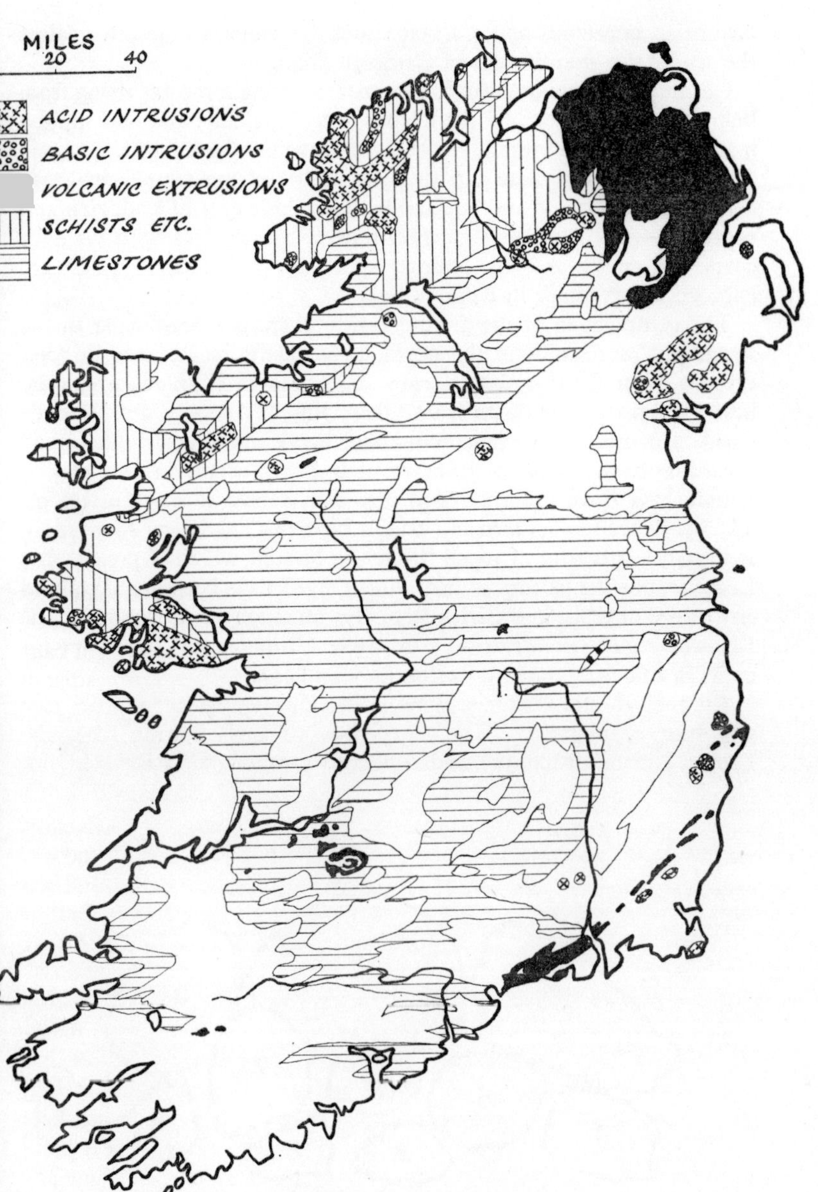

Geological map of Ireland

Cambrian quartzites and Carboniferous limestones, shielded against the sea by the granite stock of Carnsore Point.

On the western margins of the Leinster Granite hot gases rising from below have locally turned the felspar into china clay, and new molten material has seeped into the cracks, forming veins of aplite which contain small almandine garnets. In the east the overlying strata have been extensively indurated and injected with sulphide ores of lead, zinc and copper, attended by their gangue minerals, as well as with veins of coarse pegmatite and fine-grained aplite, or pure quartz, which are exposed to advantage in Killiney Bay.

The composition of the granite varies: there is more felspar in the south and more mica in the north. The quartz, sometimes in good crystals, is smoky in county Carlow and yellow in Wicklow, where the best specimens have come from Glenmalure, especially near Round-wood, also noted for cinnamon-stone, beryl and schorl. The latter according to the Geological Survey of Ireland[10] occurs in thin prisms, seldom over three millimetres in diameter, brown to black in colour. The beryls are small, green and usually opaque. The Ulster Museum in Belfast has a crystal of topaz 'from the South', which is presumably Leinster, but the locality is unspecified, and I have been unable to find any record of topaz in the Irish Republic, although its occurrence in the Leinster granite is intrinsically probable. Brindley has found spodumene in some pegmatite dykes on its west flank.[10]

Kilranelagh and Glenmacarnass in Wicklow are other localities that will bear examination. The 'auriferous streams' flowing from the Crogan Kinshela Mountains self-evidently must contain some gold, but

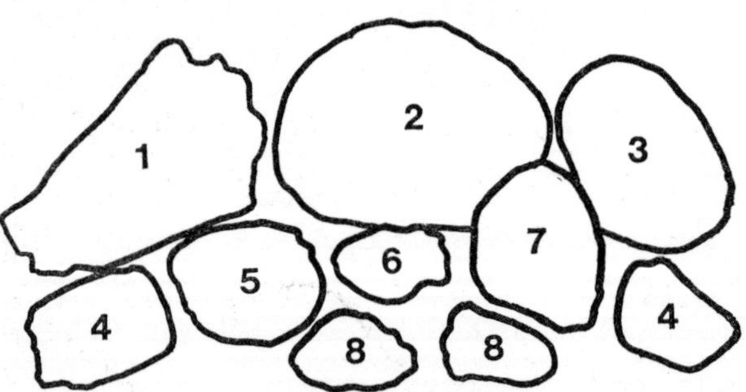

JASPER and AGATE. Key to Plate opposite: 1. *Galston, Ayrshire*; 2. *Campsie, Stirlingshire*; 3. *Sidmouth, Devon*; 4. *Jasper, unknown*; 5. *Churchill, Somerset*; 6. *Fremley Pit, Lichfield, Staffs*; 7. *Puddingstone, Herts*; 8. *Montrose, Angus*

are also credited with zircon, spinel and sapphire, while wolfram is abundant in this area. With regard to the sapphire Greg and Lettsom wrote in 1858: 'Mr Mallet, lately of Dublin, has observed small rolled fragments of corundum having a blue colour, scratching topaz and chrysoberyl, specific gravity 3·98, in the bed of a stream having its source in the Crogan Kinshela Mountains, in the County Wicklow.'[31]

The county also has jasper, jasper-agate and (chalcedony) agate at Bray Head, serpentine, epidote, found with quartz near Arklow, and fluorite of a pale violet-blue colour, said to be common in both crystalline and massive form at the Glendalough lead mines.

Which localities are reported and which not is to some extent a matter of accessibility, mining or quarrying operations, and simple luck. Somebody finds, say, beryl at a particular place, describes this in a paper, other mineralogists go there and find more beryl, but do not trouble to explore farther afield. Thus a distorted picture of the situation becomes fixed in the literature by dint of repetition.

Since, though, beryl, tourmaline and almandine-to-spessartite garnet (see p. 109) are accessory minerals of the Leinster Granite, they may be looked for in any likely pegmatite vein or druse, which with a total area of 625 square miles, to say nothing of the neighbouring outcrops and the metamorphic aureole, offers plenty of scope. A good hill walk has not hurt anybody, and you never know your luck until you have tried it.

We will now move to the extreme north of the granite, to Dalkey Island and Killiney Bay in the county of Dublin. On the former, garnet, brown tourmaline in large prisms, and fluorite may be found in druses. On the latter we may look for 'opalescent, milk-white and highly translucent' felspar, deemed 'suitable for ornamental purposes', and garnet in the form of 'small, red, brilliant crystals' in quartz veins together with beryl, slender crystals of schorl and grey-green opaque spodumene. The latter is obviously not of gem quality, nor is beryl for that matter. Apatite, however, is also an accessory mineral of granite and occurs in 'fine prisms' of a sea-green colour on Killiney Hill and in light-green transparent ones on Threerock Mountain.[31] Andalusite is abundant, but has largely decayed to sericite.[67]

A further place for fluorite is the Castleknock quarry, a few miles west of the capital. On its opposite side, at Howth, rock crystal has been found in marl, and on the beaches amber in small highly-transparent lumps of 'a rich yellow colour'.[31]

As we shall see later on (p. 65), there is also some amber in Ulster,

---

Top: SPHALERITE (blende), *Alston Moor, Cumberland*
Bottom: QUARTZ, *Durham*

GBI C

but nobody seems to know very much about Irish amber. On the other hand, I have heard tell of the red amber from the Irish Sea. This seems to resemble the red copal resin from the old Northumbrian lead mine of Settling-stones, where it is found on calcite. In any event this is more than hearsay, for I have actually come across a piece of semi-opaque carmine-red material which seems to answer the description, on a beach in Arran, Scotland.

However, to return to Dublin, amethyst has been recorded in the county without further particulars and citrine at Palmerston, westwards along the Liffey.

6.3   THE CENTRAL PLAIN AND THE WEST

The latter is in limestone country, and farther inland it is Carboniferous Limestone, the middle division of which is known as Calp, all the way to the Galway Bay in the west, and again with some intermission to the Sligo and Donegal Bays, a further tongue of limestone running northeast between Caledonian ridges almost to the very shores of Lough Neagh in Ulster. In England and Wales limestones of this age often make high dry land, but in southern Ireland they appear mainly at the bottom of synclines and are frequently associated with low wet conditions, as in the Bog of Allen and the Central Plain, smoothed and scoured by the Ice Age. The slope of the ground is low, without distinct watersheds, and the river headwaters tend to form strings of small lakes or long, twisting loughs, full of inlets and islets, where 'peace comes dropping slow' among the reeds between the sky and the water. This structure achieves in Lough Corrib and especially Lough Erne a jigsaw-puzzle intricacy.[7]

Whereas in southern Britain high ground and igneous formations are concentrated in the west, Ireland is more like a dish with upraised rims, where harder rocks keep out the sea.

The uppermost division of the Carboniferous limestone does throw up some moderate or low hills between Cashel, Kilkenny and Portlaoise, south of the Galway Bay, though even these are largely sustained by a stiffening of Millstone Grit, and again in Sligo and Leitrim in the north. But the peaks and moors of south-central Ireland are carved in Old Red Sandstone and Lower Palaeozoic rocks. Such are the Slieve Bloom, Slieve Aughty, Silvermine and Galtymore Mountains, which attain 3015 feet in their titular peak. In the Golden Vale, about Limerick and Tipperary, there is an old volcanic complex with acid lavas and basic intrusions, probably associated with the Armorican land movements and accompanied by an extensive mineralization, which has given rise to a crop of mines in the counties of Limerick, Clare and Tipperary. Fibrous and stalactitic malachite is known from the silver mines and the Lackamore mine near Newport, Tipperary, and represented at the Geological Museum in London, while azurite has been recorded in Limerick and fluorite, described as 'very fine' in several Clare mines, notably at Doolin and Lisdoonvarna.[60]

I doubt if this list is exhaustive, but these three counties and the neighbouring Kilkenny, Laoighis (Leix), Offaly and Kildare appear to be substantially devoid of gem minerals, although igneous rocks form low hills north of the town of Kildare and near Daingean in Offaly. Rock crystal, however, is reported to occur in large prisms at Castlecomer, county Kilkenny, in the Leinster coalfield.

Generally speaking the Central Plain is not a good hunting ground for our kind of game, and we may profitably pass on to western Galway beyond Lough Corrib, where Caledonian granite accounts for most of the southern area and outcrops sporadically along the coast, as well as inland by Maam Cross and Oughterard. There are also minor bodies of basic rock on the margins of the granite bosses. These granites do not rise to any great height, and the Twelve Bens of Connemara to the north owe their existence to the hard quartzite capping Dalradian schists and gneisses, in which they resemble the peaks of the North-Western Highlands of Scotland. Nevertheless the effect of the granite is clearly portrayed in the northern outline of the Galway Bay and the damming of Lough Corrib. Northwards, in Murrisk, the rocks of the Sheefry Hills are Ordovician with marginal intrusives and volcanics, yielding ground to Silurian slate and quartzites along the Clew Bay. By now, however, we are in Mayo.

The Galway granite contains garnet, fluorite and sphene as accessory minerals. Fine octahedral crystals of fluorite have come from the Inveran lead mine within the granite mass.

Grossular garnet in crystals up to about three-quarters of an inch in diameter may be found in the contact rocks, but it is usually opaque. Malachite in the form 'acceptable to the jewellery trade'[10] has been obtained in small quantities from the Tynagh lead, zinc, copper and silver mine. There is more fluorite in the Glengowla lead mine at Oughterard and at Rahoon, where it is massive.[31] Finely crystallized iridescent labradorite has been reported, and epidote occurs in basic dykes. Finally, we have the 'Connemara marble'.

J. K. Charlesworth[7] writes: 'At Recess and other localities between Galway and Clifden, the white calcite layers alternate with the mineral olivine which has been altered into light or dark serpentine, the whole uniting in a handsome marble.' Greg and Lettsom are more specific and mention Ballynahinch quarries in the west as a source of 'very fine serpentine and verde antique'.[31] The quarries at Streamstown and Creggs, north of Clifden, and at Bunowen, Glendnagh and Recess, east of Clifden, are now in operation.

6.4 ON THE NORTHERN BORDERS OF THE REPUBLIC

In Mayo the Nephin Beg Range is structurally similar to the Mountains of Connemara, and to the north-east thereof Carboniferous strata make up some lower, more fertile land south of the Killala Bay. This is crossed in the south-east by a Caledonian band, some eight miles wide, of harder rocks, mainly Old Red Sandstone near Westport and Dalradian schists farther on, pierced by a wide granite ridge, about twenty miles long in its main part, which forms the backbone of the Slieve, Gamph and Ox Mountains in the neighbouring county of Sligo. These hills hardly deserve the name of 'mountains', as they nowhere exceed 1800 feet above sea level, but are comparatively rugged. In eastern Mayo a little more granite peeps out through Silurian quartzite south of Charlestown, where a low range of hills, built of Old Red Sandstone and capped with short stretches of acid lava rolls on east-north-east into Roscommon and Leitrim towards Lough Allen.

Mayo has some serpentine about Westport and garnet and kyanite in the mica-schists, notably at Erris, but its main attraction lies in Achill, a largish offshore island, joined to the mainland by a bridge, north-west of Clew Bay. This is again quartzite and schist with quartz veins, which on the south slopes of Slievemore, half a mile west of the Deserted Village, contain some rose quartz, and between Dooagh and Keem Bay amethyst,[35] well represented in the museum collections throughout the British Isles, though the specimens in the British Museum, London, are reddish and hardly do it justice. Greg and Lettsom[31] describe the Achill amethyst as found 'in fine crystals, occasionally eight to ten inches long'. This site, however, has been known for well over a century, so that the best and most accessible material has probably been removed. On the other hand, road works in 1968 and 1969 exposed more amethyst veins and it is a fair surmise that the same veins reappear at other points of the island which are less readily accessible. In fact, some of the best collection specimens have come from coastal cliffs.

Patrick Doran has reported fine crystals of red and green tourmaline in the Ox Mountains, but nothing seems to be known about this by the Geological Survey of Ireland in Dublin.[10] His collection is now at the Ulster Museum and it does contain red and green tourmaline, though its place of origin is not specified.

Amethysts have also been found in county Leitrim and farther east near An Uaimh (Navan), which if my Gaelic is to be trusted means 'The Cave', in Meath, probably in connection with the minor igneous outcrops between it and Slane. Gypsum with some good alabaster is found near Kingscout in Cavan, just over the county boundary, at Drumgoosat, in Monaghan, and Carney Bridge, in Meath.

There may be something, at least rock crystal, in northern Longford and Cavan as well, as country rocks here are mainly Ordovician and Silurian, rather like the Southern Uplands of Scotland, and there is a sizable intrusion of granite near Bellananagh in the latter county. But the records are silent.

6.5 AND SO TO DONEGAL AND ULSTER

The high ground in the counties of Leitrim and Fermanagh is chiefly Carboniferous sandstone and shale, surmounted by Millstone Grit and rising above limestone valleys as in the south of the country, but there is a body of basic igneous rock between Lough Melvin and Lower Lough Erne, eastwards of which a block of Old Red fills most of Tyrone up to Omagh in the north. In the east the sandstones are overlain by patches of Carboniferous basalt, and between Omagh and Cookstown a large expanse of gabbro and intermediate intrusives is rimmed and pierced by smaller stocks of granite and syenite. North of this line we have two distinct types of country: east of the Sperrins and the rest, which accounts for northern Tyrone, most of Londonderry and Donegal in the Republic.[7]

The Sperrins themselves and the bulk of the land to the north and west are Dalradian schists, interspersed with quartzite and metamorphic limestone and having New Red (Triassic) Sandstone formations along the eastern edge. Thus the landscape shows close affinity to parts of the Scottish Highlands, but the less exciting ones, as the relief is much more subdued. It is a dour, grey country of sheep runs and sparse crofts, save for the fertile valley of the Foyle on the Ulster border.

I have come across a mention of tourmaline, found in granite, in county Leitrim. The 1962 edition of *The Geological Map of Ireland*, however, shows no granite within this county, although there is some gneiss and schist between Lough Gill and Manorhamilton, and a little granite may possibly outcrop there. Across the border, Fermanagh is known chiefly for a crystal of diamond reported in one of its streams by V. Ball.[1]

As we have just seen, Tyrone has a promising geology and various minerals may be expected here. Indeed, there are records of opal in felspathic porphyry east of Clogher in the south and on Barrack Mountain near Pomeroy. Rock crystal is also found in 'large detached' prisms in the Pass of Donaghmore and Tullynisken, between Pomeroy and Dungannon, while cavities of fossil shells in limestone and calciferous sandstone near Omagh are reported occassionally to be lined with fluorite.[31] The igneous complex between this locality and Cookstown contains a good deal of jasper, is highly mineralized and may well be worth a look.

The county of Londonderry is best known for 'Dungiven crystals', which may be citrine or cairngorm and attain considerable size. In fact, one specimen found at Dungiven weighed close to ninety pounds (reports of still larger ones from Blarney Castle, co. Cork, remain unconfirmed!). The Parish of Banagher and Fingle Mountain nearby are mentioned as the best hunting ground for these; but they are also to be looked for in the parishes of Upper and Lower Cumber. Rose or ferruginous quartz has been reported from Ben Bradagh Hill near Dungiven.[31]

In the west Donegal is a geological extension of the North-Western Highlands of Scotland, with deep sea-loughs and quartzite-capped peaks, but it is also intruded by large granite masses and minor bodies of basic rock, metamorphic limestone peeping out along the faults, with a larger area of Carboniferous limestone round the Donegal Bay in the south.

There are two main granite masses: a smaller one in the Blue Stack Mountains and the much larger which has provided the material for most of the Donegal Mountains and extends to the offshore islands, its fault-shifted portions reappearing along the coast farther north. Yet the highest peak, Errigal (2466 feet), which looks like a miniature Fujiyama, is gabbro-backed quartzite outside the granite area. The granite is generally described as Caledonian, but is not all of the same age and is divided into the Main Granite and the Rosses farther west, which are again subdivided according to age, composition and texture. The main accessory mineral is apatite, said to be of a brown colour;[10] but garnet, tourmaline and beryl are also present in locally variable amounts. Considerable land movements have occurred during and after the intrusions of magma, which is surrounded by zones of sometimes repeated metamorphism up to two miles wide. Pegmatites are strongly developed along the margins of the granite and at the junctions between different types of granite.[47]

Greg and Lettsom[31] refer briefly to Donegal rock crystal as 'very fine'. Well-crystallized quartz may be expected in the pegmatites. Nothing is said about its colour, though in most intrusions of this age it is brown or smoky. In fact, crystals of smoky quartz up to two inches across have come from the Owendoo River, south of Cronloughan in the Blue Stack Mountains.[19] On the other hand, the Royal Scottish Museum in Edinburgh has some green beryl from Donegal with quartz that is unmistakably amethystine, although the quality of both is very poor. Tourmaline in large crystals, up to half an inch across, occurs in granite, as well as in the metamorphic aureole. It is brown or black, but Greg and Lettsom record green tourmaline near Dunfanaghy in the north, well outside the granite area, presumably at contact with the basic intrusions in this area, which is also known for serpentine.

Donegal beryl is grass-green, never blue or emerald-coloured. It occurs in large prisms, up to several inches long, with flat endings, which are usually badly flawed, broken and resealed with milky quartz (like the Perthshire garnets, p. 46). According to J. S. Jackson, former Keeper of the Natural History Division of the National Museum of Ireland in Dublin, they may, however, occasionally attain the dignity of 'low-grade aquamarine'.[35]

Beryl is found in vein quartz and greisen at Sheskinarone near Dungloe (spelt Dunglow on most maps) in the Rosses, but the Geological Museum in London has specimens from the Gweebarra Range (there is a river of this name) and Parknatomogard to the south of this area.[60] The best hunting ground for apatite is in the south-east of the Main Granite.[47]

The Dalradian rocks of Donegal have experienced an advanced degree of regional metamorphism, upon which has been locally super-imposed the heat action of the intruded acid and basic magmas. Owing to this various crystalline minerals have developed according to the degree of alteration and chemical composition of the rocks. The most widespread of these minerals is garnet in several guises. The metamorphic aureole is well developed in the Mass district about the Gweebarra Bay in the west, where garnet, varying in composition from grossular to andradite, idocrase, kyanite, sillimanite and staurolite may be found, and along the south-eastern fringe of the Main Granite, in the Fintown-Glenkeo and Lough Gartan areas.[16] Good kyanite occurs sparsely between Glenkeo and a point north of Cashel on the east side of the Lacagh River, as well as at Carrowtrasna, to the north of Lough Gartan. Pitcher and Read[47] record diopside in calcareous (limey) rocks altered to calc-silicate granulites in the Fintown area. Greg and Lettsom mention Altnopastie for kyanite. Garnet crystals up to an inch across are not uncommon, though usually opaque.

The Geological Museum in London has some idocrase from Dungloe, while Greg and Lettsom[31] add Derryloaghan and Bunbeg on the Gweedore Bay in the north-west as further idocrase localities. At the latter it is said to occur in 'fair crystals' of a hair-brown colour together with large dodecahedral garnets of a 'rich cinnamon colour', as well as 'very large and perfect' dark green ones (andradite) in coarse crystalline dolomite. The hessonite variety of garnet (p. 109) may be obtained with idocrase from the Meenacreeve limestone quarry at Annagary. Another metamorphic gem mineral to be looked for in gneisses and highly altered schists is cordierite.

Barnes Gap, which bestrides the granite between Stragaddy Mountain and Crockmore, about four and a half miles north-west of Kilmacrenan, is noted for garnet, light-green epidote and idocrase.[31, 60] Farther to the north-west, fluorite is known from Rathmullen on Lough Swilly, at the entrance to which agates are found on the beaches about Malin Head. These are usually thought to have been brought by the glaciers of the Ice Age from Scotland and occur at many points of the north coast of Ireland. Yet jasper-agate is found in lava amgydales at Clonca on the Donegal shore, and chalcedony is fairly widespread in the igneous formations of Northern Ireland, so that this view need be only partly true.

Before leaving Donegal we may refer to the zeolites in the basic rocks near Kilrean.

6.6 NORTHERN IRELAND

The country east of the Sperrins, comprising part of Londonderry' most of Antrim and the fringes of the counties to the south, is thickly mantled with Tertiary basalts. These are part of the vast flows of Thulean Basalt, mostly submerged beneath the ocean waves, extending as far as Greenland over a total area of nearly a million square miles and contemporaneous with the volcanoes of Arran, Mull and Skye. The basalts form the Plateau of Antrim, which reaches its highest point of 1817 feet in Trostan and drops in columnar escarpments towards the sea. To the south of Ballycastle, however, in the north-east corner of Ulster there is an area of Dalradian schists, pierced by acid intrusions and rimmed with limestone and chalk, the latter of which extend all the way south along the coast and the edge of the basalts to Belfast and inland to Lurgan in county Down.

The basalt envelops the wide trough of Lough Neagh with a kind of pincer movement. The trough is floored with Tertiary sediments, followed south-westwards by Triassic strata and Carboniferous limestone. It lies at the head of a broad rift valley, which continues the line of the Scottish Midlands on a much reduced scale, just as the country to the south-east of it, covering the counties Down, Armagh, Monaghan, Louth, Cavan and parts of Longford and Meath, forms a geological extension of the Southern Uplands of Scotland. We have here the same Ordovician and Silurian strata with Devonian granites of Newry and Bellananagh in Cavan (p. 38), but, added to these, there are the Tertiary igneous complexes of the Mourne Mountains, Slieve Gullion and Carlingford, which correspond to those of Arran. Incidentally, Slieve Gullion and Carlingford are ring structures in which igneous rocks of variable acidity appear in concentric array; they may, therefore, be thought of as analogues of lunar craters. Traces of similar structure are present in the Mourne Mountains, which fall into two approximately circular parts, the lower western and the higher eastern, where Slieve Donard attains 2796 feet. Minor volcanic necks of the same age pearl out along the coast of Antrim, Scawt Hill four miles south of Glenarm being the most remarkable of these from our point of view, as here basic rocks have been intruded into and interacted with chalk, giving rise to

rare crystalline minerals. These include spinel, but according to
K. A. Jones of Queen's University, who specializes in metamorphic
minerals, it is not of gem quality.[36]

Chlorospinel has recently been reported from another Antrim intrusion at Carneal, and crystals of blue corundum have developed in
hornfels at contact with basic magma at Tiewshilltagh, as they have in
Arran (p. 41). The porphyry of the acid volcanic neck at Cushendall on
the north-east coast contains jasper and it is also abundant in conglomerate. Crystalline quartz—I believe, yellow—is known from Knock-
layd Mountain near Ballycastle, and in the colourless form of rock
crystal from Divis Hill near Belfast. Agates may be picked up near
Ballycastle and elsewhere along the northern and north-eastern shores,
but also on those of Lough Neagh. Jackson[35] suggests that amber may
occur in the Oligocene clays, which are rich in coniferous timber, south
and west of Lough Neagh, but can find no reference to Irish amber.
P. S. Doughty, the geologist at the Ulster Museum, also says that he
can find no written records of Irish amber, and the Keeper of Antiquities
inclines to the view that the material for the Bronze Age amber beads,
commonly used for personal ornaments in Ireland, came from the
Baltic. Yet Greg and Lettsom[31] expressly mention amber as occurring
in Ulster: at Craignashoke in lignite, and at Rathlin Island in coal.

The basalt amygdales contain a number of gem minerals, including
chalcedony, agate and opal. Greg and Lettsom record jasp opal and
common opal 'of different colours and sometimes lightly opalescent' at
Sandy Braes, as well as cacholong at Smulgedon, in Antrim. P. S.
Doughty writes: 'Milky opals are known from parts of Co. Antrim,
normally in the centre of flints baked by the Tertiary lavas. Occasionally
milky opals are also found associated with the amygdales in the basalts
and we [Ulster Museum] have specimens from the north coast of Co.
Antrim.'[14] The Geological Museum in London has onyx with fluorite
from the Giant's Causeway. Fluorite is said to be widely distributed in
the basalts, though nowhere common.

The Giant's Causeway and Rathlin Island are well worth a visit. In
addition to opal and varieties of chalcedony, the basalt of the former
contains olive-green and brownish olivine, both disseminated and in
small crystalline masses, while rose quartz occurs on the latter. Greg
and Lettsom record it near Belfast as well. Fairhead and Whitehouse
are other olivine localities, but Island Magee deserves special mention
here, as its olivine is described as being of a 'fine cherry-red colour',
translucent and occurring in 'large crystalline concretions in trap'
(basalt).[31] Yellowish-white apatite in doubly terminated six-sided
prisms has been reported from a basaltic dyke near Kilrost.* Finally,

* The name is given after Greg and Lettsom, but seems to contain a printer's
error and should properly be Kilroot or Kilrea.

we have the zeolites and natrolite in particular at Carn Castle, Upper Glenarm, and the Little Deer Park nearby, where it is found in 'delicate silky crystals' with calcite in 'amygdaloidal claystone'. The Giant's Causeway (Ardihannan Cove), Portrush, Island Magee (near Larne) and Cave Hill near Belfast are other Antrim zeolite localities, while Portstewart, Magilligan and Craignashoke are listed in county Londonderry.

Yet on the one hand, many of these minerals will be found at other places as well, and, on the other, there is no guarantee that, unless otherwise stated, they will be of gem quality.

As we move south into Down, we leave most of the basalt behind We may find olivine near Glasdrummond and opal in the form of hyalite at Donald's Hill and at Quarus, south of Newcastle, where it is 'pearly and iridescent'. But our main interest shifts to the granites.

Sphene occurs in mica-schist at Cariglinneen and in small crystals in syenite, in Crow Hill near Newry. The compact old Newry Granite, however, which extends for over twenty-five miles along the Caledonian trend from Down into Armagh, has nothing much to offer, although it would be surprising if it did not produce at least some rock crystal. But the Mourne Mountains, apart from 'sloping down to the sea', are well known for their druses and accessory minerals. To quote from Charlesworth's *The Geology of Ireland* (p 162):[7]

> 'The Mourne granite, prevalently grey or white, is coarsely grained so that we can detect with ease its dark quartz, its opaque porcellanic plagioclase (albite) and its shining flakes of black biotite. The margins have numerous drusy cavities . . . lined with perfect crystals of smoky quartz . . . , of rectangular white albite and tiny "books" of black biotite, less commonly topaz, fluorspar, stilbite and green beryl. Owing to these drusy cavities, well seen, for example, at the Diamond Rocks near Hare's Gap, the granite is used for economic purposes on a more limited scale than the older Newry granite. . . .'

The beryl is actually blue; prehnite has been found on the east margins of the Mourne granite and the transparent adularia felspar in Slieve Corra; the labradorite variety has likewise been recorded. There is also some amethyst, though, as stated, the Mourne quartz is usually smoky (cairngorm) and far from 'perfect': in fact it is full of inclusions and internal fractures and gem-quality crystals are extremely rare. The same is also true of the beryl. I have seen only one crystal that was partly suitable for cutting. Greg and Lettsom,[31] however, speak of Mourne beryls as 'mostly of a fine blue, sometimes quite transparent and of considerable size' and mention Slieve Corra and Chimney Rock Mountain as the places to look for them. Now their book was written over a hundred years ago, and this makes me wonder if the supply of good crystals has not been exhausted since then in the more accessible parts of the mountains. The Geological Museum in London has a clear green beryl which is labelled 'emerald' and purported to come from the Mournes, although E. A. Jobbins regards it as an aquamarine and its place of origin as highly suspect. Still, considering what Greg and Lettsom have said, it may be the Mournes after all, the more so as the Royal Scottish Museum also has some clear green-blue beryl from these mountains.

On the other hand, the Mourne topaz is invariably flawless, if not very exciting inasmuch as it is typically colourless Again, however, according to the just-quoted authors it 'may also have a faint tinge of pink, blue or green'.

The Carlingford (Co. Louth) and Slieve Gullion granite are of the same age and comparable composition. At least cairngorm occurs in the former together with black tourmaline, while grossularite and idocrase are known from the contact rocks.

This completes our bird's-eye-view of the British Isles. I have spared no effort to present as full a record of the situation as possible and some further particulars will be found in the chapters to follow, but there is a great deal of work yet to be done, especially in Ireland and the north of Scotland.

7 *What is it I have got?*

A mineral—and this includes a gemstone—is a chemical substance of fixed composition, also having certain physical properties, such as crystalline habit, hardness, specific gravity, by which it is characterized more or less adequately. When, however, these basic physical properties are different we have different minerals even if their chemical make-up is the same. As already mentioned (p. 8), graphite and diamond are a case in point. They are both pure forms of the element carbon (C), which also occurs in the less pure form of mineral coal. Graphite is opaque, black or steel-grey ('black lead'), crystallizes (rarely) in six-sided plates like mica, is very soft, making 1 on the scale of hardness, of which more later. Its specific gravity fluctuates between 2·1 and 2·3. It is no gem. The specific gravity of diamond is 3·52; it crystallizes in transparent cubes or octahedra of hardness 10 with a striking display of 'fire', owing to its high refractive index and dispersion (see p. 79). Brookite and rutile are similar paired forms of titania, or titanium oxide (TiO_2), which differ in crystalline habit, specific gravity, hardness, etc.

7.1 ABOUT CRYSTALS

Yet the distinction between different forms of the same substance is not always equally clear. Thus graphite may be either massive or crystalline, but is still the same mineral. Flint, chalcedony and quartz are classed as distinct minerals, but they are all silica (SiO_2). Flint is massive and contains clayey and calcareous (limestone) impurities; chalcedony is also described as 'massive', but is properly *crypto-crystalline*, with crystals too small to be seen separately without appropriate magnification, and shades almost imperceptibly into the crystalline form of quartz, which, too, may be massive, whereby it is meant that the crystals in it are not readily distinguishable.

These points are worth bearing in mind, but we need not worry about them overmuch in practice. Suffice it to say that there are massive and crystalline minerals, or massive and crystalline forms of the same mineral, and leave it at that.

When a mineral has no definite shape it is described as *amorphous*, which is simply the Greek for 'shapeless'. Very often, though, such an

Isotropic	Uni-Axial			Bi-Axial		
Cubic	*Hexagonal*		*Tetragonal*	*Orthorhombic*	*Monoclinic*	*Triclinic*
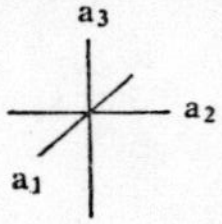	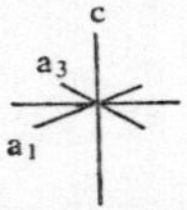 angles a-c = 90°; aa = 60° $a_1 = a_2 = a_3$; c		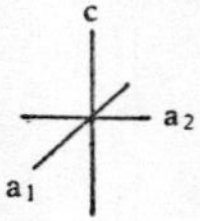	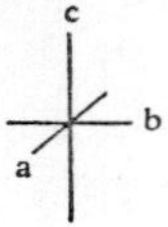	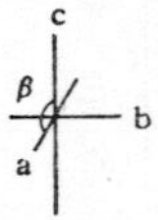	
all angles 90° $a_1 = a_2 = a_3$	6-fold symmetry	3-fold symmetry (Trigonal)	all angles 90° $a_1 = a_2$; c	all angles 90° a; b; c	β greater than 90°; other ∠s 90°. a; b; c	all angle different a; b; c
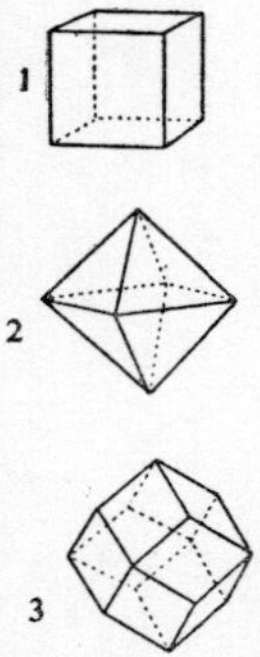	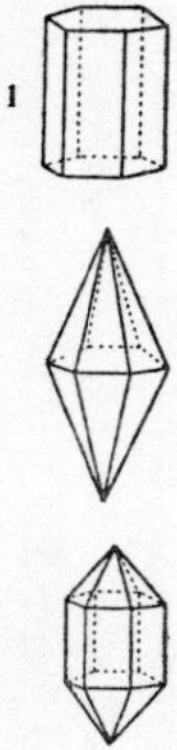	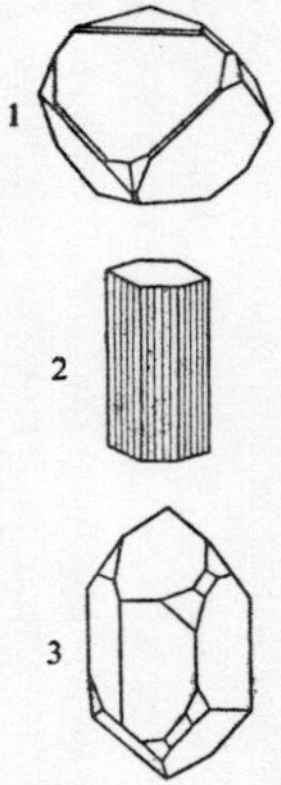	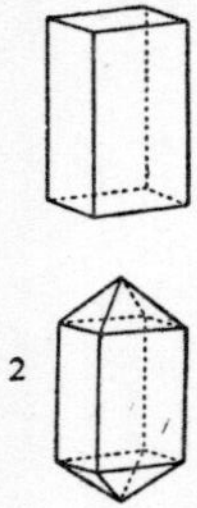	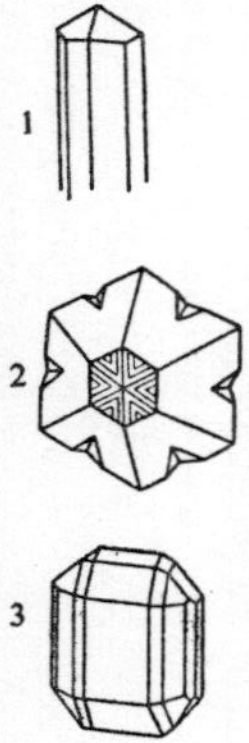	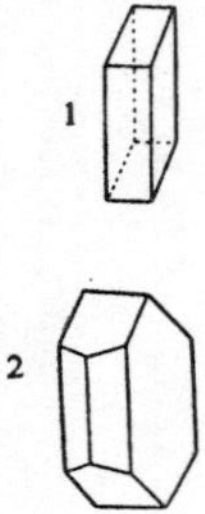	
Diamond 1; 2 Spinel 2 Garnet 3 Fluorspar 1	Beryl-Emerald 1	Ruby 1 Tourmaline 2 Quartz 3	Zircon 2	Topaz 1 Alexandrite 2 (twin) Chrysolite 3	Kunzite 1 Feldspar 2	Kyanite

TABLE I. The Crystal Systems (after G. O. Wild, *Praktikum der Edelsteinkunde*)

amorphous mineral, when deposited from solution, develops a bumpy or pommelled surface. If the pommels are large and flattish the resulting appearance is 'kidneyed', or *reniform*. When the knobs are smaller and more rounded comparison is drawn with a bunch of grapes, whence another Greek name—*botryoidal*. Haematite and chalcedony often display this structure. If a botryoid is split or cut open we shall see that inside it crystalline fibres are arranged radially, like the quills of a rolled-up hedgehog.

Radial aggregates of larger crystals which do not coalesce into a solid spherical surface are typical of many minerals; for instance, aragonite and kyanite.

Crystallography is a science in its own right, but for mineralogical purposes it is enough to master the main features of the six crystal systems: (1) Cubic, (2) Hexagonal, (3) Tetragonal, (4) Orthorhombic, (5) Monoclinic, and (6) Triclinic.

(1) The cubic system is also known as *isometric*, meaning 'of equal measure', which is perhaps a better term, for, although the cube is the simplest crystal form of this system, most of the crystals so classed are not cubical at all and have a larger even number of symmetrically disposed faces. But if we measure a fully developed crystal from centre to centre of two opposite faces or from a point to an opposite point in two directions at right angles to each other the two measurements will be the same. This amounts to saying that the crystal can be inscribed in a sphere and forms a kind of facetted bead. It has complete central symmetry.

(2) In the hexagonal group the crystal is generally elongated, i.e. it is a *prism*, hexagonal, or six-sided, in cross section at right angles to its long axis. The faces, however, are frequently of unequal length and width, and what with minor secondary facets and multiple crystallization, this statement is no more than approximately true. In particular tourmaline often looks in cross section like a bloated triangle and may be almost round, the hexagonal pattern being recognizable, if at all, only at the ends of the prism.

The central 'girdle' of the prism may be missing, so that we have two six-sided pyramids fitted together at the base; or else the form resembles a barrel (corundum), or tapers one way. More often than not, however, the prism looks like a hexagonal pencil, terminating at one or, rarely, both ends in a point, a roof-like structure, a system of small beady faces (beryl), or stark flat.

If you like to play about with axes of symmetry, the central normals to the adjacent faces of the pencil form an angle of 60°, and any of these intersects the long axis at right angles: the crystal stands upright. (See Table 1.)

(3) The tetragonal system is very much like the hexagonal, except that

the pencil is of square cross section and the terminal pyramid is four-sided, but again the 'girdle' may be missing and various complications, with faces being unequally developed or running out into triangles, bevelled points and edges, may arise.

(4) This resembles (3), but the opposite side faces stand in pairs of unequal width on the matchbox or tablet pattern, i.e. the three axes of symmetry are of unequal length, but all intersect at right angles. The number of faces in the pencil is often doubled, or trebled, however, making a complex polygon instead of a rectangle in cross section, with various further 'embellishments' until alexandrite, which is classed in this group, appears hexagonal to an unprejudiced eye. Perhaps fortunately, this gem is foreign to our shores.

(5) The basic form of the monoclinic system may be described as an oblique matchbox tilted one way. The crystal is no longer upright, but is still rectangular in cross-section; two of the bounding side faces are parallelograms, but the remaining faces are rectangles.

(6) In this system no angle is of $90°$; the crystal is inclined both frontwise and sideways, is four-sided and all the faces and cross section are parallelograms. This results in a geometrical solid which glories in the name of parallelepipedon. There are the usual complications, which largely make nonsense of what I have just said. Axinite, albite and kyanite belong to the triclinic system.

To encourage you further, I may mention that about 3000 different forms of the calcite crystals are known. The varieties are largely regional. Probably the best answer is to study the actual minerals in museum collections and become familiarized with their appearance.

Recognition is often aided by secondary features. Some crystals are grooved or striated (lined) lengthwise, others crosswise. The striations do not usually extend to the terminal faces of a prism, but these may be etched in a characteristic way. Other mineral forms are typically bevelled or have bulging faces, and so on.

Another surface property is *lustre*, or the manner in which the crystal reflects light. It may be *metallic*, which means that the mineral looks like polished metal and so opaque; *adamantine* or resembling diamond; *vitreous* or *glassy*, which denotes a reduced brilliance; *resinous*, as in some garnets; *silky*, as in some felspars (satin spar) and gemstones with fibrous inclusions (e.g. cat's eye); *waxy*, as in turquoise, chalcedony and jasper. A *pearly lustre* appears on the fracture surfaces of some stones, such as topaz. Lustre, however, can be judged properly only on clean and undamaged faces.

Another characteristic feature of many minerals is *cleavage*. Crystals split preferentially in some directions. Mica, which is readily divided into thin plates, provides an extreme example; but topaz has a marked tendency to split at right angles to the long axis. It would be foolish to use this an as identity test on a good specimen, but it may occur naturally and is also something to be guarded against. These are instances of *smooth* fracture, but in the absence of clear cleavage planes the stone breaks unevenly, yet distinctively. Thus beryl and quartz break with *conchoidal* fracture, the resulting surface recalling the inside of a mussel shell, but in amethyst the fracture is *rippled*. *Hackly* (jagged) and *splintery* are self-explanatory terms.

7.2 SCALE OF HARDNESS

The property of *hardness* is closely allied to fracture, as generally speaking the harder the mineral the less readily will it fracture. Topaz, however, stands only two grades below diamond in hardness, and hard materials can be brittle. The latter is an important distinction, for hardness is tested by scratching, not crushing. The scale of hardness devised by Mohs is a kind of 'pecking order', the question asked being, What scratches what? The scale has ten divisions, in which any mineral can be scratched by all those that follow it but by none of those that precede it. The scratch is made by drawing the point of a crystal, chip or penknife used in the test gently, without pressure, over a good sound surface of the stone to be identified, due care being taken not to damage its appearance if it is intended as a collection exhibit. If, say, the blade of a penknife is pressed sufficiently hard it is quite possible to produce a kind of 'scratch' on a mineral intrinsically harder than steel by crushing it.

Moh's Scale reads:

1. Talc or Soapstone.	6. Felspar (Orthoclase).
2. Gypsum.	7. Quartz.
3. Calcite.	8. Topaz.
4. Fluorspar (Fluorite).	9. Corundum.
5. Apatite.	10. Diamond.

The synthetic gem borazon, which is a compound of boron and nitrogen (BN), is harder than diamond. It has not been encountered in nature, which, though, does not necessarily mean that it cannot arise without human intervention. Thus in the unlikely event of your coming across a crystal (cubical habit) that scratches diamond you will know what it is.

The divisions of Mohs' scale are somewhat arbitrary and do not correspond to any fixed interval in hardness, but they are subdivided by fitting other minerals in between the successive steps and further minerals in between them. This results in fractional hardnesses; for instance, $6\frac{1}{2}$ for epidote and $7\frac{3}{4}$ for beryl. Some minerals can be scratched more easily lengthwise than crosswise, the best example of which is kyanite, or disthene ('two-strength'), whose hardness is only 5 along the prism but 7 across it.

The hardness of a fingernail is about 2, copper coin—3, window glass—5, penknife—between $5\frac{1}{2}$ and 6, and steel file—$6\frac{3}{4}$. Acquiring a piece of felspar (orthoclase) and quartz does not, however, present any special difficulty, and they are easier to carry about than glass or a steel file.

Minerals that rank less than 6 in hardness do not properly qualify as gemstones, although apatite (5) and even fluorite (4) are often cut for the sake of their transparency and beautiful colouring. They are obviously unsuitable for rings or similar jewellery, where they would be exposed to abrasion.

7.3   SPECIFIC GRAVITY

Another property of a mineral that can be determined with comparative ease, if not as readily as hardness, is *specific gravity* or *density*, which— we shall recall—is the factor by which the weight of a stone exceeds that of the same volume of water.

Archimedes was so impressed by the fact that, when immersed in a bath, his body weighed less by the weight of water it displaced that he ran naked through the streets of Syracuse shouting 'Eureka!' This is not absolutely necessary for finding the specific gravity of a gemstone, but the procedure is based on his discovery.

You weigh the stone in an ordinary way on the scale of a balance, then suspend it on a fine thread at the point of the balance beam at which the scale hangs and weigh it again, immersed in water. The first reading (A) gives you the full weight of the stone (in air), and the second reading (B) its weight less the weight of the same volume of water (C). C = A − B, and the desired density D = A ÷ C.

Gem dealers, who have to test and weigh precious stones all the time, use heavy liquids of different densities (Clerici solution, methylene iodide, etc.). If the stone floats in one liquid, but sinks in another, it must be less dense than the first liquid and denser than the second liquid, so that its specific gravity will fall between these two limits, which may be adequate as a test. A more accurate and even quicker determination can be made by means of a *diffusion column*. If we take two miscible liquids, one heavier than the other, pour the heavy liquid into a tall beaker first and then the lighter liquid over it very gently, without disturbing the heavy liquid, a column of liquid can be obtained where the density is graded upwards from that of the pure heavy liquid to that of the pure light liquid. Any stone dropped into it will come to rest at a level where its specific gravity equals that of the liquid mixture. The column can be graduated by means of appropriate specimens of known specific gravity; and, since diffusion in liquids is very slow, the accuracy of the graduation will endure for many days and even weeks.

Some of the liquids used for this purpose are not only expensive but poisonous, while others are affected by light and have to be kept in darkness. In sum total the amateur gemstone collector will be well advised to stick to Archimedes.

7.4 OPTICAL PROPERTIES

Accurate measurement of optical properties requires sophisticated apparatus, but in many cases a rough estimate by the eye may suffice for identification, especially when combined with the previous tests.

Lustre has already been considered in connection with the outward appearance of stones. Colour belongs here, too, but as already mentioned on page 8, it is an uncertain guide to the nature of the mineral, because, with a few exceptions, it varies widely in one and the same species; for instance, quartz may be violet, brown, yellow, green, blue and pink. Opacity, translucency and transparency are terms used to describe, somewhat roughly, the ability of the stone to transmit ordinary light.

Some gems, to take turquoise, jasper and malachite as examples, are essentially opaque, while chalcedony and opal are never other than translucent. Generally speaking, however, transparency, too, is a variable property. Quartz, topaz, beryl, sphene are frequently opaque, which may disqualify them as gems, if not necessarily as collection specimens. On the other hand, such minerals as felspars, rutile, sillimanite and dioptase, which are typically opaque or at most translucent, occasionally become sufficiently clear and transparent for cutting.

The colour of the transmitted light, or of the light reflected back from within the crystal, may differ from that of the surface reflection, or else the colour changes with the angle of viewing and illumination. These effects are related to *dichroism* (p. 9) and may aid identification. A high refractive index betrays itself at a glance as sparkle, but requires a special optical instrument to be measured. The matter will be considered somewhat more fully in the next chapter, but the hints given here should be adequate for most practical purposes.

8 Taking it a step further

It is human to categorize and generalize. This is an aid to understanding, but there is an element of arbitrariness about any classification, which must be allowed for. Reality refuses to be tailored to Man's convenience.

What is a 'mere mineral' and what a gemstone?

We have already discussed the distinguishing marks of the gem. The difference is roughly the same as between a 'weed' and a 'flower'. Yet the dandelion is objectively beautiful, and the sight of a field full of dandelions in bloom will delight the artist's, if not the farmer's, eye. So too haematite and iron pyrites are but utilitarian ores of iron (oxide and sulphide thereof respectively), but they are hard and lustrous, will take high polish, and are sometimes used in jewellery. Such marginal cases apart, many minerals that are far too soft to qualify as gemstones are beautifully coloured and a joy to behold.

Is the collector in the field coming across one of these to be denied the pleasure of possessing himself of it? The description of non-gem minerals goes beyond the scope of this book, and the interested reader must be referred to other works, of which there is no shortage. Nevertheless, some identification tests of a more general nature and not particularly applicable to gemstones may be of interest here.

8.1 STREAK

One of these is the so-called *streak*.

The streak is the colour of the mineral in powdered form. It is commonly obtained by scratching the mineral against a hard surface, such as an unglazed tile, called the *streak plate*. The colour of the streak is frequently very different from that of the compact mineral. For instance, massive haematite is black or iron-grey, but its streak is cherry-red; cobaltite, which is an arseno-sulphide of cobalt, is silver-white with a reddish undertone in crystalline form, but its streak is grey.

The streak is, in fact, what we get in a miscarried test for hardness when the tested mineral is crushed by applying too much pressure (p. 72), or when the testing material is softer than the tested and leaves a mark of itself upon it instead of a scratch. The blade of a penknife drawn over a quartz crystal will leave upon it a metallic line: this is the streak of steel.

Obviously, to obtain a streak, we must use a streak plate that is harder than the materials to be tested. An emery cloth or paper will do for anything short of diamond and corundum (hardness 9), with which it is itself coated; carborundum paper will do for corundum as well. The procedure, however, is not very useful for gemstones, which are generally hard and crystalline, as the streak of a transparent crystal is usually white and correspondingly unrevealing. On the other hand, pyrite, known as 'the fool's gold', and marcasite, or white iron pyrites (which is used in jewellery), have a greenish black streak, while that of a true gold nugget is golden, knowing which we will not be fooled by appearances.

8.2   FLAME TEST

Powdered mineral is also used in another kind of test, which is a rough form of spectral analysis, and relies on the fact that chemical elements, when heated to incandescence, emit light of definite colours or wavelengths. They also absorb light of the same wavelengths when present in a transparent mineral (Kirchhoff's Law), so that the test is possible in reverse, of which more later.

The apparatus of a *flame test* comprises a piece of thin platinum wire (about 2–3 inches) embedded at one end in a glass handle to protect the hand from the heat, and a bunsen burner, which is quite simply a gas jet and failing which a spirit flame may do, and a little hydrochloric acid, to keep the wire clean. This equipment is not all that expensive, except for the platinum wire, which is a lasting investment, and will provide some good fun.

The wire can be easily welded into a short piece of thin glass tubing of the kind used by chemists. The glass will soon turn plastic in the bunsen flame and the wire be brought to white heat; when it is inserted into the glass in this condition and cooled the tool has been forged and all is set for the magic.

The wire must be chemically clean, which is ensured by dipping it into the acid and then putting it into the flame. If the flame stays uncoloured and undisturbed the wire is ready for use; if not, the operation must be repeated. The clean wire is allowed to cool, then a little powdered mineral is picked up on it and it is introduced into the flame. If any of certain elements is present a flash of beautiful colour will light up the bunsen. The flash is often so short-lived that the test must be repeated, to make sure of the colour. Its intensity will otherwise depend on the amount of the powder on the wire and the proportion of the colouring element in the mineral.

Brick-red is a sign of calcium, magenta of lithium, crimson of strontium, orange-yellow of sodium, yellowish-green of molybdenum, blue-green of zinc, greyish blue of antimony, pale-sky-blue of arsenic or lead, strong sky-blue of copper, lilac of potassium, etc.

8.3   BORAX BEAD TEST AND SPECTRAL ANALYSIS

The same apparatus will do for the *borax bead test*.

For this purpose a small loop is made round a pin or a similar pointed object at the end of the wire. The loop is dipped into borax and inserted into the flame, where the borax melts into a bead filling the loop. If it fails to do so at the first go, try again until it does. The bead is colourless, or should be if the borax is pure, but when a little powdered mineral is placed upon it and it is reheated a colouring, which is often vivid and depends on the composition of the mineral, may appear. The colouring will vary according to whether the flame is *oxidizing*, i.e. blue or colour-less, or *reducing*, i.e. white or yellow.

These tests are more suitable for ores than for gemstones, but this is only a matter of degree, for many gem minerals are also salts of metals and in crude state may even be used as ores; for instance, zircon is a source of zirconium, sphene of titanium, beryl of beryllium, spodumene of lithium. The only difficulty is that the tests involve the physical destruction of some of the stone, which is not practicable in the case of a dressed gem and may be awkward in that of a good-quality crystal. It is, therefore, more usual to determine the chemistry of a gem from its *absorption spectrum*, which is, moreover, very sensitive to the presence of even minute impurities that could not be detected by the relatively crude flame test. The method, however, is applicable only to trans-parent, or at least translucent, gemstones.

As we will recall, every substance absorbs the light of the same wave-lengths as it emits when incandescent. If, then, a strong beam of white light is shone through the gem and observed with a *spectroscope*, which spreads or *disperses* the light into a continuous rainbow ribbon, dark gaps will appear in the ribbon, and these uniquely correspond to the chemical elements and compounds present. This involves no great difficulty, but spectroscopes are comparatively expensive and rather more than an average collector is likely to indulge in. Should, however, he or she do so, after all, there are technical treatises where the matter is dealt with in detail. A brief outline will be found in Rudolf Börner's *Minerals, rocks and gemstones*.[4]

8.4   REFRACTIVE INDEX

X-rays are used to study intimate crystal structure, and this method has been recently invoked to establish the authenticity of the diamonds produced artificially in 1880 by the Glasgow chemist J. B. Hannay who heated a suitable chemical mixture in a sealed iron tube. This was necessary owing to the minute size of the crystals. In larger specimens it is enough to measure the *refractive index*, which as we already know goes together with dispersion to the making of 'fire', by means of the optical instrument called *refractometer*.

Reflection of light in a stone

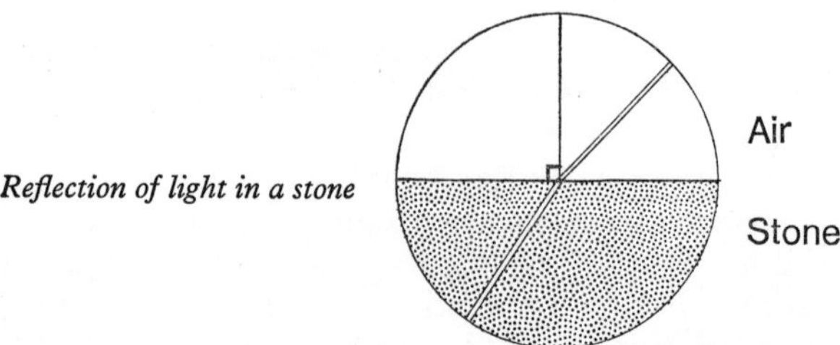

Refraction is the bending of a ray of light when it passes from one transparent substance (optical medium), say air, into another, say gemstone, and is due to the fact that light moves in them at different velocities. The *angle of incidence* is the angle between the ray and the normal (direction at right angles) to the boundary between the media at the point where the ray strikes it. The *angle of refraction* is that between the selfsame normal and the refracted ray after it has crossed the boundary. The refractive index of a gemstone, or other mineral, is the ratio of the sines of these two angles (see above) when air is the first medium.

The light moves faster in the air than in the stone and in passing from the stone into the air is deflected away from the normal to the boundary. If the angle of incidence continues to increase a point will eventually be reached where the angle of refraction exceeds 90°, so that the ray is bent back into the stone. This is called *total internal reflection*, and the angle of incidence at which this happens is the angle of total internal reflection. It is this angle that the refractometer measures, only that an oil of a high refractive index is used, which introduces a further complication, and the boundary where reflection takes place is between oil and the stone; but we need not go into all this.

It should be clear, however, that with a high refractive index total internal reflection will readily occur, so that when a facetted gem or crystal is moved now one, now another facet on the inside will reflect the light back into the eye, giving the sparkling effect of 'fire'. Another important ingredient of this effect, however, is dispersion, which we have encountered in the spectroscope. White light is a mixture of all the colours of the rainbow, but the refractive index is different for different colours (wavelengths of light), so that the total internal reflection will not occur for all of them simultaneously, sometimes the red or the green light only being cast back, the play of light being thus supplemented

with that of colour. The refractive index as given in the tables corres-
ponds to the yellow light emitted by sodium in the bunsen flame.
Dispersion or *dispersive power* is expressed by the difference between the
refractive indices for the violet and red light. For diamond the respective
indices are 2·451 and 2·407, so that it has a dispersion of 0·044. Its
refractive index is 2·42. In combination these properties are responsible
for its lively fire. It is, however, surpassed in both respects by synthetic
colourless rutile, which has a refractive index of 2·90, and another
artificial gem, strontium titanate.[39]

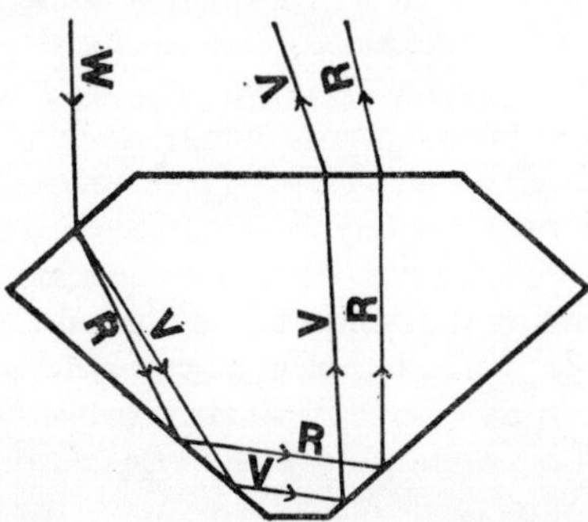

*Dispersion and total internal reflection of
light in a brilliant*

The refractive index of sphene is only 2·06, but it shares with rutile
the property of *birefringence*, in other words a ray of light is split in it
into two unequally refracted rays. The refractive index for the second
ray is 1·91. This serves to multiply internal reflections, and when we
look through such a crystal we see double. The same effect is present to
a marked degree in the more common calcite.

8.5   DICHROISM AND OTHER PROPERTIES OF GEMSTONES

When a doubly refracting, or *birefringent*, stone is coloured the colours of
the two rays often differ. In green sphene the one is deep green and the
other reddish brown; in aquamarine a pale yellowish-green is seconded
by a pale blue, but in a true emerald the colours are yellowish green and
bluish green, which affords a means of distinguishing between the pale
specimens of this precious stone and the semi-precious aquamarine.
This is described as *dichroism* and can be accurately ascertained by
another instrument, called *dichroscope*, where the primary and secondary
beam can be isolated, but may be noticeable to the eye when the gem is
viewed under different angles.

Gemstones are better conductors of heat than glass and so are colder to the touch than their glass imitations, known as *paste*. Some acquire an electric charge when heated, and are described as *pyro-electric*, which is characteristic of topaz and tourmaline. Many crystals are *piezo-electric* and are set into vibration by electro-magnetic waves, which forms the basis of a cat's-whisker receiver.

An interesting property of some minerals that is not altogether beyond the reach of an amateur collector is *fluorescence*. They are incited to luminescence by the invisible ultraviolet radiation, and glow with unearthly colours when illuminated by a dark ultraviolet lamp. The Natural History Division of the British Museum in South Kensington, London, and some other museums have special 'magic caves' where fluorescent minerals can be made to perform by switching on the 'dark lamp'. The latter, incidentally, is not altogether invisible and appears to the eye to emit a faint violet glow. There exist portable ultraviolet lamps, and these have been used by collectors to spot fluorescent minerals at night. Fine crystals of scheelite, a calcium tungstenate, used to be fairly common on the dumps of the disused Carrock or Wolfram Mine in the Lake District, but have now to be dug for, as the more accessible specimens have been eliminated by this method:[56] scheelite fluoresces lilac. It is not properly a gem mineral, but fluor or fluorite, from which the word fluorescence is derived, usually emits a deep violet 'velvet' glow in ultraviolet light, although some varieties fluoresce in blue, green or red, or else fail to fluoresce at all. They may also *phosphoresce*—continue to shine after the u-v lamp has been switched off.[21]

Incidentally, fluorescence is not limited to minerals. Natural teeth and dentures fluoresce in different colours, and so do butter and margarine, so that if you are afflicted by the inability to distinguish 'Stork' from butter there is a useful hint for you.

9 *The Royal gems*

Gemstones may be arranged variously: according to colour, which is often done, but has manifest drawbacks (p. 8); according to general appearance—crystalline, massive, transparent, opaque, and so on; preciousness, chemical composition or geological antecedents. There may be something to recommend all of these alternatives, but it is usual to start with diamond as the gem of gems. A good emerald may be more pricey, more exclusive, but there is nothing to beat the vulgar evocative power of the Cullinan or the Koh-i-Nor. These are the true jewels of crowns, for which human blood, being cheap and common, may have been spilt in profusion. Rubies and sapphires come next over the monarch's head.

So too do they in Mohs' table, where they stand at 9, immediately after the diamond's 10, with nothing in between. Diamond is, of course, the hardest natural substance, but the frivolous test of putting it on an anvil and giving it a good whack with a hammer will reduce it to crumbs, for, though hard, diamond is also brittle. Somewhere, perhaps on the Moon or Mars—anyway nicely out of reach—perfect crystals of natural borazon may gleam in a spacious cave, to challenge the primacy of diamond. But our eyes are on the British Isles, and it so happens that both diamond and corundum, at least in its blue guise of sapphire, occur within our shores, if only just, in geologically similar circumstances.

Chemically there is nothing wonderful about either gem. Diamond is a crystalline form of the element carbon, by no means uncommon as coal or black lead (graphite). Corundum is similarly crystalline alumina, or aluminium oxide, Al_2O_3, which forms about 15·5 per cent of our igneous rocks and in the rough form of emery is used as industrial abrasive, as is rough diamond, or bort. All that is needed to turn them into gems is heat and pressure.

9.1 MANUFACTURING GEMS

The heat of the oxy-hydrogen flame, equal to $+2200°$ C, is adequate alone for ruby. The technique of making artificial rubies was developed towards the end of the last century and perfected by Verneuil of Geneva by 1904. In his process powdered alumina with an admixture of 1·3 per cent of chromic oxide as colouring agent is shaken through a fine sieve into a downward stream of oxygen, which then meets a stream of hydrogen gas in an amount somewhat in excess of that needed to burn it to water (H_2O). As the gases are ignited in a refractory chamber, a 'boule' of red corundum begins to grow on a moveable support below the flame and is gradually nursed into anything up to 300 carats. When removed and cooled, the boule is split by a smart blow 'into two roughly symmetrical halves' (see *A guide to the collection of gemstones in the Geological Museum*, p. 26),[39] which shows that smartness pays, for 'three asymmetrical halves' would be hard to bear.

Sapphires were a harder nut to crack, but were eventually obtained by substituting a little magnetic iron oxide and titanic acid for chromic oxide as the colouring matter. Vanadium yielded green stones which turned red in lamplight like alexandrites and were miscalled 'synthetic alexandrites', accordingly. 3 per cent of nickel oxide produced yellow sapphires, corundum of any colour other than the ruby-red being called 'sapphire'. Fine sapphires and rubies, including the star varieties, have been produced in recent times by the Linde Air Products Co. of San Francisco, who have also developed a secret method of growing synthetic crystals of emerald, previously obtained in Germany. Quartz, tourmaline and some other gemstones seem to be easy as pie.[75]

Colourless 'white sapphire', with a refractive index of 1·77 and a low dispersion, makes excellent optical lenses. Jewel bearings, as a look inside your watch will reveal, are made of pink or colourless synthetic corundum, which is also used in scientific instruments and for thread guides in textile machinery. Synthetic gemstones, however, are so unpopular with the jewellers and fetch such low prices that seemingly they are not worth the trouble of manufacturing. Yet in a cut specimen it requires microscopic examination to distinguish a synthetic from a natural gem.

9.2   DIAMOND

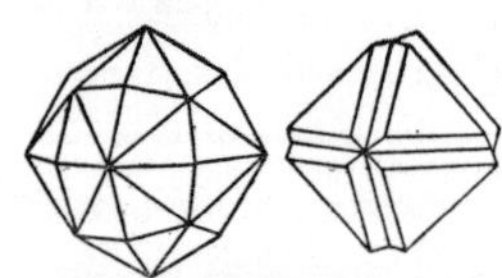

Carbon being combustible, diamond cannot be produced so simply by heat alone, not even in a reducing ambience; it also needs high pressures. This is the main difficulty of obtaining 'synthetic' diamonds (synthesis being a reaction in which two or more chemical elements are combined and diamond being plain carbon, the term 'synthetic' is inapplicable). Most early attempts failed, but J. B. Hannay's dangerous experiments resulted in 1880 (p. 77) in some minute crystals recognizable as the genuine article. In 1954 the General Electric Company of America did better and produced a diamond crystal 1·2 mm long. The process has been developed commercially since then, but the problem of high pressure has never been completely mastered and the artificial diamonds are generally of 'dust size', less than 0·1 mm in diameter, which makes them suitable only for feeding into metal in grinding and cutting tools.

As we have seen on page 61, a loose diamond crystal of fair size is said to have been blundered upon in the county of Fermanagh, in Ulster, but this report is described as 'unsubstantiated' by J. S. Jackson of the National Museum of Ireland, in Dublin.[35] A similar story is told about Ben Hope, in Sutherland, Scotland, and is equally unconfirmed. Perhaps it was the same diamond ? Or was it zircon, which is also recorded on Ben Hope ? Nevertheless, J. G. Goodchild in the Supplement to the second volume of Forster M. Heddle's famous *Mineralogy of Scotland* mentions the latter having told him that small diamonds were to be found three miles north-east of Ben Hope.[33]

On the other hand, diamonds, albeit very small, at Craigman, five miles west-south-west of the Ayrshire town of New Cumnock are no hearsay. Here a seam of coal was invaded by magma, which converted some of it into graphite, and at contact with the igneous intrusion, where the heat was most intense, tiny crystals of diamond have developed.

The Ayrshire diamonds may be too small to be anything but a mineralogical curiosity, but volcanic activity was widespread in the British Isles on several occasions, in the pre-Cambrian, Ordovician, Devonian, Carboniferous and Tertiary times, when the requirements of diamond formation must have been met. Although generally speaking the ground has been gone over with a fine comb, we have seen that large parts of the county of Inverness north of the Great Glen have not been properly surveyed yet and mineral discoveries continue to be made.

9.3 CORUNDUM

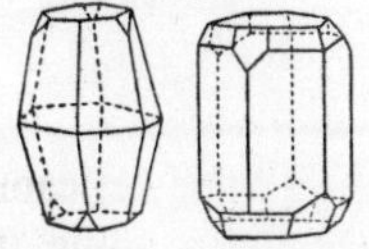

The sapphires of Arran did not come to light till the twenties of our century and this within a couple of miles of the island's capital and popular holiday resort of Brodick, in a place that had been literally crawling with geologists for generations. The sapphires occur in small platy crystals at the junction of granite and slate, which has been baked to hornfels, in Glen Rosa. Once more they are mostly unworthy of a lapidary's attention, but I have been told that a few fair-sized crystals have been found.[24, 67]

Corundum may form in limestone or slate by contact metamorphism, but the prerequisite is at least a local scarcity of silica; otherwise some silicate of aluminium will replace corundum. Thus corundum is typically associated with basic igneous intrusions, such as the basaltic dykes of Mull and Ardnamurchan. It appears, however, that the Arran granite becomes more basic on the margins, probably owing to the absorption of material from the surrounding rocks, which explains the anomaly.

The Mull sapphires I have seen were tiny and could at first sight be mistaken for the dark biotite mica, as their blue colouring is not readily recognizable in the parent rock. According to W. J. MacCallien,[37] however, they 'sometimes reach a size of half an inch across'. A Geological Survey memoir lists several localities on the Island where sapphires can be found, as well as Glebe Hill in Ardnamurchan on the Scottish mainland, where they are said to be deep blue and 2–3 mm in diameter. In addition, Heddle[33] has recorded diminutive sapphires in Glen Clova, Aberdeenshire.

Small crystals of blue corundum also occur in hornfels at Tiewshill-tagh, in Antrim,[36] not to mention those 'auriferous streams' of Wick-low,[31] in Ireland, and John Postlethwaite in *Mines and Mining in the Lake District*[48] mentions corundum, qualified as a 'variety of sapphire', in the Carrock Mine. I paid it a brief visit in the summer of 1969, also Roughtengill on the Caldbeck side of the same hill, where I came across some millimetre-size pale-blue crystals in a rock. Before, however, I could obtain a hand specimen the crystals were completely shattered by the vibrations from the hammer blows, so that there was nothing to show for my pains. As R. K. Harrison,[32] an Institute of Geological Sciences petrologist, has put it in a letter to me, 'The blue variety of corundum is . . . of fairly widespread (though sparse) occurrence in minute particles, occurring in the "heavy" crops of arenaceous rocks . . . X-ray diffraction methods are essential for positive identification', to which you are welcome.

There is no record of green, violet or yellow corundum from the British Isles, which does not necessarily mean that they do not exist. I am informed by M. W. Strong, apparently on the authority of B. N. Peach and J. Horne, that rubies occur ten miles south of Dundonnell in the Little Loch Broom area of the North-West Highlands. But nothing is known of this at the Royal Scottish Museum in Edinburgh or the Institute of Geological Sciences in London, and the original report remains untraced.

Anyway corundum belongs to the hexagonal system. The crystals are often barrel-shaped with flat endings, but may also be bipyramidal, with the two pyramids joined at the base, though the Scottish sapphires assume the form of hexagonal plates. There is some difference between the crystallization of sapphire and ruby, the hexagonal structure being less clear in the latter and the crystals often assuming a tabular form with characteristic triangular markings.

The origin or the red and blue colourings has already been indicated on p. 81 f, but that of other colours remains doubtful. The natural green sapphires, unlike the synthetic stones, do not change to red in lamplight and are sometimes described as 'Oriental emeralds'. Similarly yellow sapphires are dubbed 'Oriental topazes' and violet ones 'Oriental amethysts', which is highly confusing and cannot be wholly ascribed to a desire to 'ennoble' a cheaper stone, for at least amethyst and topaz are more common than corundum. The practice would rather seem to stem from a firm traditional association of certain colours with definite gem species.

Ruby is more highly valued than sapphire, blue or otherwise, especially when of a deep-red hue touched with violet which goes by the name of 'pigeon blood'. Such stones hail from the crystalline limestones of Mogok, in Burma, which together with the river gravels of Ceylon are the main source of gem varieties of corundum.

Corundum is dichroic: the ruby giving in a dichroscope a violet to dark red and a pale red image with a yellowish undertone. The corresponding colours for sapphire are clear blue and greenish blue. This provides a means of distinguishing cut gems from other similarly coloured stones, garnet and red tourmaline (rubellite) in the first case, and blue tourmaline (indicolite) and kyanite in the second. The hardness of 9, the specific gravity, which varies from 3·94 to 4·1, and the refractive index (1·76–1·77), provide other criteria of identification.

As already stated, there is nothing, bar the artificial silicon carbide (carborundum), in the scale of hardness between corundum and diamond, and the gap is quite wide withal.

9.4 MORE ABOUT DIAMONDS

The basic crystal form of diamond is the cube, which develops into octahedron and dodecahedron (12-sided solid), often with bulging faces, striated edges and triangular etchings. The specific gravity of 3·50–3·57 is below that of corundum, but the refractive index, which varies from 2·42 to 2·43, is much higher, as is also the dispersion, which gives the diamond its lively fire, unrivalled by the various 'pseudo-diamonds', except possibly the colourless zircon.

The colour varies within a wide range, but is usually a pale bluish. The South African stones, however, are yellowish. Yellow, brown, red, green, blue and 'black' diamonds are also known—and the latter are not just coal! The Blue Hope is a famous blue diamond from the mines of Golconda in India, which have long yielded the pride of place as a source of diamonds to Africa and South Africa in particular.

It is from the Priemier Mine, near Pretoria in the latter country, that came the largest-ever Cullinan Diamond. The rough stone, which was only a part of a single crystal, weighed a little short of 1 lb 6 oz. It has resulted upon cutting in two big, seven smaller and 96 still smaller brilliants, the main piece being a pendeloque weighing nearly a quarter of a pound, than which there is no larger cut diamond in the world.[39]

The native British diamonds and sapphires are tiny and often doubtful. If we want something bigger we have to turn to 'Cornish diamonds', 'Bristol diamonds', or more generally 'Occidental diamonds', all of which are plain colourless quartz, or rock crystal. After all, Pliny's 'diamonds' were just that!

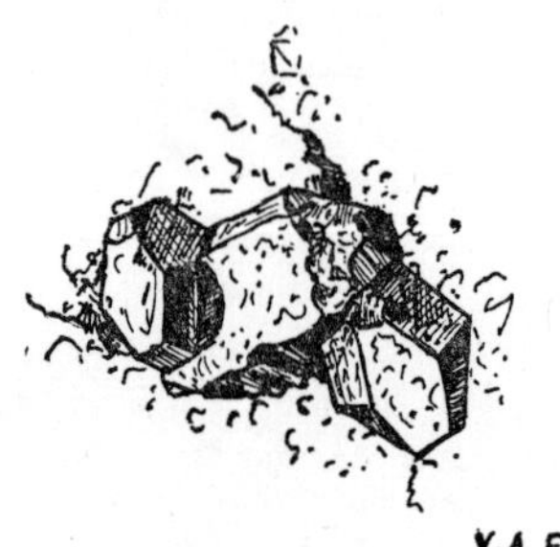

Zircon in matrix, Perthshire

10 Cross-course spar

'Quartz' is a handy contraction of the unwieldy German *Querklufterz*, meaning 'cross-cleft-ore'.[59] The Cornish miner had a similar idea when he called it *cross-course spar*, which, being also a little heavy on the tongue, he cut down to *spar*, although the mineral has another local name, *cann* or *kann*, as well. Anyway it is no ore, even if it forms stringers crossing the lode.

Cross-course spar, or call it what you will, is highly ubiquitous: it occurs in igneous, metamorphic and sedimentary rocks alike, as a main constituent, veinstone, or a filling in hollows, where it has been deposited from alkalized solutions. As we may recall (p. 7), its substance is silica, or silicon oxide, SiO_2, and so in a class with alumina, but even more common. Indeed, silica accounts for 61 per cent of the Earth's crust, although it is mostly chemically bound in various silicates, which include many gemstones and are exemplified by felspar. Only the unbound excess of silica appears in the crystalline form of quartz or the massive guise of chalcedony, opal (with water), and, when impure, hornstone, jasper, flint and chert, which will be considered in more detail under another heading.

So much for the reasons why, but a tidy mind may be driven to despair by the sloppy use of the words *crystalline* and *massive*. I have just said, truthfully, that quartz is crystalline, but am later on going to follow the common usage in speaking of 'massive quartz'. What is meant in the latter case is that the crystals are so jumbled together that they are not readily distinguishable and form a single mass, to express which there is no simple adjective. Moreover, even chalcedony is cryptocrystalline (p. 68), in other words its crystalline structure is concealed, the crystals being too small for the naked eye. In quartz itself the size of crystals varies almost *ad lib*. They may make a lining of fine diamante grains on a rock joint, or exceed a foot in length, the largest known crystal, found in Madagascar, having been twelve feet long.

10.1 MODES OF OCCURRENCE

Sand is made substantially of rounded grains of quartz, which in sandstone become cemented into rock, and this in turn may be metamorphosed into quartzite, a solid mass of coarse quartz. Quartzite, as also most of vein quartz, is usually white, though some Irish quartzites are purple, and veins are often tinged with yellow or ginger-red by limonite or haematite (ferruginous quartz), more rarely carmine-pink (rose quartz), green (prase), blue (sapphire or azure quartz), or violet (amethyst quartz).

Vein quartz is typically opaque or translucent and when white rather like frosted glass. It may sometimes be confused with another common veinstone—calcite, which though is much softer (3 on Mohs' scale), can be cut with a penknife and scratched with a copper coin, feels soapy to the touch, and breaks either into clean glittering faces or floury crumbs, whereas the fracture of quartz is conchoidal (p. 72). Opaque or feebly translucent white quartz is not reckoned a gemstone, but it has occasionally been polished into white beads. When, however, it becomes semi-transparent with a slight bluish tinge it is known as milky quartz, which is quite good-looking in the form of beetle-like cabochons, as also are the coloured varieties.

A quartz vein may be worth examining for 'steam cavities' or druses, called *vuggs* or *vughs* in Cornwall and *loughs* in the north of England, which will generally contain well-developed crystals. If the druse has been exposed to the weather the crystals will probably be opaque and discoloured, as the coloured varieties of cann fade upon long exposure to strong sunlight, but deeper into the rock the druse crystals may be clear and possibly coloured, even in a white vein. For the same reason druses filled with clay or rock rubble are the more likely to yield gem-quality material.

A druse may be of any size, from a small chink to a chamber. Obviously large crystals cannot have grown in a tiny hollow, but the walls of a big cavity may be lined with small crystals. This depends on the nature of the vein and the surrounding rock. A *vugg* in Dolcoath mine, in Cornwall, described by Rule in 1818, was '20 fathoms long by 3 fathoms high and 1 to $1\frac{1}{2}$ fathoms wide and contained carbon dioxide gas'.[13] (So clearly not a 'steam' cavity!) Those were the days. Still, not all is lost. Within my own lifetime E. H. Shackleton[56] 'well remembers entering one of such loughs in the Force Crag mine (Lake District). It was the size of a small room, lined from floor to ceiling with the purest white barytes and resplendent with glittering crystals of sphalerite which shimmered like diamonds in the light of our acetylene torches.' Sphalerite is a learned name for zinc blende, which is not usually considered a gem; nor is barytes, or heavy spar, for that matter, though its crystals

---

Top left: JET, *Whitby, Yorkshire*
Top right: CALCITE, *Frizington, Cumberland*
Bottom: AMBER. Large boulders, *Cromer Beach, Norfolk*; small boulders, *Bridlington, Yorkshire*

may be coloured and, if transparent as well, look quite attractive—it is too soft, 3·0–3·5 on Mohs' scale.

The main mineral of Dolcoath mine, however, now disused, is cassiterite, or tin oxide, SnO_2, which is quite hard (6–7) and occasionally forms transparent crystals of a rich amber yellow, which are wholly 'gemworthy', although these do not occur in the British Isles. It is accompanied by quartz and tourmaline as gangue minerals (p. 12).

Cross-course spar, together with felspar and mica, is the essential mineral of granite and some other igneous rocks, but is substantially absent from the basic ones, save for such occasional oddities as quartz gabbro. It is, therefore, in granite country that good quartz crystals are mainly to be sought, especially if the rock is coarse-grained and penetrated by veins of aplite and pegmatite, which are often 'vuggy'. Vuggs may also be expected at the junction of granite with other igneous rocks, including granite of a different age.

Silica is the last to crystallize out of the molten granite mass, so that by the time quartz crystals start growing there is not much room left for them to grow into. This is why the large 'porphyritic' crystals are usually felspar and good quartz crystals are very rare in 'live' granite, unless it be very coarse, or of giant grain, i.e. pegmatite. By the same token, however, when the cooling rock contracts and fissures open in it they are usually filled with quartz, which is also caught up with magmatic left-overs and mineralizing emanations, so that quartz veins may carry metals and rare minerals.

10.2   VARIETIES OF QUARTZ

The quartz in granite may be dull or clear and glassy, in which case it is known as *rock crystal*, if well formed; smoky, of a greyish-brown hue, sometimes touched with purple; yellow, from lemon to ochre, when it is called *citrine*; brown, from sherry to dark ale, as in the Cairngorms, where at least two fifty-pound crystals of this kind have been found, and hence named '*cairngorm*'; or nearly black and opaque, termed *morion*. Some authors do not distinguish between smoky quartz and cairngorm. Indeed, all these varieties may shade into one another imperceptibly, but there is a definitely grey kind of quartz that may be properly described as smoky, as well as the definitely brown cairngorm. I have a vague childhood memory of granite with pink quartz, seen in some unrecognizable place, possibly in Scandinavia.

Top: HAEMATITE, *Nigel Mine, Furness, Lancs*
Bottom left: FLUORITE, var. bluejohn, *Castleton, Derbyshire*
Bottom right: BERYL, var. aquaramarine, *Mourne Mountains, Ireland*

GBI D

As a rule, however, the pink *'rose quartz'* is found in veins or small 'concretions' in other rocks. It seldom forms fully developed crystals, which tend to be 'misty'. This is also true of the green *prase* and the blue *'sapphire quartz'*. Nor does amethyst usually occur disseminated through granite. It will rather be found in a druse or as a bright purple streak running through the middle of a white quartz vein. It also lines

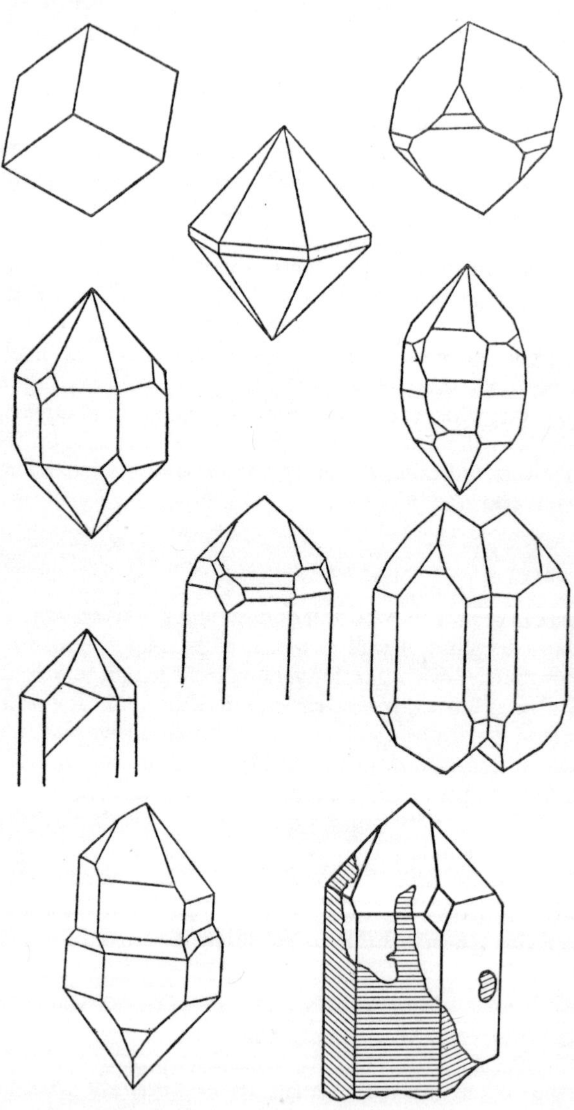

the hollows, known as *geodes*, in potato-stones, which look very much like grimy potatoes and are formed in limestones, subjected to the circulation of hot alkaline water, which washes out the soluble rock and replaces it with chalcedony, crystalline quartz or other minerals, as in the Mendip conglomerates of Somerset or in Glamorgan.

The colouring matter of the *amethyst*, which is now thought to be colloidal iron, is often unevenly distributed, as also happens in the brown varieties, whose colour is similarly ascribed to colloidal silicon.[29] Not infrequently—and most disappointingly—there is a blotch of burning violet at the cloudy base of the crystal, the rest of which is plain colourless glass. On the other hand, the uniformly tinted specimens are more often than not of a pale lilac hue, and deep colour is rare. It may vary from wine-red through purple to pure violet and bluish-violet. Other things being equal, dark stones are the more prized.

There are some structural differences between amethyst and the garden varieties of cann, the former breaking with a characteristic rippled fracture, which is also the hallmark of 'true citrine', a gem of somewhat rare occurrence, but may be present in colourless crystals as well. This is rather confusing. The explanation of the colourings, while not untrue, also seems oversimplified. Both amethyst and cairngorm, when subjected to heat, turn yellow* and so would be citrines. Prolonged exposure to sunlight seems to have a similar effect. The Arran 'smokies', known locally as 'Goatfell stones', generally vary from purplish grey to brown, but I have come across loose crystals of a beautiful yellow hue, somewhere between champagne and lemon, which have presumably been derived from the ordinary kind. On the other hand, crystals of cairngorm from the Central Cairngorms are distinctly reddish and some dark specimens look like burgundy against the light. Cornish citrines are often associated with cassiterite, which does not seem to be a coincidence either, while the yellow and ginger tones of ferruginous quartz are indubitably due to haematite.

Much of the so-called 'rose quartz' picked up on the British and Irish beaches is flesh-pink massive ferruginous quartz. But the real McCoy is of a carmine-pink hue, due to titanium, and rather rare in our parts, although it is listed in two Cornish localities (St. Michael's Mount and Wheal Buckets), in Black Middens, Aberdeenshire, Scotland, and on Achill and Rathlin Islands in Ireland. Titanium in the form of needle-like crystals of rutile, known as *flèches d'amour*, is a not infrequent inclusion in rock crystal.

Aventurine quartz is spangled with little flakes of mica. This is not to be confused with sunstone, a translucent or semi-transparent variety of felspar similarly spangled with haematite and also known as aventurine

* There is a recently found Brazilian variety of amethyst, which on being heated assumes a green colour and is marketed under the name of *vermarine*.

felspar. Small internal fractures are responsible for the iridescent lights in rainbow quartz, while fibrous inclusions of crocidolite, a variety of asbestos, produce a shimmer, which in stones cut *en cabochon* gives a moving band of light. The natural colour of crocidolite is blue, and if unaltered is passed on to the stone. This is the sapphire quartz or azure quartz, also called pheasant's-eye, which it is said to resemble in cabochon form; often, however, the crocidolite is oxidized to a 'fine golden-brown', which transmutes the pheasant into a cat. The proper cat's-eye being a variety of chrysoberyl, this is quartz cat's-eye. But I have not finished with eyes yet. Prase, or fancifully 'mother-of-emerald' (which it is not), is a leek-green quartz tinted by actinolite and in a cabochon it, too, may show a chatoyant band of light, which makes it a falcon's-eye. I had a kind of notion that falcons' eyes were red; but I must admit that I am not much of a falconer, and only once in the Monadhliath hills of Inverness did a flight-weary peregrine choose to spend a few minutes seated on my ski-mittened hand.

10.3 BRITISH AND IRISH LOCALITIES

However, at least blue and green quartz are to be found in Cornwall (e.g. the Penandrea mine, North Roskear, near Redruth), and cat's-eye in the Vale of Llanberus, in Wales, and in Scotland. Milky quartz is known from several Cornish mines, and that from North Roskear is described as 'massive bluish' by J. H. Collins.[8] Blue or opalescent quartz is abundant in gneiss between Scourie and Loch Broom, in the North-West Highlands.[44] Rough amethystine quartz is of fairly widespread occurrence from the Scilly Isles onwards in veins in granite and metamorphic rocks; good crystals are rarer. Still, before we turn up our noses at British amethyst, it may be worth mentioning that according to Heliodorus, who flourished in the third century A.D., 'British carved amethysts must have been quite well known in Egypt', though apparently they were not as good as those from Nubia.[6] In those days Britain was the far more exotic of the two countries. These amethysts most probably hailed from the Cornish tin mines.

Today the best Cornish amethysts are to be found near St. Just and Land's End, but especially on St. Austell Moor, where much of the felspar in the granite has decomposed to kaolin, releasing the harder constituents from its grip. There is some amethyst in the area of Okehampton, at the edge of Dartmoor, and in the potato-stones from the conglomerates of south Devon, the Mendips and the Bristol and Glamorgan hills. Good amethyst is said to occur in north Wales, also in Derbyshire, Staffordshire, in the Lake District along the coast, and on the Anglo-Scottish border.

Scotland's variegated petrology has expectedly produced quite a few amethyst veins, in granite, metamorphic rocks and occasionally in sandstone, where it has been affected by igneous dykes. Most of the amethyst is massive, of variable quality and severely localized. As we have seen, it can be looked for in several Scottish counties. The Loch Morar amethysts have been mentioned on p. 49. They seem even to have a proper 'dragon' to guard them in the shape of the recently reported rival to 'Nessie', said to be given to chewing oars. If, however, it is a real plesiosaurus, on which subject in the words of Eric Linklater 'my mind is as open as perfect ignorance can make it', it would be interested in fish rather than gemstones. The celebrated Heddle Collection at the Royal Scottish Museum, in Edinburgh, also contains a very good amethyst geode from the Old Red Sandstone lavas near Montrose. The Cairngorm mountains and the far Shetlands, too, include amethyst among their attractions.

In Ireland Achill Island is well known for its amethysts, which are rivalled and perhaps surpassed by the lilac stones from the quartz veins in the west of county Cork, and on Kerry Head, Ballyheige, at the mouth of the Shannon.[31, 35]

Clear rock crystal may be found in any granite and almost any quartz vein, as well as in potato-stones. Only by way of example in Cornwall it occurs in the Delabole Slate Quarries, St. Teath, and at Tintagel 'in nests in the slate-stone, embedded in a yellowish-white clay, like mud, and sometimes as black as wet soot . . .'. So on p. 187 in the *Manual of Mining*, published at Truro in 1825,[73] but apparently this description remains correct.[52]

The position with regard to citrine, on the other hand, bears comparison to the case of rose quartz. As I see it, *citrine* is a lemon- or saffron-coloured stone, and it has been mentioned that it is supposed to break with a rippled fracture like amethyst. This would make it quite rare, rarer perhaps than amethyst itself, with which it is often associated. Yet pale cairngorm and pale ferruginous quartz are not readily distinguishable from the citrine thus defined and are usually spoken of as citrine. In any event true citrine is found in Cornwall on St. Michael's Mount (out of bounds to collectors), at Marazion, Carn Brea and Restormel; also on Dartmoor. I have found yellow quartz crystals of a lemon hue in the Caldbeck Fells, in the Lake District, as well as in quartz veins in schist in Perthshire, Scotland, and have already referred to those from the Isle of Arran (p. 91). Pale sherry-tinted cairngorms can be picked up in any cairngorm locality, including the Cairngorms themselves.

Cairngorm is characteristically a Scottish stone and much used in Highland brooches, though all-too-often imported from Brazil. But it occurs in England and Ireland as well. It has been recorded in Cornwall and on Dartmoor in Devon. I have seen a pale cairngorm crystal, some three inches long and three-quarters of an inch thick, from the Meldon Quarry, near Okehampton.

We have seen in Chapter 6 that yellow and brown quartz of good quality is known from several Irish localities, though the cairngorms from the Mournes, Carlingford and Slieve Gullion are usually badly flawed. But the best material, including the somewhat legendary ninety-pound crystal, hails from Dungiven in county Londonderry. In the English Lake District, Cleator Moor and Shap Fell have yielded fine fullblooded cairngorms. Across the border there are large granite masses in Kirkcudbrightshire, and the Highlands are bespattered with bright red on the geological map. Most of these areas have some cairngorm or morion.

The Cairngorms and Arran are the first on the list, but the granites of Lochnagar and many Aberdeenshire quarries, as well as the Gourock Quarry in Renfrewshire, North Rona in the Hebrides, Ben Loyal and Quinag in Sutherland are well known as cairngorm localities. Jet-black morion also occurs in association with agates near Montrose in Forfarshire and near Luthrie in Fife.

10.4 MINERALOGICAL CHARACTERISTICS

As repeatedly stated, the hardness of all quartzes is 7; they cannot be scratched by steel. Specific gravity hovers about 2·65. Clear cleavage planes are absent; the crystals splinter irregularly or break with conchoidal and, in the case of the 'mineralogical amethyst', rippled fracture. They are weakly birefringent, with refractive indices of 1·55 and 1·54. Dispersion being also weak, quartz has little fire. The lustre is vitreous (like glass) or greasy. A fully-developed crystal is a six-sided (hexagonal) column (prism) terminated at both ends by regular pyramids, bounded, coincidentally with the prism faces, by six isosceles triangles, whose sides are one half again as long as the base. The crystal is typically lined, or *striated*, across the column. Such perfection, however, is rare: the various faces are often unequally developed, subsidiary rectangles and triangles pop up on the corners, several crystals may coalesce, which results in very complicated shapes. In druse crystals, which grow out of a rock wall, the bottom pyramid is usually absent. But bipyramidal crystals, with or without a narrow prismatic girdle, are likewise encountered, as well as are, if seldom, pseudo-cubical ones (see p. 90).

A connection exists between crystal shape and the mineral impurities responsible for the colour. Cairngorms and amethysts are often strongly striated, but in rock crystals the striations may be absent altogether. Amethyst crystals are typically uncomplicated.

There are at least two high-temperature varieties of crystalline silica:

cristobalite and tridymite, the latter of which occurs in the lavas of
Antrim, Northern Ireland. It is clear, occasionally milky; crystallizes in
bevelled hexagonal plates; has a lower specific gravity of 2·27; and is also
a little softer than quartz, the hardness fluctuating between 6·5 and 7.

Cairngorm, Arran

11 Granite accessories

It was in a remote part of the Cairngorms, over Glen Avon, one sunny August afternoon. The distances were pale slate-blue beneath strings of pearly cloud, and the near hillsides green-purple and green-brown, shimmering with small scree and hung with the perished silk of waterfalls, rocks rising in dark triangles from pools of shadow. Bouldery terrace succeeded bouldery terrace after flights of springy turf, but the summit seemed to recede with each step up. Suddenly my eyes lit upon a grey weathered boulder. A green streak ran right across it—a vein of beryl.

The stuff was of good colour, almost emerald-green in parts, but massive and barely translucent, jumbled with felspar. No clear crystals at all. Somewhere among those fields of boulder-scree the vein would be continued, become 'vuggy'. The Cairngorms had yielded crystals of beryl and topaz up to a foot long.

The 1795 *Statistical Account of Scotland* spoke of 'pellucid stones, of the nature of precious stones, equally transparent, beautiful in their colour, and some of them, particularly the emerald, as hard as any oriental jem of the same kind' found in the Cairngorms But my time was short and luck did not serve. And one needs luck; a schoolgirl once rode on the chairlift up Cairngorm, got off at the top station, stooped and picked up a one-inch gem-quality beryl from the path where thousands had walked.

Sometime in the eighteenth century *Cailleach nan Clach* (The Old Woman of Stones), who used to flit like a wraith through the corries at the foot of beetling crags, searching, searching, searching, had a dream. She saw a huge crystal beckoning to her from the rocks of Beinn a' Bhuird, near Braemar. She noted well the place and wasted no time. At first light she was on her way up through the cool pine forests, and . . . she found it! The famous Invercauld Cairngorm weighs 52 lb, and is now on show at Braemar Castle.[70]

In any search time is a very important factor, and the Cailleach was not otherwise gainfully occupied, although, no doubt, she managed to scrape up a living from her stones, as did many Cairngorm ghillies, some of whom, Seton Gordon maintains, 'died from drinking water from gravelly burns'.[72] My authorship includes *The Cairngorms on Foot and Ski*,[68] so that these mountains are very familiar to me. In fact, I used to live there many years ago. This, though, was before my interest in gemstones had been seriously aroused, and my visits since then have been comparatively brief and chiefly in winter. In the crowded south prophetic dreams are rarer than emeralds, and, alas!, I have never found any 'oriental jem' of this description, only some cairngorms, rock crystals and a waterworn stump of topaz in the 'Blue Hills' (Cairngorms) of Scotland. On the other hand, I have come across a beautifully clear twinned crystal of blue-green aquamarine, about a quarter of an inch long (now in the British Museum), in a perfectly empty druse on Am Binnein, and two even smaller, but flawless, dark sapphire-blue beryls in Glen Rosa, in the 'Grey Cuillin' of Arran.

Fluorite occurs in granite druses, e.g. on Shap Fell in Westmorland, so does apatite, and cassiterite in Cornwall; even sapphire and diamond are known from some foreign granites, while veins of metalliferous quartz and pegmatite may hold almost anything, including gold and platinum, or more likely pyrite and antimonite. Typically, however, and not unexpectedly the accessory minerals of acid igneous rocks are silicates: beryl, euclase, phenakite, spodumene, zircon, topaz, tourmaline and garnet. This does not mean to say that these minerals are confined to the granite clan; indeed, they may be formed by regional or contact metamorphism as well. But most granites contain at least one of them.

II.I BERYL

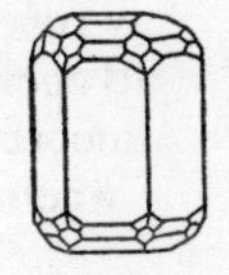

Beryl is a composite silicate of two light silvery metals, beryllium and aluminium, $Al_2Be_3(Si_2O_6)_3$, alloys of which are important in aircraft and spacecraft industries, so that coarse beryl is valued as a source of beryllium. W. F. Davidson of Penrith (Cumberland) has found a $9\frac{1}{2}$-lb beryl, now in the British Museum, in Knoydart, Inverness-shire.[11] J. H. Collins[8] mentions an American crystal which measured 4 ft. 3 in. by 2 ft. 8 in. by 1 ft. 10 in. But this is a mere baby! A coarse crystal of beryl unearthed at Albany, Maine, U.S.A., was described as the 'size of a cottage' and weighed 18 tons.[37] There is some massive beryl about St. Just in Cornwall; it is, however, more familiar as a gemstone.

Standing at $7\frac{1}{2}$–$7\frac{3}{4}$ on Mohs' scale, beryl is somewhat harder than quartz, which it resembles in hexagonal crystal form, except that its prisms are lined lengthwise and not across, and commonly end up flat. Sometimes the end face is bevelled at the edges or develops pretty, small subsidiary facets, and very occasionally the crystal looks like a sharp pencil grooved at the point. The fracture is conchoidal, without clear cleavage, the lustre glassy or greasy, as in quartz. The refractive index is somewhat higher across the prism (1·59) than along it (1·57). The dispersion is low—again like quartz. So, too, is the specific gravity, which varies between 2·65 and 2·75 depending on fluctuations in chemical composition, to which the differences of colour are due.

Beryl may be colourless, like rock crystal, or white, like vein quartz, as found in the granite quarries of Mabe and Constantine in Cornwall. Collins[8] lists 'red, grey . . . , iridescent, or opalescent' as further alternatives. The more usual varieties of gem beryl, however, are blue, green, yellow and pink or mauve, opalescence occurring in the yellow, or *golden*, *beryl*. The pink or mauve beryl is known as *morganite*. The different colours may be arranged in bands in the same crystal, as is also the case of topaz and tourmaline. Such banded crystals, in green, white and mauve, are said to be found on the east side of Cairngorm, but I have yet to see one.

All coloured beryls are dichroic, which provides one way of distinguishing between emerald and aquamarine, as well as between true beryl and other similarly coloured stones masquerading under such fancy names as 'oriental emerald', which is a green sapphire, 'Brazilian emerald', which is a tourmaline, 'Siam aquamarine', which is a zircon, and so on.

This confusion of nomenclature extends into the beryl family itself. The blue and green-blue stones are called *aquamarine*, which is well and good, except that pale green specimens are likewise so described, although at other times they are referred to as *heliodors*, which is an alternative name of golden beryl as well, and may actually be pale emeralds. Yet *emerald* is a somewhat different substance, some of the aluminium being replaced by chromium according to the formula $Be_3AlCr_2(Si_2O_6)_3$, and so it has a different spectrum and in a dichroscope gives a pale yellowish green and a bluish green image, while the corresponding colours for aquamarine are 'usually' pale yellow and pale sky-blue.[4] Emerald is also slightly heavier and softer. Pale specimens do not fetch a high price, whereas aquamarines are expected to be pale. Now you know—I hope (I am not sure that I do).

Apart from the features just mentioned, the jeweller's emerald is distinguishable by its deep shamrock-green colour, and the only British locality where such stones appear to be found is the Cairngorm Mountains. (The doubtful case of an Irish emerald from the Mournes is mentioned on p. 67.) The leek-green stones are classed as heliodors, and the yellow beryls are usually slightly greenish in hue.

Green beryl, presumably of the aquamarine variety, occurs in the Dartmoor granites. Lustleigh is mentioned in this connection. On the other hand, the beryls from the Meldon Quarry near Okehampton I have seen were blue. I have several pieces of Dartmoor veinstone, which contains a bewildering variety of minerals, extremely difficult to identify owing to their minute size and imperfect crystallization. However, green and yellow material with the structure of beryl seems to be present, although the dark-green hexagonal crystals appearing in section are probably tourmaline. The small Cornish beryls from St. Michael's Mount and Mabe are blue. There is a record of beryl[48] in the lavas of Walla Crag, near Keswick, in the Lake District, but no particulars are given.

In Scotland, beryl occurs, apart from Arran and the Cairngorms, in Aberdeenshire granites: Rubislaw Quarry—yellow and occasionally over a foot long; Pitfoddels Quarry—green; Pass of Ballater—yellow; also near Belhelvie and Keig Bridge. I have seen large turbid yellow-green beryls from Struy Bridge and we must not forget that $9\frac{1}{2}$-lb crystal from Knoydart (p. 97) in the county of Inverness. Beryl is also found in Kincardineshire, at Kinloch Rannoch, Perthshire, and on Ben Loyal, Sutherland. I would not regard this list as exhaustive.

Blue beryl is not particularly scarce in the Mountains of Mourne, in Ulster, while the green variety occurs in large masses in the Rosses granites of Donegal. The quality and colour of these stones are generally poor, but clear specimens have been found.[31, 35]

11.2 EUCLASE AND PHENAKITE

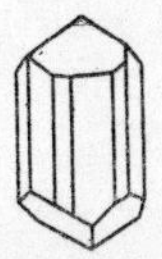

Euclase, a rare hydrated silicate of beryllium and aluminium, $Al(OH.Be_2SiO_4)$, one crystal of which has been confirmed at Cligga Head, Cornwall,[46] is closely comparable to beryl (hardness $7\frac{1}{2}$, specific gravity about $3\cdot1$, refractive index $1\cdot67$–$1\cdot65$), but belongs to the monoclinic system. The colouring is pale and varies from blue to green, being reminiscent of aquamarine.

Phenakite

There is also a plain silicate of beryllium, Be_2SiO_4, called phenakite. It is described as a 'gemstone of little importance (often confused with quartz)',[39] which it indeed resembles in crystalline habit, except for the absence of transverse striations and the presence of narrow vertical faces along the edges of the prism. It is also harder ($7\cdot5$–$8\cdot0$) and heavier ($3\cdot0$). Phenakite may be colourless, pale yellow or pale pink. It has been recorded near St. Agnes, in Cornwall.[52]

11.3 SPODUMENE

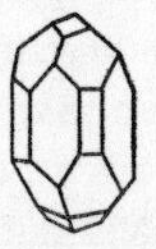

Spodumene is another variation of the theme of beryl, in which lithium, the lightest of all metals, replaces beryllium—$AlLi.Si_2O_6$. It is, however, somewhat heavier than beryl ($3\cdot1$), as well as being a shade softer than quartz ($6\frac{1}{2}$–7), which it somewhat resembles, although its striated prisms are monoclinic. The crystals are often large and may be looked for in granite and gneiss pegmatite. The coloration varies from amethystine purple through lilac and pink to yellow and emerald green ('lithia emerald'). The pink variety is known as kunzite and the green as hiddenite. Spodumene is dichroic and birefringent (refractive index 1·68 and 1·66), with somewhat more fire than either beryl or quartz. It has been recorded, without particulars and it seems doubtfully,[41] in the Peterhead granites[4, 59] in Aberdeenshire, and at Killiney near Dublin and in some pegmatites on the west flank of the Leinster granite (Brindley), in Ireland.[10]

11.4 SPHENE

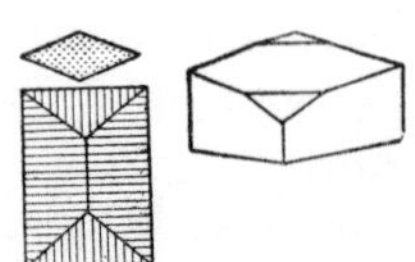

The likewise monoclinic sphene is a different type of mineral, being a combination of a titanate and silicate of calcium, $CaTi(O|SiO_4)$ Its wedge- or lozenge-shaped crystals occur in acid igneous rocks, but also form by contact metamorphism in limestone. Sphene is comparatively soft $(5-5\frac{1}{2})$ and heavy (3·45–3·53). Its further distinguishing marks are adamantine lustre and fire, which rivals that of diamond and is due to high dispersion, combined with birefringence and refractive indices of 2·06 and 1·91, exceeding those of most natural stones (see pp. 77 ff). The colours are yellow, green, brown, red-brown and black, but good clear crystals are rare, and even these are slightly cloudy. The occurrence of sphene in Wales (p. 25) and Scotland (p. 38) has been noted.

11.5 ZIRCON

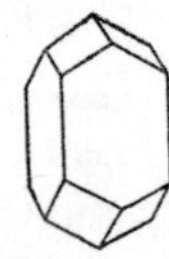

Zircon is comparable to sphene in fire. Its birefringence, with refractive indices of 1·99 and 1·92, is even higher, and one sees double through a zircon crystal or cut gem. The dispersion (p. 79) of 0·038 is somewhat below that of sphene (0·051) and diamond (0·044), but still at the top of the list. This is how colourless zircon, misleadingly dubbed 'Matura diamond', can sometimes be passed off for the genuine article, or, more honestly, be used to enhance a small diamond, which is mounted embedded in a larger but cheaper zircon. Zircon, however, is readily distinguishable by its high specific gravity of 4·33–4·75 and much lower hardness, ranging from 7 to $7\frac{1}{2}$. These limits reflect the varying perfection of crystallization, seemingly of radioactive origin. The 'low-type' zircons are lighter, softer and less refractive than the fully-crystalline 'high-type' ones. The former are usually greenish and can be converted into the high type by heat treatment; this also alters their colour to a greenish blue and makes them dichroic, which natural zircons are not. Most of the colourless 'Matura diamonds' on the market have likewise been obtained by heating.[39]

Yet even without such artifices the chromatic range of zircon is unusually wide. Pale yellow stones are known as jargoons, and red or brown ones as hyacinths or jacinths, but there are natural green and purple varieties as well.

Zircon is a straightforward silicate of zirconium ($Zr.SiO_4$), a metal used in the manufacture of refractory materials and electric equipment. The crystals belong to the tetragonal system and commonly assume the form of pointed prisms of rectangular cross section.

Zircon is finely disseminated through many gneisses and granites, for instance, in the Lake District[56] in the form of minute inclusions, but well-developed large crystals are relatively rare. It has been recorded in *xenoliths* (external rock fragments engulfed in the magma) in the Great Rocks Dale Dyke in Derbyshire.[27] The occurrence of zircon in Ireland is subject to doubt (p. 57), but W. J. McCallien[37] lists several Scottish zircon localities after Heddle,[33] to wit: Strontian on Loch Sunart in Argyll; Elie Ness in Fifeshire; Brann a'Bharra in Lewis, Scalpay and Tiree in the Hebrides; Milton in Glen Urquhart, Loch a'Bhruthaich and Struy Bridge in Inverness-shire; Burn of Palnure in Kirkcudbright-shire—in granite boulders; Mam Ratagan above Loch Duich, Glensgaich near Achnasheen and the head of Allt Graad on Loch Glass side in Ross-shire; and, finally, Beinn Laoghal (Ben Loyal) and Ben Hope in Sutherland. Again I doubt if even Heddle's lifelong dilligence could have sufficed to survey all of the vast solitudes of the Northern High-lands. At any rate zircon has been recorded since in the Triassic sandstones of Morayshire,[21] and I have found good red zircons near Trinafour, in Perthshire.

II.6 TOPAZ

I am not sure about sphene. I can half-sense it glittering somewhere in a corner in the *Arabian Nights* or Omar Khayyam. But zircon, spodumene, phenakite, you do not call that sort of thing a real gem, do you? They are upstarts without pedigree or emotional appeal. Now topaz, that is different: it touches the heart of imagination with the hand of antiquity. And, of course, it is yellow (as the 'poet' says, 'The topaz is yellow, the sapphire blue, the emerald green, and so are you'). Hence a crop of false topazes: Scotch, Spanish, Oriental, Occidental, and even plain 'quartz topaz', all of which are citrine, save for the 'Oriental topaz', which is a sapphire.[4, 26, 59]

So it comes as something of a shock to learn that British topaz is typically a pale sky-blue or colourless. To be sure, there is some yellow topaz as well; also green, brown and wine-red in the corries of Beinn a'Bhuird, where the crystals are often multicoloured.

As a fluoro-silicate of aluminium, $Al_2[(FOH)_2SiO_4]$, topaz is charac-teristic of, though not limited to, *greisen*, which—it will be recalled—is

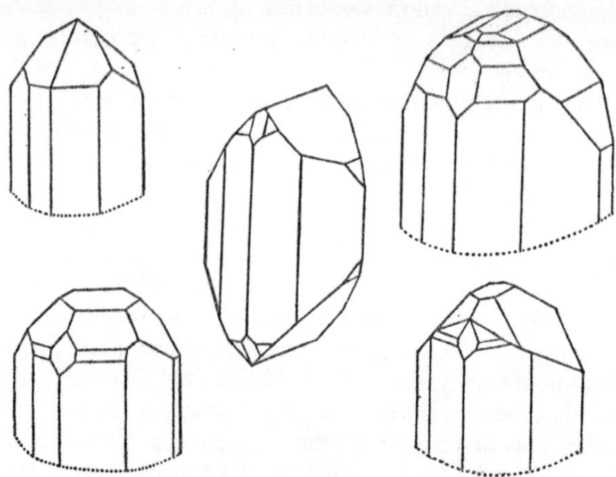

granite penetrated and altered by hot fluids rich in fluorine. In greisen (grysen) felspar is largely eliminated and replaced by white mica and partly by topaz, fluorite being another typical accessory, with tourmaline and apatite as possibles. The replacement of felspar by mica gives such greisenized rock a soft crumbly texture, which is a bonus to the rock-hound.

Apart from granite proper, topaz is also found in the metamorphic aureole round acid igneous intrusions and as a gangue mineral in tin veins.

All this points to its presence in the Cornish and Devonian granites, and in association with these, and rightly so, although topaz crystals are rare and do not reach anything like the size of those from the Cairngorm pegmatites. They are usually colourless or pale blue and, characteristically of topaz, seldom flawed. The Cornish localities are: St. Burian, Lamorna Cove, St. Michael's Mount, Tremearne, Constantine, St. Agnes. Dartmoor is not usually listed, but Lundy is.

I have no clear record of topaz from the English North, but it occurs as a rock-forming mineral in North Wales. In Scotland the Cairngorms are the principal source of topaz, the largest crystals having been found on Beinn a'Bhuird. Honey-coloured topaz has also been reported from the glacial erratics of Brodick Bay, in Arran—I have found none—and Machrihanish in Kintyre. The reports of topaz finds on Harris in the Hebrides, and on Lochnagar in Aberdeenshire are unconfirmed. In Ireland clear colourless topaz is known from the Mourne druses, where it occurs together with blue beryl and smoky quartz.

The Geological Museum in London contains a water-worn topaz boulder from Brazil weighing 29½ lb. Smaller, but still impressive topaz 'chuckies' have been found in the Cairngorms. In fact, topaz is a good 'crystallizer', and occurs in bold, well-developed prisms of the ortho-rhombic pattern, striated lengthwise. These may be long or short, occasionally twinned and terminate in a square pyramid or roof-like structure, which may develop subsidiary facets, but, unlike those of quartz or beryl, the large terminal faces need not coincide with the side faces of the prism (*see* opp.). Topaz has perfect cleavage at right angles to the long axis of the prism and splits very readily in this direction. For this reason it must be handled very carefully and shielded against strong vibration. The lustre is vitreous. Like most gemstones, topaz is doubly refractive (refractive indices 1·63 and 1·62) and has a little more fire than beryl or quartz; most coloured stones are dichroic, but this is not apparent to the unaided eye. The hardness is, of course, 8, and specific gravity fluctuates between 3·5 and 3·6.

Tourmaline and garnet are complex silicates of variable composition; they occur as accessories in some English and Irish granites (see Chapter 4), but may be considered primarily metamorphic. Apatite is another gem mineral present in many granites, for instance, at the eastermost tip of the Dartmoor boss and in the south-east of the main Donegal granite, but it is not a silicate and has an affinity to fluorite, which too is among the granite accessories, and may be best discussed in connection with it.

11.7   FELSPARS

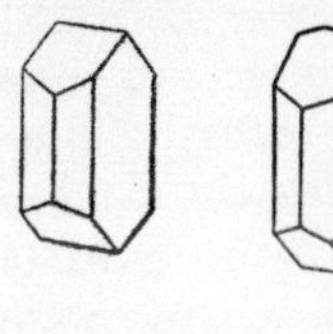 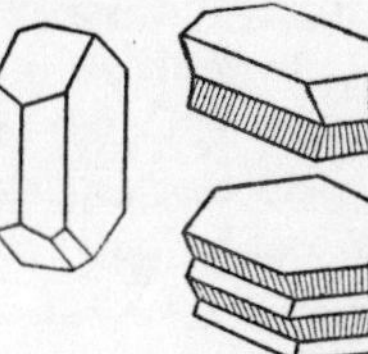 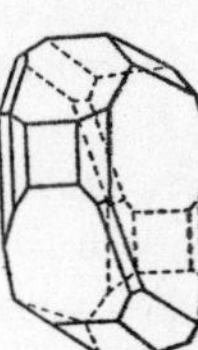

Felspar, or feldspar, is no mere accessory, but an essential ingredient not only of granite, but of most igneous rocks, and may form by metamorphic processes as well. As a gemstone, however, it is only marginal and used mainly in manufacturing glass and porcelain.

Chemically felspars, of which there are a bewildering variety, are silicates of two metals, one of which is aluminium and the other potassium (K), calcium (Ca) or sodium (Na), the latter two being largely interchangeable and often present together in variable proportions. For the most part felspars are opaque and look rather like bone with a pearly lustre, to match which the crystals also bear a vague resemblance to coffins. Orthoclase, or potash felspar ($KAl.Si_3O_8$), is *usually* mono-clinic. Plagioclases belong to the triclinic system and range in composi-tion from pure soda felspar (albite) to pure lime felspar (anorthite) through various mixtures of the two. They are typically opaque, but orthoclase may be translucent or transparent and provides the main gem varieties, for which the hardness of 6 is adequate. Plagioclase may be harder, up to $6\frac{1}{2}$. The colour varies, flesh-pink being reserved for orthoclase and red and yellow for plagioclase, while both may be white, grey or green.

The transparent orthoclase is called adularia and occurs in Cornwall on Snowdon, in North Wales, and in the Mountains of Mourne in colourless form, but I have also come across some colourless transparent felspar in Arran (Scotland). Such stones are not reckoned 'gemworthy', but yellow adularia from Madagascar may be admired in cut form in the Geological Museum in London. Better known is moonstone, said to bring luck to those born in June. This is adularia enclosing thin lamellae of albite, which in a cabochon produce a shifting blue sheen. There is one place in Cornwall, glorying in the name of Gluvias Burnt-house near Penryn, where moonstone is said to have been found, but this report is clouded by doubt.[8] On the other hand, I have before me a piece of Arran granite with smoky quartz, a little biotite mica and a cream-coloured sub-transparent felspar, which seen at some angles displays a lovely satin sheen that could be shown to advantage in a suitably fashioned stone.

Amazonstone or amazonite, a green or blue-green triclinic kind of potash felspar (microcline), has been reported from Sutherland.[77] Sunstone, or aventurine felspar, has already been mentioned on p. 91.

Plagioclase affords one ornamental variety, labradorite, represented massively in Labrador as the name implies, but also present in Antrim, Ulster, and in the English Lake District. Owing to small lamellar inclusions, labradorite shimmers with moving blue, green and yellow, occasionally red, lights, like the wing of some exotic butterfly. But to bring out these beauties, the stone has to be properly cut along the planes of cleavage, usually in flat slabs, and as found in nature wears a grey-green greasy look, like Kipling's Limpopo River.

12 Fruits of heat and pressure

Rocks decay and are reformed, new crystals, often of a different kind, taking the place of the old as the mighty hand of nature folds and twists the coat of the Earth or pours molten magma into its seams and tears. The coat is solid rock and tremendous pressures are needed to fold it. The temperatures of the magma reach and exceed 1000° C. Pressure and heat often generate different minerals. Since, though, the friction involved in moving millions of tons of rock may also be a source of great heat, it is safer to leave it to the geologists and mineralogists to disagree at leisure which mineral is due to what.

On the other hand, it is not too difficult to distinguish between regional metamorphism, due mainly to pressure, and contact metamorphism round igneous intrusions, where heat is the main factor of transformation. The former extends over large areas and affects ancient strata, while the latter's range is limited from a few inches to about a couple of miles, depending on the mass and heat of the invading magma, as well as on the rate at which this heat is dissipated and this in turn on the depth below the surface. Reality, however, is always more complicated than textbooks, and the mountain-building processes of which the folding of the rocks is a sign and portent also give rise to igneous intrusions, so that the two types of metamorphism often overlap.

Heat and pressure turn sandstone into quartzite, limestone into marble. But typically the rocks which have been subjected to great pressures in the course of land movements become layered, or foliated, so that they readily split into thin slabs or sheets. Such rocks are called *schists* (p. 11). Although the general effect of metamorphism is to 'ignify' sedimentary formations, regional metamorphism affects igneous rocks as well. Granites are altered to granulite and eventually assume the banded structure of gneiss, though this is also the end product of pressure metamorphism of sedimentary rocks. Basic igneous rocks are transformed into 'greenstone', or, more accurately, hornblende and epidiorite schists and serpentinite. Schists, quartzites and gneisses make up most of the Scottish Highlands and Islands, appear massively in the north-west of Ireland and patchily in England and Wales (see Chapters 4, 5 and 6).

When I was small and in bed with high temperature, which, alas!, was not infrequent, I used to get a peculiar sensation as though the blanket were enormous, miles long and wide, and all horribly kinked and folded. This was inexpressibly sickening, and the tortured intricacies of fold and foliation of the Dalradian schists have something of the same quality. It has taken millions of years of pushing, pulling and twisting to achieve such rock texture, and the pressures involved increased with the depth below the surface. Since the Caledonian mountains were first levelled down more or less completely and then their stumps were up-raised and dismembered by streams and glaciers into the present Highland bens, the height of the rocks exposed in these bears no relation to the depth at which they had originally lain. This depth, however, is generally the greater the farther away to the north-west we move from the Highland Boundary Fault. The degree of transformation follows a parallel course, from slate through phyllite, a silky foliated rock with flakes of sericite, and mica-schist to gneiss. The Irish Caledonides show a similar trend. This simple pattern, though, is greatly compli-cated by the changes due to the heat of the later (Devonian and Tertiary) igneous intrusions.

Each metamorphic stage is characterized by certain minerals. Garnet (almandine) first appears in the phyllites, and mica-schists being joined at the next stage by staurolite and kyanite in the mica-schists and gneisses, the two latter minerals being replaced by sillimanite and by cordierite in the most highly metamorphosed gneisses; but garnet persists to the end. Diopside, corundum and idocrase are further possible gem minerals belonging to this stage, while beryl and tour-maline may appear in the mica schists of appropriate chemistry. Indeed, tourmaline is found in Scotland together with kyanite in Glen Clova, Mull and Unst.

12.1 TOURMALINE

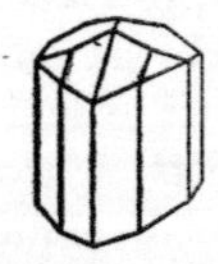

Tourmaline is a highly complex silicate of boron and aluminium with varying proportions of magnesium, iron and the light alkali metals (sodium, potassium and lithium), which affect its physical properties. The specific gravity ranges from 2·94 to 3·24 and hardness from 7 to $7\frac{1}{2}$. The crystals belong to the hexagonal system and usually take the form of long prisms of roughly triangular cross-section with rounded corners; they are strongly lined lengthwise, so that the side facets are partly lost in the grooves, and the hexagonal pattern asserts itself only in the terminal facets, when present, which may not coincide with the side ones and lack symmetrical correspondence between themselves. Like topaz, tourmaline is pyro-electric, and, if heated or rubbed, will attract dust, chaff or small bits of paper.

Optically it is glassy, has little fire, owing to low dispersion and refractive indices (1·62–1·64) only slightly above those of quartz, but it is strongly birefringent and markedly dichroic. A crystal of tourmaline looks very dark when viewed along the prism, and pale across it. For this reason it is usual to cut dark specimens with the 'table' (the large frontal face of the gem) aligned with the edge of the prism, and conversely at right angles to the prism in pale stones, which stand to gain by enhancing their colour.

The colouring varies widely with composition and is not due to minor impurities as in many other gemstones. The common iron-tourmaline, or *schorl*, is usually black or brownish-black. It is one of the main constituents of the Cornish and Devonian granites, and some fine crystals have come from Bovey Tracey in the latter. Most of the Scottish tourmaline is also schorl, e.g. in Glen Clova, and so are the Irish tourmalines from Altnadua near Castlewellan, County Down, and the Donegal and Leinster granites. Schorl is not a gemstone, and the difficulty with the reports of tourmaline is that they do not generally specify what kind of tourmaline has been found. There may be some excuse for this in the fluidity of composition of tourmalines, which shade into one another by imperceptible gradations, like felspars or garnets (to be considered later on), so that different varieties may be expected side by side. This is particularly true of pegmatites and mineral lodes, whose chemistry may depart considerably from that of the country rock.

In writing about the St. Austell granite C. S. Exley[22] says: 'Round clear *topaz* is present in all granites except the biotite-muscovite variety, as is *apatite*, which, though usually rounded and very clouded, may also be anhedral [ill-formed] and clear, enclosed by felspar. . . . Primary *tourmaline* is brown, sometimes zoned with blue, and may be interstitial or replacing felspar, while secondary tourmaline is blue-green, acicular and often grows on primary crystals. It is rare in the fluorite-granite. . . .'

It will be recalled in this context that the St. Austell granite is largely kaolinized, so that the harder crystals have been released from the grip of the decayed felspar and can be extracted with ease. The rock is traversed by numerous veins, or *stents* as these are locally known, and will contain druses, where large crystals ought to have developed.

Postlethwaite[48] mentions tourmaline among the minerals at the Carrock Mine in the Lake District, and, indeed, I have some black and brown tourmaline from there, but nothing of gem quality. I suspect that tourmaline may be present in some other north English localities as well, but have no definite proof of this.

Most of the Irish tourmaline is also brown or black, but we may recall (p. 60) that red and green tourmaline has been reported from the Ox Mountains and green from Dunfanaghy in the north of county Donegal.[31]

W. J. MacCallien[37] gives without qualification, after Heddle, a longish list of Scottish tourmaline localities, already reproduced in Chapter 5. But there is no reference to coloured tourmalines, and in the museum collections it is all schorl.

Yellow and brown tints are characteristic of magnesium. Alkali metals yield green, red and colourless varieties, but the possible permutations are legion. Good green tourmaline, fancifully described as Brazilian emerald', although its hue is distinctly different from that of. 'true emerald—darker and not so clear—is considered the most valuable *Rubellite*, sometimes known as 'Siberian ruby', makes a closer approach to ruby. The blue or greenish-blue tourmaline is called *indicolite*, and the colourless variety is *achroite*; other colours have escaped christening. Multi-coloured crystals, usually red and green, are not uncommon.

As already indicated, the position with regard to the gem varieties of British and Irish tourmaline is somewhat obscure. I know of no British tourmaline cut as a gem, but my knowledge is not exhaustive. Collins[8] mentions green tourmaline 'on the flanks of Carn Marth', in Cornwall, and near Okehampton, in Devon, the latter of which I can confirm from personal experience (p. 22). Achroite has been found in Cornwall, notably in the Roscommon Cliffs near St. Just, Unanimity Mine in Gwennap, and RocksHill near St. Austell. The Geevor Mine near Trewellard, which is still in operation, has also produced some achroite in 'large prisms ... trikingly zoned in orange', as well as blue and yellow tourmaline.[13] R. D. Penhallurick[45] has found some crystals tentatively identified as achroite at Meldon (Okehampton), where rubellite and indicolite have been reported as well.

12.2   THE GARNETS

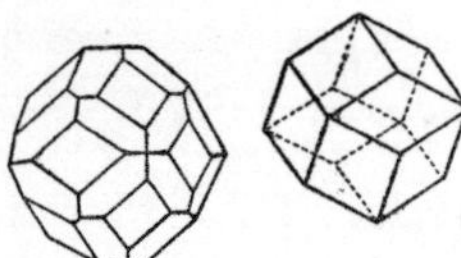

The garnets differ from the tourmalines mainly in the absence of boron; aluminium may or may not be present with other metals; but they share a fluidity of composition, there being no clear boundaries between different kinds of garnet. The 'other metals' are somewhat different: iron, magnesium, manganese, calcium, chromium and titanium. Typically a garnet is a double silicate, for instance the purplish-red almandine, or precious garnet, is an iron-aluminium garnet and the olive-green grossularite is a calcium-aluminium one. The specific gravity ranges from 3·4 to 4·3, hardness from 6 to 8, and refractive index from 1·7 to 1·9, so that garnets have considerable fire. They are singly refracting and non-dichroic. Another unifying feature is the cubic crystalline habit; the cube as such is rare and the most characteristic form is a twelve-sided regular bead. The lustre is resinous. The colour with which the word 'garnet' is traditionally associated is red or brown-

Name	Chemistry	Colour	Hardness	Specific Gravity	Refractive Index
Almandine or Precious garnet	Iron-aluminium silicate	Ruby-red to purple	$7\frac{1}{2}$–8	3·83–4·20	1·78–1·82
Andradite	Iron-calcium silicate	Brown to brownish-green	$6\frac{1}{2}$–7	3·80–3·90	1·88–1·89
Demantoid	Variety of above	Green	$6\frac{1}{2}$–7	3·80–3·90	1·88–1·89
Grossularite	Calcium-aluminium silicate	Pale olive-green	7–$7\frac{1}{2}$	3·60–3·70	1·74–1·76
Hessonite or Cinnamon stone	Variety of above	Honey to orange-red	6	3·50–3·70	1·74–1·76
Melanite	Titanium-calcium silicate	Black	$6\frac{1}{2}$	3·83–3·86	1·8–2·0
Pyrope	Magnesium-aluminium silicate	Deep red	7–$7\frac{1}{2}$	3·65–3·80	1·74–1·75
Spessarite or Spessartine	Manganese-aluminium silicate	Brownish-red to orange	6	3·98–4·25	1·80–1·81
Uvarovite	Calcium-chromium silicate	Green	7	3·4–3·55	1·84

TABLE 2. Classification of garnets

ish-red, but it may be yellow, brown, orange, green, purple, violet, pink, black, and there exists a colourless 'water garnet' as well. Indeed, the only colour that is definitely out is blue.

Although garnet is an accessory mineral of granite and occurs also in volcanic rocks, it may be described as a metamorphic mineral *par excellence* and is commonly found in the metamorphosed clayey sediments, limestones, dolomites and basic igneous formations.

The family of garnets is best presented in tabulated array.[4]

It must be remembered that any such summary can be approximate only, for, as stated, garnet varieties, like human types, shade into one another imperceptibly. Thus the chemical formula of andradite, one of the most variable types, is $Ca_3Fe\ldots_2(SiO_4)_3$, where '...' stands for other metals. There are further varieties, considered rare and of foreign occurrence, such as *topazolite*, a yellow calcium-iron garnet. J. Phemister, however records a 'yellow garnet' of unspecified composition, which 'frequently develops perfect crystal outline', in the South Terras mine in Cornwall.[13]

Garnets which were used quite extensively in early Anglo-Saxon jewellery are usually thought to have been of foreign, probably Scandinavian, origin. Yet garnets are by no means uncommon in the British Isles, and, although mostly of mineralogical rather than gemmological interest, there are exceptions galore to 'confirm' this doubtful 'rule'.

In our travels round the British Isles we have called, however briefly, on the main British and Irish garnet localities.

Garnets of the andradite, grossularite and hessonite variety are to be found in association with the Cornish and Devonian granites. For the most part they are massive and poorly crystallized, but at least the cinnamon-stones from Botallack near St. Just in the former county are translucent, and some specimens suitable for cutting could be found among them. I have also seen clear almandines in the granite of St. Michael's Mount. The black melanite variety is reported from about Lanlivery and Lostwithiel. The other principal source of English garnets is the Lake District, [48, 56] where almandines are to be found in the Borrowdale volcanics and grossularites and andradites in the metamorphic aureoles, notably of the Shap granite, whose druses may also contain garnets. Again these are usually turbid, but I have come across some small, clear green crystals on Shap Fell.

Garnets are of widespread occurrence in the Scottish and Irish micaschists and metamorphic limestones and as accessory minerals in the Leinster, Galway and Donegal granites. The pyrope garnets from Elie Ness in Scotland, popularly known as 'Elie rubies', are definitely of gem quality, and at least some good stones may occasionally be found elsewhere. Uvarovite, generally rare but sometimes 'gemworthy', may be looked for in the chromite-bearing rocks of Unst and Fetlar in the

Shetlands. Heddle[33] has recorded the colourless water garnet at two localities in the county of Banff.

12.3   STAUROLITE

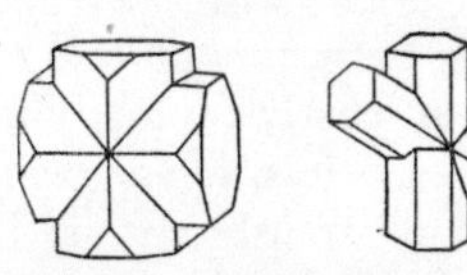

As regional metamorphism progresses, almandine garnet is joined by staurolite, which it somewhat resembles in being a complicated hydro-silicate or iron and aluminium of variable composition, hardness 7–7½, specific gravity 3·7–3·8, and a reddish-brown or blackish-brown colour. But its crystalline habit is very different. Not only does it form six-sided prisms according to the orthorhombic prescription, but these are usually spliced crosswise in 'staurolite twins', giving the effect of a cross. Although typically opaque, it may be translucent and achieve sufficient transparency to be cut as a gem.

The 'habitat' of staurolite is very similar to that of garnet, and, in fact, they often 'live' side by side in the Scottish Highlands and in Donegal.

12.4   KYANITE

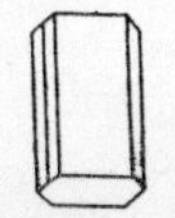

Another gem mineral to be sought at the same address is kyanite, also known as disthene, which is the Greek for 'two-strengths', for the hardness as measured across the triclinic prism comes at 7, but at barely 5 lengthwise. The crystals are frequently arrayed in rosettes, for instance, in the Shetlands, which together with The Ross of Mull and Kinloch Rannoch have produced some of the best material.

Kyanite is a silicate of aluminium of the formula Al_2SiO_5 with a variable proportion of ferric oxide, which is responsible for its characteristic blue colouring. But other metallic constituents may alter this to red, green or yellow. The colour tends to be patchy, as in amethyst, with parts of the crystal water-clear or opaque, white or grey. Kyanite is dichroic and doubly refracting (refractive indices 1·73 and 1·72). It is a fairly heavy stone, having a specific gravity of 3·60–3·68.

An increase in metamorphic heat will turn kyanite to sillimanite or fibrolite of identical chemistry, but somewhat lighter (specific gravity 3·23) and crystallizing in the orthorhombic system, most commonly in felt-like fibres (whence the alternative name) or thin needle-like prisms. It is, indeed, the high-temperature form of the same substance, andalusite being the low-temperature and kyanite the high-pressure form. Andalusite has a further variety, which contains carbonaceous matter and is known as chiastolite, macle or cross-stone from the cruciform pattern it displays in cross section.

12.5 ANDALUSITE

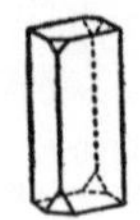

Andalusite is harder than sillimanite, 7 to $7\frac{1}{2}$ as against 6 to 7. The specific gravity is 3·1–3·2 and the crystals are likewise orthorhombic, but usually rather thick and very simple: a quadrangular brick with bevelled corners. The lustre is vitreous in both, though that of sillimanite is described as 'fat' and of andalusite as 'pearly'; it may also be dull in the latter case. Andalusite may be colourless, olive-green, brown or reddish-yellow. Commonly opaque or translucent, it is doubly refracting (refractive indices 1·63 and 1·64) and strongly dichroic in clear specimens, the same crystals looking brownish-red along the prism and green at right angles to it.

Andalusite is conjured up in clayey sediments by metamorphic heat and may be looked for on Dartmoor and at its edge near Okehampton in Devon, where it occurs in the form of chiastolite in altered slate at Ivybridge and with axinite, of which more anon, at Holestock; also in Cumberland, Scotland and Ireland (Leinster granite aureole). It may occasionally be found in granite druses.

12.6 SILLIMANITE

To return to sillimanite, it has a distribution similiar to that of kyanite and extends from mica- and hornblende-schist into gneiss, where it overlaps with cordierite, which marks the last stage of regional metamorphism. It is common in the Scottish Highlands and Donegal.

Sillimanite is birefringent (refractive indices 1·63 and 1·65) and dichroic. The colouring is faint: greyish-yellow, greyish-green or brownish. Crystals of a pale sapphire-blue are used as gemstones, but you may see cut specimens of a greenish hue at the British Museum.

12.7 CORDIERITE

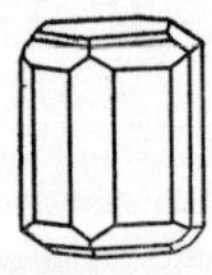

Cordierite, also known as iolite, dichroite and water-sapphire, is a double silicate of aluminium and magnesium, part of which is replaced by ferrous iron, with water of hydration. The specific gravity fluctuates between 2·58 and 2·65. The lustre is greasy or vitreous as in the case of sillimanite; the crystal system is also the same but the prisms are short, stumpy, the side faces numbering ten or more, and rounded at top and bottom. Not remarkably, when found in the rock (which may be granite), they are too dull and turbid for cutting, but, if free to develop, are translucent or transparent, doubly refracting (refractive indices 1·54 and 1·55) and strongly dichroic, whence, of course, the name of dichroite. The colour is blue-grey or yellowish, but owing to dichroism the crystal may look a deep signal-blue in one direction, pale yellow at right angles to it and nearly white at right angles to both. This property can be exploited to advantage by using a suitably oriented, deep table cut.

The main cordierite localities are the Scottish Highlands, Donegal and Cornwall. The best foreign stones come from Ceylon, Burma and Madagascar.

12.8 GLAUCOPHANE

A rather rare similarly circumstanced mineral is glaucophane, found in the soda-rich mica-schists of Anglesey east of the line drawn from Malldraeth to Red Wharf Bay.[63] This complex hydrated silicate is not usually listed among gemstones, but I do not see why, for it has an adequate hardness of 6–6½ and often an attractive deep-blue colour, becoming nearly black in the darker specimens. It is translucent and would make a good cabochon. Glaucophane may be massive or crystalline, forming hexagonal prisms of the monoclinic system, with perfect fracture along the crystal faces and a specific gravity of 3·0–3·1.

Metamorphic alteration of lime-rich rocks may give rise to calcium garnets and one or more of the following silicates, depending on the composition of the rock itself and of the magmatic emanations: axinite, idocrase (or vesuvianite), diopside and epidote. Axinite contains boron and may be accompanied by tourmaline. If phosphorus is present apatite may result, and fluorine or hydrofluoric acid in the gases from the magma may produce fluorite and topaz. Apatite and fluorite, however, are not so much metamorphic as pneumatolytic minerals, due to the chemical action of hot gases, apart from being accessories in igneous rocks, so that they do not properly belong here. Nor are they silicates. Tourmaline and topaz have already been considered (pp. 106 and 101).

12.9 AXINITE

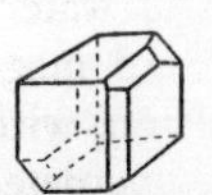

Axinite is a complex boro-silicate of calcium and aluminium with a variable proportion of iron and manganese. It may be massive, but is characteristically crystalline, forming thin translucent plates with very sharp edges (like an axe), less frequently brick-like or columnar bodies, belonging to the triclinic system. The crystals are brilliant and deeply grooved, almost corrugated, break very easily and must be handled with care. The hardness ranges from 6½ to 7, and specific gravity from 2·63 to 2·70. The colour is clove-brown to plum, but may also be greyish to greenish. The appearance of the crystal varies with the angle of viewing owing to strong dichroism, changing from violet or bluish to brown, greenish or greyish. Axinite is doubly refractive (refractive indices 1·68 and 1·69) and has more fire than topaz. It may be facetted or cut *en*

cabochon, but seldom adorns a jeweller's display window. You can, however, admire some cut specimens at the Geological Museum in London.

I can have found no record of axinite in either Scotland or Ireland, but the mineral is not uncommon in the metamorphosed 'killas' (p. 15) of Cornwall and Devon, where clove-brown crystals up to $1\frac{1}{2}$ inches across have been found. They may, though, be rather difficult to extract, as they are often solidly embedded in hard metamorphic rock, largely made up of massive garnet. Axinite is also known from Caernarvonshire, in Wales.[53]

12.10   IDOCRASE

The chemistry of idocrase is even more complicated than and not unsimilar to that of axinite, but it does not contain any boron, to make up for which variable amounts of ferric oxide, manganese oxide, magnesia, potash and soda may be present, affecting the colouring and specific gravity. Idocrase may be massive or granular. The crystals belong to the tetragonal system, and commonly take the form of short thick prisms. The lustre is glassy, greasy on a broken surface, which is not hard to come by, for, like axinite, idocrase is brittle and lacking in regular cleavage. The hardness is $6\frac{1}{2}$, specific gravity between 3·3 and 3·5. The stone is transparent or at least translucent, weakly birefringent. The predominant colouring is brown or greenish-brown, but yellow, red-brown and blue varieties are not unknown.

Idocrase occurs in the Loch Tay limestone, in Perthshire, Scotland. The Irish localities are mainly in Donegal, where the stone has a 'hairbrown' colour,[47] but it is also present in the metamorphic aureole of the Carlingford granite (county Louth).[36]

12.11   DIOPSIDE

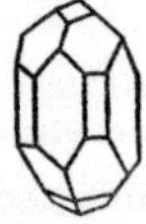

It is often associated with diopside, a straightforward calcium-magnesium silicate, $CaMg.Si_2O_6$, characteristically pale to bottle-green, but also colourless, grey or yellow. Ferrous iron appears to be the main source of colour.

The mineral is weakly dichroic and doubly refracting (refractive indices 1·67 and 1·70). It may assume lamellar, scaly or massive form. The short prismatic crystals, often twinned, belong to the monoclinic system and have grooved side faces. The fracture is hackly, but cleavage is good and often lamellar. The hardness varies from 5 to 6, and the specific gravity from 3·27 to 3·31.

Diopside occurs in mica-schists, metamorphosed limestones and dolomites in the Scottish Highlands and in Donegal, in the aureole round the granites, with idocrase, kyanite, epidote and garnet.

12.12 EPIDOTE

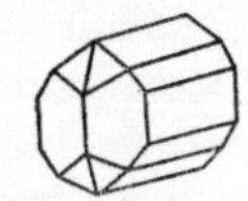

Epidote is of fairly widespread occurrence, although its crystals often look like blades of grass pressed flat against the stone—for instance at Marazion, in Cornwall, or in the Meldon quarries, in Devon. But quite large crystals occur in the British Isles, usually as long bars striated lengthwise, not unsimilar at first sight to those of tourmaline, although tourmaline belongs to the hexagonal and epidote to the monoclinic system. Epidote, however, is softer—hardness 6–7—and somewhat heavier—specific gravity 3·35–3·50—than tourmaline. It is brittle, has perfect cleavage along the prism and conchoidal fracture.

The range of colour is quite wide: the stone may be dark green, bluish-green, blackish-green, brown, yellow. There is also a red variety, called withamite, which may be found in druses in Glen Coe,[31] in the Scottish Highlands, and pink zoisite, which is common in the Moine rocks of the Highlands, though not in gem quality.[44] Epidote is strongly dichroic, and the green specimens give in a dichroscope a green and a dark-brown image. A mainly-blue trichroic variety, called *tanzanite*, has recently been discovered in Tanzania.

Cornish epidotes are green or brown. Dark-green epidote occurs with garnet at the Copper Hill Mine near Redruth; Lamorna Cove and Botallack are some other Cornish localities.[8] [52] Epidote has also been reported from Jersey and Guernsey, where it is found in granite; from the Worcestershire side of the Malverns; Dolgelley and the Vale of Llanberis (olive-green), in Wales; from Skiddaw and Carrock Fell, in the Lake District; Arklow, county Wicklow, Knockmahon mines, county Galway, near Kilmacrenan, county Donegal, in the Irish Republic; counties Antrim and Londonderry, in Ulster.[31] It may be looked for in the epidiorite schists, of which it is one of the main constituents, in the Scottish Highlands, and a number of other places in Scotland. Yet, though epidote is not rare as a mineral, crystals that are sufficiently large and clear are hard to come by.

12.13 SPINEL

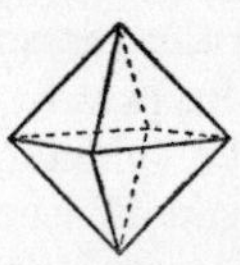

Spinel, the little brother of corundum, is another typically metamorphic mineral, found in dolomitic and magnesian limestones and similar rocks in contact with igneous intrusions, but also as an accessory mineral in basic and ultrabasic rocks, such as dunite, for instance three-quarters of a mile of Loch Coruisk, in the Isle of Skye.[41]

Precious spinel is an oxide of magnesium and aluminium of the formula $MgAl_2O_4$, but both magnesium and aluminium may be wholly or partly replaced by other metals, so that spinels form a group of minerals of variable composition, not unlike the garnets or felspars. These other spinels are not considered 'gemworthy', but, since the variation in composition is continuous, it is not always easy to say where the one ends and the others begin. This accounts for the wide range of variation in specific gravity (3·5–4·1) and colouring. Reddish and red-brown hues are the most common, but the Scottish spinels are typically bluish-grey to greyish-blue. Yellow, purple, greenish, blue and brownish-black stones are also known. Pure green spinels, however, are rare.

Red spinels are sometimes called *ruby spinel* and when pale *balas ruby*. It may be worth noting that the two large stones in the British Crown Jewels formerly believed to be rubies are, in fact, spinels. One of these, mounted at the front of the English Crown, was originally given by Pedro the Cruel to the Black Prince in 1367, and was worn by Henry V at Agincourt. The other, known as the Timir Ruby, is the largest known spinel in the world and weighs 352 carats. It was presented to Queen Victoria in 1851.[64, 67]

However, to return to the colours, purple stones are referred to as *almandine spinels*, orange-to-yellow ones as *rubicelles*, blue as *sapphire spinels*, while *pleonastes* or *ceylonites* are the green-to-black varieties. The blue colour in synthetic spinels is due to cobalt, but in natural stones it is ascribed to chromium and occasionally to zinc. FeO is responsible for the pale green shades and Fe_2O_3 for the red ones.

Spinel is non-dichroic and singly refracting, with a refractive index of 1·72 in most natural stones and 1·73 in the synthetic ones, but the blue zinc spinels reach 1·75. The hardness is 8, and all spinels belong to the cubic system, characteristically crystallizing in octahedra, occasionally twinned, with a vitreous lustre and conchoidal fracture. The cleavage is very poor. Spinel is usually disseminated through the parent rock in small grains, and in the Scottish and Irish specimens the crystal shape is not clearly apparent; they do not appear to be of gem quality.

Apart from the already mentioned locality in Skye, spinel has been reported in Scotland from a point about two-thirds of a mile north-west of Beinn a'Chaprill, Balvraid in Glenelg, where it occurs in metamorphic limestone, and two-thirds of a mile east of Sgaith Beinn, all of which are in Inverness-shire; also from Croc Led Beg, in Sutherland.[41] B. N. Peach *et al.*[78] mention diopside and serpentine in the rocks of Assynt, affected by magmatic heat, these minerals being also present in 'the corresponding rocks from Skye, together with a violet spinel' (p. 454). It will be recalled that spinel occurs in the Crogan Kinshela Mountains in Wicklow and in the metamorphic aureole of Scawt Hill in Antrim.[36] I have no record of its being found in England.

13 Grubbing about in lodes and gangues

Nature is neither chaotic not arbitrary—man often is. Yet, self-evident as this may seem, the order of nature is natural: it comes about because within certain limits the parts of which the world is structured are standardized at various levels, and so, too, are the forces that act between them. Thus the resulting situations fall into repetitive patterns, and this makes possible the formulation of the so-called 'laws of nature'. There is, however, a basic difference between the natural order of things and the bureaucratic order of concepts, which are only words scrupulously defined, introduced by man for his own convenience: the relationships in the latter are logical or semantic, and for logic or semantics nature cares not a fig. This is why any systematic description leaves something to be desired, and exceptions are said 'to confirm the rule' (the devil, they do!).

In the present instance I have tried to arrange the description of minerals according to their mode of occurrence, for when a rockhound is confronted with a certain type of rock in the 'field', his practical concern is what manner of minerals or gems this may contain, rather than how these would fit into Dana's System of Mineralogy, which is to be found in *Dana's System of Mineralogy*[29] in a library, or in a carefully arranged exemplifying collection in a museum. If, however, we take, say, fluorite, it may occur as a *primary* accessory mineral in granite, as it does on St. Austell Moor in Cornwall, or as a *secondary* replacement mineral, formed after the main rock mass has consolidated, as in the Triassic sandstones near Elgin;[21] it may be found in limestone, as in Derbyshire, or in basalt, as in Antrim. The issue, therefore, boils down to what is the typical or most frequent mode of occurrence of fluorspar. On the balance it may be described as a *pneumatolytic* mineral, which means a mineral formed by the action of *mineralizing fluids*—and a fluid is either a gas or a liquid (a semantic relationship!)—exhaled by molten magma. Generally these fluids will be hot, but high temperature only serves to accelerate a chemical reaction, and in a particular case a mineral could be precipitated from a cold solution. The situation is further complicated by chemical weathering, some minerals being subject to 'spontaneous decomposition', more often than not through the weak but persistent reaction with carbonic acid, which is formed when carbon dioxide from the air is dissolved in water.

It is fairly obvious why pneumatolytic or decomposed minerals will generally develop along fractures and in cavities, but a whole body of rock may be penetrated by magmatic exhalations, and, for instance, granite may be greisenized as a result (p. 16), while chemical decomposition may take place long after the magmatic emanations have ceased.

The minerals we are concerned with in this chapter are either typically pneumatolytic or secondary, often occur as gangues in metalliferous lodes, and in some cases are themselves ores.

13.1 FLUORITE

Fluorite, fluor, or fluorspar, is the first on the list. It is calcium fluoride, CaF_2, often found as a gangue mineral in lead, zinc and copper lodes,

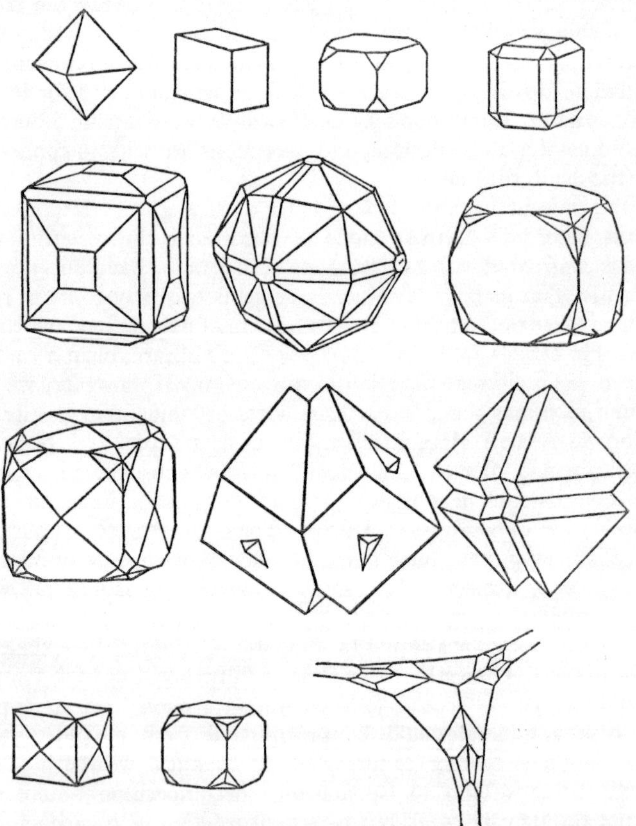

in metamorphic limestones, etc. It is, of course, one of the markers in Mohs' scale, with hardness 4, which is the lowest admissible in a gem-stone. In fact, fluorite would certainly have failed to qualify as one save for its wide range of beautiful colourings. It is too soft for use in rings and similar personal jewellery where it would be readily scratched and tarnished. The pure mineral is a colourless glass and in this form is used for optical purposes, but various impurities, among which the rare-earth metals seem to be the most important, may impart to it any colour of the rainbow, from the violet through blue and green to yellow and red, including such hues as amber and smalt-blue which the rainbow cannot boast. The colour can often be changed by heating.[21]

The stone may be opaque, translucent or transparent; massive or crystalline. The massive variety, of which the Derbyshire bluejohn is the best known example, is used for ornamental objects, such as vases, ashtrays and the like. Clear crystals of outstanding colour have occasionally been cut as gems.

Singly refracting, with a refractive index of 1·43, fluorite is singularly lacking in fire. Nor is it dichroic. Yet a crystal viewed at some angles sometimes shows a second colour, usually some shade of violet. This seems to be due to the property of fluorescence, described on p. 80. Since ordinary sunlight includes ultraviolet rays, these will excite a fluorescent glow in the crystal.

The crystals are isometric, most commonly cubes or octahedra, frequently twinned or intergrown; but more complicated shapes occur (*see* opp.). The lustre is glassy, fracture conchoidal, cleavage along the cube faces perfect, and, unlike most crystalline material, which gives a white streak, that of fluorite is colourless. Its specific gravity falls between 3·1 and 3·2.

Fluorite occurs widely in the British Isles, and the main localities have been considered in Chapters 4–6 in some detail.

13·2 APATITE

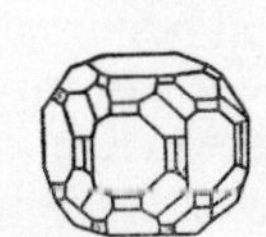

It is arguable whether apatite should be put into this chapter or regarded as an accessory mineral of acid igneous rocks; indeed, it is both that and a pneumatolytic product, and may occur in basic rocks (gabbro) to boot. But it is not a silicate and is chemically related to fluorite. It is a complicated fluoro-chloro-hydro-phosphate of calcium, where fluorine and chlorine are interchangeable and may be present jointly or separately, yielding fluor-apatite and chlor-apatite respectively. This description makes it clear why apatite may be found in metamorphic limestones together with fluorite; but it is also associated with cassiterite (tin oxide), iron ores and serpentine.

The British occurrence of apatite is far more restricted than that of fluorspar. In Cornwall and Devon it is mostly found in granite and tin lodes.[8, 13, 31, 52] Yellowish-green crystals occur with garnet and axinite near Botallack. Bluish or greenish specimens have come from the Godolphin Bridge mine and Tremearne; fine blue ones from Luxulyan. Stenna Gwynn, St. Stephens and Crinnis are some other Cornish localities. In Devon cream-coloured apatite in crystals up to two inches in length used to be obtained from a quarry near Bovey Tracey, but the supply appears to have been exhausted. There is also some apatite at Bovey Heathfield and Chudleigh. Pale yellowish-green apatite, occasionally in fair-sized crystals, has been found on quartz at the Carrock mine in Cumberland.[48, 56]

Green apatite has been reported from Deeside and Ross-shire in Scotland. In Ireland apatite is the main accessory of the Donegal granite where according to the Geological Survey of Ireland it is brown; but a green variety is present near Killiney, county Dublin.[31]

In fact, green is the most usual colouring of apatite, but it may also be colourless, yellow, blue or pink. The hardness is, of course, 5; specific gravity 3·15–3·23 (Börner).[4] Apatite is doubly refracting (refractive indices 1·63 and 1·65) and has more fire than quartz or aquamarine, but the comparative softness restricts its use as a gem. The crystals with a vitreous lustre, conchoidal fracture and poor cleavage, belong to the hexagonal system and frequently form prisms terminated by pyramids and reminiscent of quartz, bipyramids, many-faceted beads or thick plates. They may attain considerable size. But the mineral occurs in the massive, mammilated or fibrous form as well.

13.3   CASSITERITE

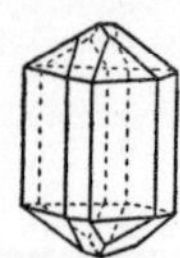  As stated, apatite may keep company with cassiterite, which again is commonly associated with zinc blende, galena, pyrite and other ores. Cassiterite, or tinstone, is a straightforward oxide, SnO_2, and belongs in its crystalline aspect to the tetragonal system. The crystals vary greatly in appearance, from comparatively simple prisms ending in pyramids to very complicated faceted solids. These, being typically brown or brownish-black, may recall garnets at first sight, from which, though, they are readily distinguishable by their great weight (specific gravity 6·8–7·1) and the brilliance of their striated faces (the lustre of garnet is resinous). It is the latter that has earned them the miner's name 'diamond tin'. The hardness is 6–7 and the streak white to pale yellow.

The Geological Museum in London has some cut specimens of

transparent tinstone on display. These are of a bright brownish-yellow colour with a good show of fire, for the refractive indices of cassiterite, which is birefringent, are 1·99 and 2·09 respectively, and the mineral is dichroic withal. The stones are foreign, and so far as I know the Cornish 'diamond tin' never attains to comparable limpidity. Even so the crystals are translucent, with a kind of reddish-brown inner glow, which could look quite handsome behind the dark, brilliant facets of a cut gem.

13.4   SPHALERITE

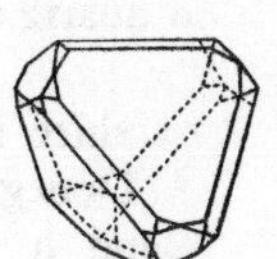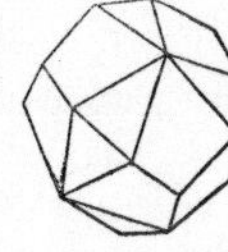 A frequent companion of cassiterite, zinc blende, or sphalerite, stands at barely $3\frac{1}{2}$–4 on Mohs' scale and is not usually considered a gemstone. Yet the Geological Museum has a cut specimen of it, too. This is grey with a brownish undertone, of a colour that may be found in zircon, andalusite or diopside. Sphalerite, however, even though it is known to miners as 'Black Jack', may also be yellow, brown or red. I am not quite sure of the origin of that cut stone, but I have seen some quite transparent, honey-brown crystals of sphalerite on Loch Tayside, in Scotland. Blende has been mined in Cornwall, Cardiganshire, Derbyshire, Cumberland, Perthshire; but at least some will be found in most lead mines, and if you look for good clear crystals for cutting you do not need tons of it.

A simple sulphide, ZnS, sphalerite belongs to the cubic system and typically crystallizes in tetrahedra with bevelled edges and points or in garnet-like beads. The lustre is adamantine or resinous; the streak—yellowish, white or 'leather-brown'; specific gravity 3·9–4·2.

13.5   HAEMATITE

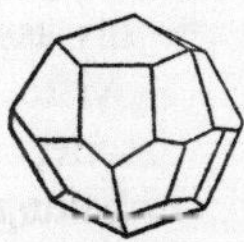 With specular haematite, or kidney ore, you are on traditional ground. Ornaments of carved haematite have been known in Babylonia and ancient Egypt, and in modern times it was, like jet, used for mourning jewellery, although the fashion has now died out. But it is still cut in the English north and used for such articles as cuff-links, and the Germans are particularly fond of it. Haematite polishes to a semblance of stainless steel. It is quite hard: $6\frac{1}{2}$.

In nature it is most often found in the massive form of kidney ore, which looks like a kind of hellish iron boils on quartz or calcite. If such a 'boil' is broken or cut open it will be seen to have a fibrous radial texture. But there is also a soft scaly 'micaceous haematite' and crystal-line 'specular iron'. In the latter guise it is assigned to the hexagonal group, which does not always find a very clear expression in its rhombohedral, pyramidal of many-faced bead-like crystal shapes, but does not really matter, as these shiny metallic bodies are not readily confused with anything else, especially if it is borne in mind that the streak is cherry-red or red-brown. Hence, indeed, stems the Greek name *haematite*, which may be Anglicized as 'bloodstone' (not to be confused with a variety of jasper known under this name); and in its earthy variant haematite is red, for it is Fe_2O_3, or just rust!

North Lancashire, Cumberland and the Forest of Dean are the great places for haematite, but it is widely distributed in penny packets as a secondary mineral through limestones, sedimentary and metamorphic rocks, and is often found, as are many other ores and metals, in quartz veins, e.g. in Pembrokeshire (p. 25).

13.6   RHODONITE AND RHODOCROSITE

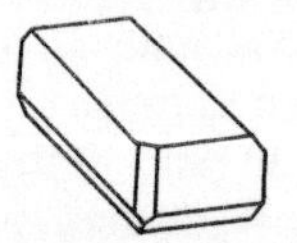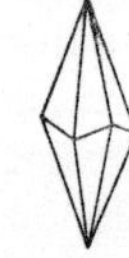 Rhodonite and rhodocrosite are two manganese minerals that may be looked for in lead-silver and zinc lodes and veins, often jointly, as rhodocrosite is derived largely from the chemical weathering of rhodonite and other manganese ores, by virtue whereof it also figures as a replacement, or *metasomatic*, mineral in limestones. The two share a pleasing rose-red colouring, shading into flesh-pink or red, the different shades being arranged in the massive form of the stones in concentric wavy bands, as in an agate. This structure shows to advantage in small ornamental objects and cabochons.

Both of these rosy stones occur in Cornwall and Devon. In a charming and useful little book, *A Collector's Guide to Minerals, Rocks and Gemstones in Cornwall and Devon*,[52] Cedric Rogers recommends the country south and west of Launceston, near Treburland and Tavistock, in this connection. Greg and Lettsom[31] pinpoint a 'manganese quarry' $1\frac{1}{2}$ miles southeast of Callington, in Cornwall, and Upton Pyne and Black Down near Tavistock, in Devon, as rhodonite localities. The year, however, is 1858, and the situation may have altered since then. Rhodonite has recently been reported from the Meldon Quarry near Okehampton. It is also known from the Leadhills, in Scotland. But I should be greatly surprised if it were found nowhere else.

Rhodonite, or manganese spar, is a silicate of manganese with a variable proportion of iron and calcium, $Mn(Fe,Ca).SiO_3$. Its specific weight is bracketed between 3·4 and 3·7, and hardness between $5\frac{1}{2}$ and $6\frac{1}{2}$. It is translucent or transparent (refractive index 1·66–1·67) with a glassy lustre, which becomes pearly on fractures. The fracture is conchoidal, but rhodonite has perfect crystalline cleavage and can be readily split into blocks. The streak is white. Crystals, though large, are infrequent and usually badly flawed; they are of triclinic habit, tabular or prismatic. Thus rhodonite is used mainly in its massive guise as an ornamental stone.

Rhodocrosite, or diallagite as it used to be called, is a plain carbonate of manganese, $Mn.CO_3$, somewhat lighter (specific gravity 3·3–3·6) and at 4 on Mohs' scale a good deal softer than rhodonite. Its streak is reddish-white. Though typically translucent and rose-red, rhodocrosite may be opaque, grey, brownish, or colourless. It forms small, sharp bipyramidal crystals in druses; the habit is hexagonal. More often, however, it will be found as a thick botryoidal encrustation. The lustre is glassy, fracture conchoidal, cleavage very good, so that the stone is easy to work.

13.7 CHRYSOCOLLA

Just as the pinks and reds may mark out the manganese family, so do the greens and blues that of copper. Analogies are seldom perfect, but chrysocolla, which is a hydrated silicate of copper, $CuSiO_3.nH_2O$, and a product of weathering of copper lodes, may be thought of as a copper counterpart of rhodonite, while malachite and azurite are those of rhodocrosite.

The colourings of massive chrysocolla vary from emerald-green through blue-green to sky-blue, and the hardness from 2 to 4, depending on the amount of water of hydration (n). Opaque and translucent on thin edges, with a fatty or silky lustre, chrysocolla is commonly found as thin seams and amorphous encrustations. I have seen it in the Caldbeck Fells of Cumberland, and it may be looked for among the copper minerals of Cornwall.

13.8 DIOPTASE

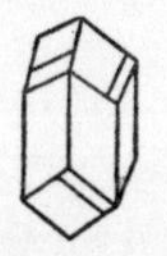

Dioptase, or 'emerald copper', with a formula $Cu_3(SiO_3)_3.3H_2O$, is a crystalline variant of chrysocolla, with which it keeps company. I have found some tiny crystals of dioptase on the Caldbeck Fells, so that the mineral is definitely of British occurrence, even if the best specimens come from South-West Africa, the Republic of Congo or Katanga. According to *Chambers's Technical Dictionary* 'when first found it was used as a gemstone'. Its later eclipse may be ascribed to the comparatively low hardness of 5, for it is an attractive, transparent or translucent mineral of a rich green hue. The birefringent crystals (refractive indices 1·64 and 1·70) with a vitreous lustre belong to the hexagonal system and may be prismatic or rhombohedral, but, unfortunately, are usually small. The fracture is conchoidal, cleavage good, streak green or greyish-blue, specific gravity 3·27–3·35. Occasionally dioptase is found in calcite veins and cavities in limestones and dolomitic limestones, but it is rare.

13.9 MALACHITE AND AZURITE

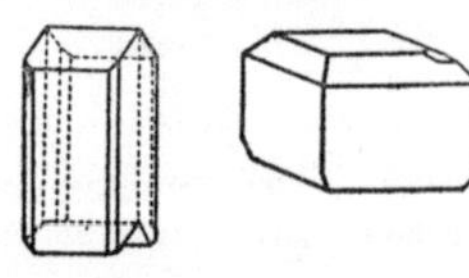

Malachite and azurite, or chessylite, are the green and blue carbonate of copper respectively. Chemically they are made up of the same ingredients, but differently proportioned, the formula of malachite being $Cu_2[(OH)_2|CO_3]$, and that of azurite $Cu_3[OH|CO_3]_2$. With a specific gravity 3·9–4·1 malachite is slightly heavier than azurite which stands at 3·7–3·9. Azurite is of a deep royal blue colour with a cobalt-blue streak, and malachite ranges from emerald to blackish green, while some English crystals I have seen were almost olive-green. The streak is light green. Both these minerals are opaque in the massive and translucent or opaque in crystalline form, which belongs to the monoclinic system and is gemmologically of little account. However, azurite crystallizes in thick plates or stumpy prisms and malachite in long thin ones. They also differ in lustre: azurite has an enamelled look, seldom achieved by malachite, which inclines to dullness. Typically both occur as massive, botryoidal to reniform encrustations on other minerals or rocks. They may be intermixed in a handsome mosaic, and malachite is usually banded in different shades. When compact, they are used as ornamental stones, though good pieces make handsome cabochons.

Yet, although the earthy, friable variety of malachite is quite common and copper-bearing rocks are often stained green and blue with malachite and azurite, these good pieces are not too easy to come by. I have found a few in the Lake District and in Cornwall, and it will be recalled that very good malachite has been obtained from the Cooshen mine, near Skull, and the Tynagh mine, county Galway,[10] in Ireland. Many other localities have been mentioned in Chapters 4–6.

13.10 TURQUOISE

Turquoise is another secondary mineral, arising from chemical weathering. It is a somewhat complex hydrated phosphate of copper and aluminium, often found with limonite and chalcedony in aluminium-rich rocks, especially trachytic lavas. In Britain it is known in the pale-blue form of rashleighite from the kaolin clays of St. Austell Moor, in Cornwall, but I have before me a piece of stone of the proper turquoise green-blue hue which I have found on the Caldbeck Fells. It has the waxy lustre, has conchoidal fracture and is not scratched by felspar and itself scratches copper and glass, as turquoise should and chrysocolla should not.

According to Börner,[4] turquoise is sky-blue, blue, bluish-green, greenish, sometimes yellowish, cryptocrystalline and may be classed as amorphous for practical purposes. It hardness varies from $5\frac{1}{2}$ to 6, and specific gravity from 2·5 to 2·9 with the fluctuations of chemical composition. Although opaque at first sight, it is transparent in thin section with a refractive index of 1·6–1·65. The streak is white.

Another similar stone is variscite. A hydrated phosphate of aluminium, it is of an apple-green to emerald-green colour and a shade softer than turquoise ($4\frac{1}{2}$–$5\frac{1}{2}$). It occurs as nodules in crystalline limestone, but I have no record of its being found in the British Isles.

13.11   SCHEELITE

The gemstone display at the Geological Museum in London includes a cut specimen of scheelite of a brownish-yellow hue.

Scheelite is calcium tungstate, $CaWO_4$, of a pale greenish or yellowish colour. It occurs in pneumatolytic veins, but also in pegmatites and thermally metamorphosed limestones, and may be looked for in the tungsten (wolfram) mines of Cumberland and Cornwall. It may be massive or crystalline, translucent or opaque, rarely transparent, of hardness $4\frac{1}{2}$–5. The crystals are tetragonal, bipyramidal or plate-like, striated, and recognizable by their relatively high weight (specific gravity 5·9–6·1); they are rather brittle, breaking with an uneven conchoidal fracture, and have an adamantine or resinous lustre. The fluorescence of scheelite has been referred to on p. 80. The streak is white.

13.12   HEMIMORPHITE

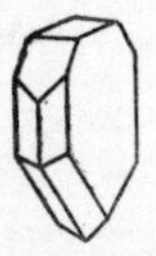

Scheelite is one more example of a mineral, not usually esteemed a gem, which may yet look quite attractive when transparent and of good colour. The blue and yellow hemimorphite (also known as calamine) from the Leadhills (Scotland) has been mentioned on p. 39 as another possibility.

It is a zinc ore, a hydrated silicate of zinc to be exact, found in association with zinc, iron and lead sulphides in Somerset, Derbyshire and Cumberland, in addition to the just-mentioned locality. The mineral may also be colourless, green or brown. Its hardness is 5 and specific gravity 3·3–3·5. It crystallizes in the orthorhombic system and is remarkable in that the two ends of a doubly terminated prism differ, whence the name, which may be anglicized as 'half-shaped'. The crystals are transparent or translucent, with a glassy exterior, have conchoidal fracture and good cleavage.

13.13 ALABASTER

Alabaster has been referred to as an ornamental stone. It is a fibrous form of gypsum, which is a hydrated sulphate of calcium, $CaSO_4.2H_2O$, of a low hardness, 2, so that it can be carved with a knife, and specific gravity 2·3. It may be white or pink and is translucent or sub-opaque.

13.14 PYRITE AND MARCASITE

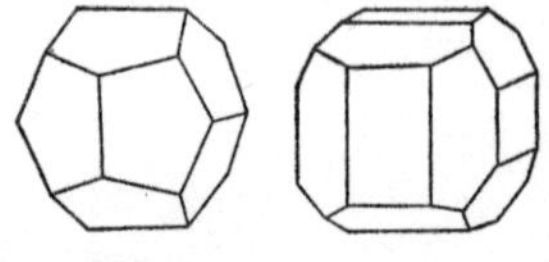
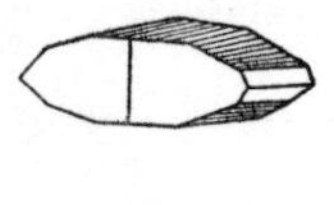

'The fool's gold', or iron pyrites, has been used in ornaments since great antiquity, and large pieces of it polished as mirrors have been found in the graves dating from the old South American civilizations. Fool's gold still retains a limited use in jewellery. It is usually set in silver in such articles as brooches, cufflinks and tie pins, as is haematite. Both are cut in flat rosettes, both are opaque, hard and metallic, except that haematite is silver-grey and iron pyrites is pale to golden yellow. They even occur together.

Fool's gold is iron disulphide, FeS_2, known in two forms: *pyrite* and *marcasite*. The hardness of both falls between 6 and $6\frac{1}{2}$, but pyrite, or iron pyrites, is much more common, crystallizes in the cubic system—cubes, octahehdra and complex multi-faceted 'beads'—is somewhat heavier, 5·0–5·2 as against 4·8–4·9 for marcasite, and of a darker colour, ranging from brassy to bronze yellow. The fracture is conchoidal, messy, but the cleavage is good in some specimens. The crystals are striated and brittle. There is nothing much it can be confused with, except chalcopyrite, which, though, is much softer—only $3\frac{1}{2}$–4 on Mohs' scale—or gold, which is malleable and still softer ($2\frac{1}{2}$–3). As a matter of fact, pyrite often contains some gold.

Marcasite, also known as white iron pyrites, is paler with a greenish cast, belongs to the orthorhombic system and forms tabular crystals, often repeatedly twinned in twig-like aggregates, short pseudo-hexagonal prisms and radial nodules. It will be recalled that marcasite is found in chalk in south-west England, near Ilfracombe in Devon, in Derbyshire and elsewhere. It has an uneven fracture and no recognizable cleavage. Both types of pyrite have a greenish-black streak. When used in jewellery, pyrite is also described as marcasite.

14 In the basic clan

On the face of it there may not seem to be a great deal of difference between the 65 per cent of silica where the acid igneous rocks end and the 55 per cent below which the basic clan begins. This, however, is only a convenient indication of a more general change in composition, and more particularly of the increase in the proportion of iron and magnesium, to which the dark colouring and high specific gravity of the pyroxene and amphibole minerals characteristic of the basic rocks are due. These minerals are usually opaque withal, although bronzite is a translucent pyroxene, reported from the Lizard, in Cornwall, and is sometimes cut as a gem. Spinel, apatite and garnet may occur as accessories in some gabbros; and basalts, for instance in Antrim, contain labradorite felspar. An outcrop of dunite in Skye contains spinel in grey-blue grains. Nepheline is a possibility, if a somewhat dim one. Otherwise, however, the main basic gem is olivine. It is indeed a wide-spread rock-forming mineral, and such ultrabasic types as dunite and peridotite largely consist of it. Thus olivine is to the basic rocks what quartz is to the acid ones.

The cavities of basic lavas and tuffs often house zeolites, of which prehnite and natrolite have been mentioned in our tour of the British Isles. Zeolites are double hydrated silicates of alkaline metals, generally transparent, but lacking in striking colouring and of inferior hardness, so that they make at best second-class gems.

The 'spontaneous' decay, due to the action of magmatic water, of hornblende, augite and olivine in ultrabasic formations, yields serpentine, which, though, may also arise in other rocks rich in magnesia, such as hornblende schists, dolomitic and magnesian limestones where it is associated with marble, calcite, apatite and fluorite.

14.1 OLIVINE

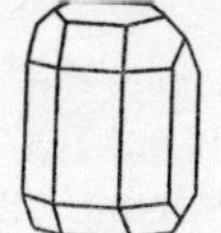

However, to return to olivine, this is a double silicate of magnesium and iron, $(MgFe)_2.SiO_4$, moderately heavy, of specific gravity 3·35–3·46, and a hardness ranging from $6\frac{1}{2}$ to 7. As the name indicates, its characteristic colouring is olive-green, but it may also be yellowish-green (chrysolite), dark-green (peridot), brown, and on Island Magee, in Ulster, 'large crystalline concretions' of olivine in basalt have a 'fine cherry-red colour'.[31]

The crystals belong to the orthorhombic system, are prismatic, often rounded at the ends, or thick and tabular with the large face vertically lined. The stone is dichroic, which is especially marked in the dark-green specimens of the peridot variety, and doubly refracting (refractive indices 1·65 and 1·69).

There has been some confusion between olivine proper and an alumino-borate of magnesium ($Mg.AlBO_4$), called *sinhalite*, which accounts for most of the yellow and brown stones. This is somewhat heavier (specific gravity 3·47–3·52), a shade less hard ($6\frac{1}{2}$), and has higher refractive indices (1·67 and 1·71) than olivine; but these differences are marginal and the two minerals are difficult to tell apart in a hand specimen.

A Guide to the Collection of Gemstones in the Geological Museum[39] says on p. 41 about olivine, 'specimens of sufficient size and transparency have been found in the parent rock at only one locality, namely the Island of St. John, in the Red Sea, where crystals occur in the cavities of an olivine-rock, of *dunite*, which is much decomposed and serpentinized'. This statement sounds a little too categorical, though it may be justifiable from the professional jeweller's viewpoint. Perhaps, however, we need not fix our sights quite so high in thinking of the British Isles, which may yet contain 'gemworthy' crystals of olivine. I have never seen the red ones from Island Magee, but I have before me a waterworn lump of basic lava from the Sound of Bute (Scotland). The purple groundmass contains nodules of red jasper, soapstone and olivine. On the surface the latter has been serpentinized, but deeper into the rock it remains unaltered and of a clear olive-green colour. Similar nodules occur in the Carboniferous basalts of Derbyshire, and, as noted on p. 29, D. Rushton[53] has seen well-formed crystals of olivine in basalt at the Calton Hill quarry, in Staffordshire. D. S. Freir[76] lists peridot amongst the gemstones of Sutherland. Cedric Rogers[52] inclines to discount the reports of olivine crystals on the beaches of the Lizard Peninsula, in Cornwall which, though, may yet be there. The rocks of Arthur's Seat near Edinburgh contain olivine, and crystals of this mineral have been recorded elsewhere, for instance, near Glasdrummond, in Antrim.[31]

14.2   SERPENTINE

Olivine goes with serpentine, which is by no means uncommon in Britain. It is found in Cornwall, Anglesey, along the Highland Boundary Fault from Loch Lomond to Stonehaven, at Portsoy, on Iona, in the Shetlands, and in some other Scottish localities. In Ireland the 'Connemara marble' of Galway is a serpentine rock (serpentinite), which is also known from the counties, Wicklow, Mayo and Donegal.

The mineral serpentine is a hydrated silicate of magnesium,

$Mg_6(OH)_8Si_4O_{10}$, always of secondary origin. It does not form crystals and occurs in the compact or fibrous (asbestos) form. It is typically some shade of green. The precious serpentine is translucent and quite soft, $2\frac{1}{2}$ to 3 on Mohs' scale, as in the 'Iona marbles', which are green to olive-green in colour, have a greasy lustre and feel soapy to the touch, a property shared by all serpentines. The refractive index is bracketed between $1{\cdot}49$ and $1{\cdot}57$, and specific gravity is $2{\cdot}50$ to $2{\cdot}65$ or so. There exists a pale green translucent variety, called bowenite, which is much harder ($5\frac{1}{2}$) and resembles jade. The deep-green mottled serpentine, which occurs in Connemara, is known under the name of *verd-antique*.[31]

More often, however, serpentine is found in the crude form of 'common serpentine', or serpentinite, of hardness four or thereabouts, and containing lime, iron oxides and other impurities. This is a rock rather than a mineral, variously veined and spotted in green, black, grey, red, yellow and white, so as to resemble, when polished, the skin of some snakes, whence probably the name. Common serpentine is used as an ornamental stone.

14.3   JADEITE

Another ornamental mineral, recorded in Sutherland (D. S. Freir)[76], and with serpentine at the Lizard (H. G. F. Smith),[59] is jadeite. It is essentially a sodium-aluminium silicate, $Na(AlSi_2O_6)$, of the pyroxene family, with variable proportions of calcium, magnesium, chromium and manganese, which are responsible for the colour variation. It is usually green or whitish with emerald-green patches, but may also be off-white or pale mauve. Crystals of jadeite are extremely rare, and it is typically massive and very tough, of hardness $6\frac{1}{2}$–7 and specific gravity $3{\cdot}2$–$3{\cdot}5$, breaking with a splintery fracture, although sometimes with a tendency to split into plates. The stone is opaque or translucent, and when sufficiently so doubly refracting (refractive indices about $1{\cdot}65$ and $1{\cdot}68$). It fuses in a bunsen flame, which it colours yellow.

14.4   BRONZITE

Bronzite is a further pyroxene known from the Lizard (Rogers)[52] and of widespread occurrence in basalts. It is a variety of enstatite, from which it differs in a higher proportion of iron, conforming to the chemical formula: $(Mg, Fe)_2Si_2O_6$. The crystals, which are seldom fully developed, belong to the orthorhombic system, are translucent or opaque with a silky bronze-like sheen, due to minute inclusions of flaky ilmenite—a mineral common on the Moon. The colour of bronzite varies from brown to green, the latter being typical of enstatite, a green transparent variety of which is known from Transvaal: the hardness is $5\frac{1}{2}$, specific gravity $3{\cdot}2$–$3{\cdot}5$. Bronzite is usually cut *en cabochon* ('beetle cut').

14.5 LABRADORITE

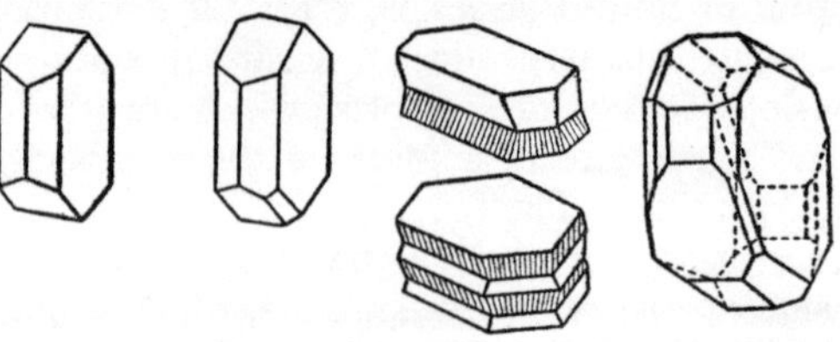

Felspars have been considered in Chapter 11 in connection with granite. While, however, orthoclases are characteristic of acid rocks, plagioclases are mainly to be found in the basic formations. It will be recalled that the former are potash felspars and the latter oscillate in composition between the pure soda felspar, called albite, and the pure lime felspar, anorthite. Labradorite is a variety of plagioclase containing between 50 and 70 per cent of anorthite, known from Cornwall, Derbyshire, Cumberland and the Antrim basalts. It resembles opal in that at certain angles it may display an iridescent play of colour, mainly in green, pale and dark blue, but also red and yellow, while at others it looks a dirty grey-green. Such labradorite, when suitably cut and polished in flat slabs, is used as an ornamental stone. At least some of the Ulster labradorites are iridescent. Very occasionally labradorite becomes sufficiently transparent for step-cutting, a specimen of which may be seen at the Geological Museum in London.

14.6 NEPHELINE

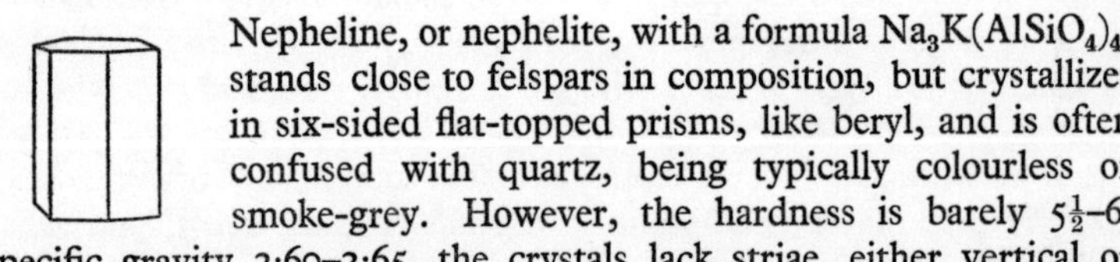

Nepheline, or nephelite, with a formula $Na_3K(AlSiO_4)_4$, stands close to felspars in composition, but crystallizes in six-sided flat-topped prisms, like beryl, and is often confused with quartz, being typically colourless or smoke-grey. However, the hardness is barely $5\frac{1}{2}$–6, specific gravity 2·60–2·65, the crystals lack striae, either vertical or transverse, have a greasy-to-vitreous look, break with conchoidal fracture, and are readily cleaved at right angles to the main axis, whence the flat ends. Nepheline is found with soda felspars and melanite (see p. 109) in basic igneous rocks, such as basalts, but also in syenite. It is not normally reckoned a gem, but good transparent specimens could be cut to an effect comparable to, say, that of zinc-blende.

14.7 DATOLITE

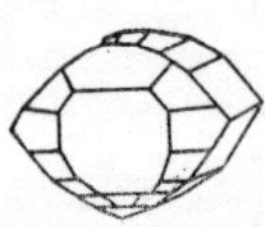

On the other hand, datolite, although softer (5–$5\frac{1}{2}$) has been used in jewellery, mainly on the strength of its livelier colour, which includes green and yellow shades, although it may also be grey or colourless. The short prismatic crystals have complicated shapes, based on the monoclinic pattern, have conchoidal fracture and no cleavage; specific gravity 2·9–3·0, refractive indices 1·62 and 1·67. Chemically it is a hydrated boro-silicate of calcium, Ca(OH|BSiO$_4$), and occurs in basic rocks. It has been reported from the Lizard, Cornwall. It may be associated with another monoclinic mineral, tremolite, found in serpentinite and metamorphosed limestone. Datolite fuses in a bunsen flame, which it colours green.

Ilmenite, mentioned in connection with bronzite, is another basic accessory. It is usually opaque, black or brown, but sometimes translucent. It is a titanate of iron, FeTiO$_3$ (titanic acid is not particularly strong!). It is not much of a gem, but another titanic mineral rutile, TiO$_2$, one of the three crystalline forms of titania (titanium oxide), may be found with ilmenite, apatite, kyanite, etc. in veins in gabbros and norites, and deserves consideration.

14.8   TITANIA MINERALS

Synthetic rutile surpasses diamond in beauty, although it yields to it in hardness. The natural stone, however, is usually classed as an ore rather than an ornament. Nevertheless, its hardness of 6–6½ is wholly adequate, and at least translucent, if rarely transparent, crystals occur. The colouring varies from black and brown through reddish-brown to blood-red, and with the remarkable fire of rutile (p. 79) even a translucent stone of this colour will be attractive.

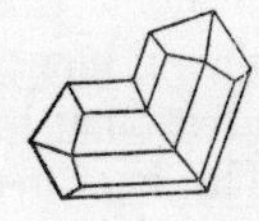

RUTILE is readily recognizable by its weight (specific gravity 4·2–4·3) and pale-yellow or green streak. It crystallizes in the tetragonal system, forming short prisms, often twinned, terminated by four-sided pyramids. Rutile may, though need not, be accompanied by the other forms of crystalline titania: anatase and brookite; and it will be recalled that all three varieties occur in sizable crystals in Wales.

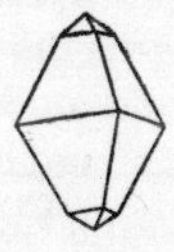

ANATASE is honey-brown, brown, hyacinth-red or blue-black, sub-transparent or translucent, softer (5½–6) and lighter (3·8–3·9) than rutile. The crystals of tetragonal habit may assume the form of sharp pyramids, tabular slabs or bipyramids. They have perfect cleavage and a messy fracture. The lustre is adamantine, resinous or metallic; the mineral is birefringent, with refractive indices well above those of diamond, namely 2·48 and 2·56.

BROOKITE is of the same hardness, but heavier (4·2–4·9), crystallizes in vertically lined tabular crystals according to the orthorhombic prescription. The streak is yellowish-white to brown; the colour yellowish-brown or red brown, occasionally black. The disposition of the crystals, which are transparent or at least translucent, is solitary;

they occur singly in cracks and druses and may be quite large, gleaming with adamantine lustre. They are brittle and uncleavable.

Rutile is a primary mineral, whereas anatase and brookite are secondary, arise from the decomposition of other titanium compounds, and may become concentrated in quartz veins, as has happened at Tremadoc in North Wales (p. 26).

14.9   ZEOLITES

In our geological tour of the British Isles we have seen that zeolites, represented by prehnite and natrolite, are to be looked for in the cavities of basic lavas. The presence of these two minerals between Botallack and Wheal Cock near St. Just in Cornwall at the edge of the granite coincides with a body of dolerite, which is halfway in grain between gabbro and basalt. Zeolites are also known from the Lizard and Stenna Gwynn near St. Austell. Natrolite is found in decomposed basalt in Staffordshire. As we have seen in Chapter 5, prehnite and natrolite occur in the Scottish Carboniferous basalts, which may also contain analcite and chabazite. Prehnite and natrolite have been recorded in the Tertiary basalts of Skye and Antrim, and another zeolite—phillipsite—is known from the latter. The Braid Hills near Edinburgh are a further natrolite locality, and an attractive flesh-pink variety of this stone may be found in basic tuffs, in Glenfarg, Fife.[31]

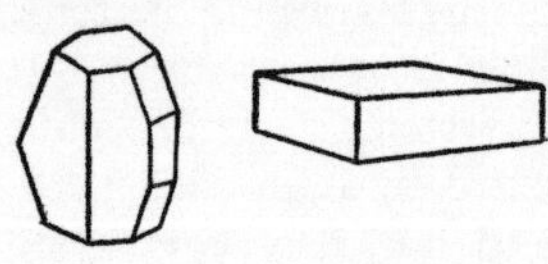

The Cornish PREHNITE is usually pale green,[8] but the colour of the mineral ranges from full green to yellow, and it may be white or colourless as well. The hardness varies from 6 to $6\frac{1}{2}$, and specific gravity from 2·8 to 3·0. Single crystals are rare, belong to the orthorhombic system and are typically tabular. More commonly, however, prehnite assumes the form of botryoidal concretions. It may be transparent or opaque. The lustre is glassy, waxy or pearly. Refraction is double with indices 1·61 and 1·65. Prehnite is brittle with distinct cleavage and uneven fracture. Chemically it is a hydrated double silicate of calcium and aluminium (zeolites are such compound silicates with one or two alkaline metals and aluminium), and has a somewhat complicated formula: $Ca_2Al_2(OH)_2.Si_3O_{10}$. Apart from natrolite and other zeolites, it tends to keep company with epidote.

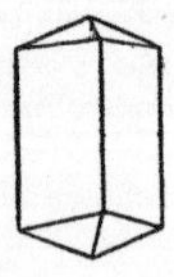

NATROLITE, a hydrated silicate of sodium and aluminium, is somewhat lighter (2·2–2·4) and softer (5–$5\frac{1}{2}$). It, too, observes the orthorhombic rules, but, unlike prehnite, often forms simple square prisms ending up in low four-sided pyramids. It may also be massive or fibrous. It has perfect cleavage and conchoidal fracture and often displays a characteristic silky sheen, like some felspars, from which it can be readily distinguished by being fusible in the light of an ordinary match. The refractive index is rather low ($1\cdot48$–$1\cdot49$) and the stone has little fire, so that only the pink variety has been cut as a gem for the sake of its colour. The greyish or yellowish specimens have little to recommend them.

The same goes for *analcite*, which may be milk-white, greyish or colourless, usually transparent with a vitreous lustre, and may be massive or crystalline, the crystals being cubical, rather like garnets to look at. The fracture is conchoidal, hardness $5\frac{1}{2}$, specific gravity $2\cdot2$–$2\cdot3$.

Chabazite and *phillipsite* are softer, at $4\frac{1}{2}$ on Mohs' scale, of comparable specific gravity, transparent or translucent and vitreous, being hydrated silicates of calcium-sodium-aluminium and calcium-potassium-aluminium respectively. Chabazite is hexagonal, crystalline, and ranges in colour from nil to reddish-brown; phillipsite is monoclinic, yellow, colourless, white or grey, the crystals being not unlike those of orthoclase, but often arranged in rosettes or crosses, like staurolite.

Although basic rocks may be described as being anti-silica, massive chalcedony and sometimes crystalline quartz concretions may form in basaltic amygdales, and in Antrim opal has developed in the flints overflowed and baked by basaltic lavas.

15 Scotch pebbles and their kin

The name 'agate' comes from Achates in Greece, which establishes an ancient and noble pedigree, but 'Scotch pebbles' are also agates and seem to have been so called in punishment for their not being Oriental or otherwise exotic. Or is it that what ranks as a mere pebble in Scotland will pass for a gem in other lands?

It is fine reading about fancy gemstones and perhaps dreaming of caves or, more modestly, druses where varicoloured crystals gleam, resplendent; but quite another thing finding any such. This may happen, even by chance, but the best way of propitiating the fickle gods of fortune is by experience, knowledge and perseverance. If, on the other hand, you have neither the time nor the inclination to explore far-off lonely places, you may yet confidently expect to pick up on a suitably chosen beach a pebble or two, which when dressed will make a pretty bauble.

15.1 MINERALOGICAL CHALCEDONY

The pebbles will most probably be some kind of mineralogical chalcedony, which includes Scotch pebbles and is crypto-crystalline silica (SiO_2) deposited from solution. Such silica may be of any colour, translucent to opaque, depending on various admixtures and impurities, which differ from each other as paint does from dirt. Chalcedony has a dull waxy lustre, a hardness of $6\frac{1}{2}$–7 and a specific gravity between 2·59 and 2·61. The streak is white, regardless of the colour of the stone as a whole. The crystals are too fine to be distinguishable without optical magnification, but may be visibly aligned in a texture resembling bristles in a tight brush, ranged at right angles to the surface. The refractive index, when measurable, is 1·54–1·55. Being deposited from solution, chalcedony tends to assume layered, botryoidal or stalactitic forms. When the layers differ in transparency and/or colour a banded structure results.

If the bands run more or less flat and parallel to one another we have *onyx*. Frequently, however, silica is deposited on the walls of a small cavity, or amygdale, in cooling lava, from outside inwards until the amygdale is more or less completely filled. Such an amygdale filling, or *concretion*, is frequently banded, the bands following the walls onion-fashion in closed concentric envelopes. The outcome is an agate. Since silica is usually a good deal harder than the enclosing rock matrix, it eventually weathers out of it as a Scotch pebble, much as flints, which, too, are an impure form of chalcedony heavily contaminated with lime, do out of chalk.

The banding may be coarse and diffuse, or fine and sharp, hundreds of layers being packed into an inch. Fine bands must obviously follow one another closely, usually in plain concentric curves (as seen in section), but the spacing tends to increase towards the centre of the concretion, which is often filled with a transparent mass of coarsely crystalline quartz, or may even be hollow and lined with crystals. A potato-stone is a large hollow structure of this kind, the crystal-lined cavity being called a *geode* (p. 91).

Two ladies of my acquaintance, the Misses Corbett, of Street, Somerset, as girls were on holiday with their mother at Sidmouth, Devon, where they were amusing themselves by throwing stones from the beach into the sea and watching the splash. One stone of about half-loaf size felt rather light, and when thrown hit a boulder and broke in half. One half was lost in the waves, but the other was hollow and lined with beautiful amethysts. It was subsequently sold to a jeweller in Birmingham for a doubtful price of ten shillings. If you are in that part of the south English coast try the beaches about Seaton. You may be lucky. I have found a small geode lined with fine dark-purple amethysts in the Mendip Hills of Somerset. The Scottish beaches in Ayrshire, Perthshire, Angus and Kincardineshire may be even more productive. In Ireland agates occur along the northern and northeastern shores.

15.2 AGATES

However, the matter of localities has been given attention in Chapters 4–6, and, to return to our agate, a close concentric banding, widening inwards and ending up in a more or less rounded mass, recalls an eye in cross section, for which reason such stones are known as *eye agates*. The word 'amygdale' denotes an almond-shaped cavity. The cavity originates as a gas bubble in creeping viscous lava on the point of setting, and the creep of the lava tends to stretch the originally round hollow into the shape of an almond, which adds to the eye effect.

A finely banded agate with layers of regular curvature can be readily split into small dish-like parts, which make excellent bearings for chemical balances and other precision instruments.

Not all amygdales, however, are almond-shaped; they may be round or angular as well, to say nothing of irregular cracks, and the banding follows suit. The walls of the cavity may have a highly complex structure and this, too, is passed on to the layers of chalcedony grown upon them. This results in various kinky patterns, the lines not infrequently recalling bone sutures on a skull (if you are familiar with skulls), or castellations. Such agates are referred to as *fortification agates*. Yet the orientation of the bands need not be consistent throughout the stone. For instance, I have a Scotch pebble from Angus where two sets of bands stand at right angles to each other. All this can yield most complicated and attractive designs, described by the general term of *landscape agate*, and when the colouring obliges as well the effect can be very beautiful.

On the other hand, the concretion may be wholly innocent of banding, or else the bands be present only in its outer skin, the rest being a milky crystalline mass of no particular distinction. Otherwise good specimens may be spoiled by cracks or hollows. Thus there is many a slap twixt the find and the lap.

The process of growth of an agate is visualized substantially thus: as the lava cools, alkaline hydro-thermal (for which the English is hot-water, but does not sound so good) solutions of silica percolate through the porous structure. The cavities become filled with silica gel, which is silicic acid, and absorbs water. Through this gel various solutions diffuse, and if two different solutions meet they precipitate some of their solutes (dissolved material) in so-called Liesegang rings. Different solutions contain different mineral admixtures, and so rings of different colours and/or degrees of translucency are formed. Sometimes, though, there are no conflicting solutions, and so no rings. Eventually the rock cools, the gel hardens to stone.

A *moss agate* is translucent chalcedony enclosing something that looks like a piece of green moss. But the name is a double misnomer, for the stone is not layered and so no agate, nor is the thing inside it moss in the way 'dragons in amber' are at least real insects, if not dragons. The material of the 'moss' is 'green earth', or delessite, derived from the ferro-magnesian minerals in the basic lava and often lining the amygdale. In a *mocha stone* the dendrite (tree-like shape) is manganese dioxide, instead of delessite. Some moss agates of both types are 'pseudo' inasmuch as the inclusion is not a true dendrite, but a crack filling. It is easy to see why moss agates may often be expected to be found with other types of chalcedony.

15.3   JEWELLER'S CHALCEDONY, JASPER, ETC.

While, however, the mineralogist uses the term *chalcedony* generically for cryptocrystalline silica, regardless of colour or structure, it is reserved by the jeweller for the greyish and bluish translucent varieties. The yellow-to-brown stones are known as *sards* and the flesh-pink-to-red ones as *carnelians, cornelians* or *carneols*. These colourings are due to iron oxide, whereas the apple-green of *chrysoprase* is attributed to nickel hydroxide, and the darker green of *plasma* to ferrous oxide and hydroxide. An increasing admixture of clayey and ferruginous matter changes translucent chalcedony first into the semi-opaque *hornstone*, which looks very much like horn and is often banded (good specimens will be found along the Menai Strait, in Wales, near Portsoy in Banffshire and Montrose in Angus), and then into fully opaque *jasper*.

Jasper may be of any colour, variegated or 'self', but is typically red. Delessite may colour the jasper a dark green, and when the stone is spotted with red we have *bloodstone* or *heliotrope*.

All these varieties may form agates, by themselves or intermixed, with a further contribution from amethyst, prase and sapphire quartz, which offers great possibilities for attractive colour combinations. Such names as carnelian-agate, jasper-agate, etc. are self-explanatory in the light of this information.

The silica in the agate, however, is often of an opaque milky variety, rather like bone china when pure white, although it may also be tinted yellow, pink, green or violet, for which there is no adequate gemmological term. *Porcellanite* gives a good description of this type of stone, but this name is more usually applied to the kind of jasper formed by the heat metamorphism of clays and shales.

15.4   ARTIFICIAL COLOURS

More often than not the natural colourings of agates are gentle and subdued, and most of the brightly-tinted specimens of commerce have been produced by artificial treatment.[39, 55, 59]

The simplest case is that of the jeweller's *onyx*, where black and white bands alternate. The successive bands in an agate differ in porosity and when soaked in a liquid will absorb some of it in different measure. In fact, the hard compact silica absorbs practically none. The procedure, therefore, is to soak a promising stone for days and even weeks in hot syrup or honey, subsequently wash and steep it in warm sulphuric acid, which burns the sugar or honey to carbon and then is itself rinsed away.

The bright blue colouring is similarly produced by soaking first in a solution of a ferric salt and then in one of yellow prussiate of potash (potassium ferrocyanide), which precipitates in the pores a deposit of Prussian blue. *Swiss lapis* is obtained in this way from red jasper and is not to be confused with the genuine *lapis lazuli*, which is a complicated alumino-silicate of calcium and sodium with some sulphur and chlorine, and may be formed at contact of crystalline limestones with granite. The traditional sources of lapis are Afghanistan and Iran, but it is also found in Italy and Chile. I know, however, of no record of lapis lazuli in the British Isles, although there certainly are instances of limestone being invaded by granite magmas.

The dun-coloured banded tuff from Cumberland, mentioned on p. 33, should be admirably suited for chemical staining. Green hues can be obtained by soaking in solutions of nickel salts or in chromic acid and heating. The ferrous oxide of iron yields carnelian tints, and so may be used to convert an insipid layered chalcedony into a pseudo-*sardonyx*, which differs from onyx in being alternatively banded in red and white or yellow.

Many artificial colourings tend to fade in strong sunlight, but they can usually be fixed by an appropriate heat treatment, or 'burnt in'. The onyx black and the Prussian blue, however, are permanent.

The idea of artificially staining agates originated in Italy, and the story is that the secret of making onyx was passed by an Italian to a German whilst both were in prison in Paris. This formed the foundation of the great agate industry of Idar-Oberstein, originally based on local material, but now relying chiefly on the stones imported from Brazil. To quote from Michael Weinstein's *Precious and Semi-Precious Stones*[67] (p. 120): 'The cutting of most of these stones is done by means of steel laps, the surface of which is coated with bort. They are finished by the use of large sandstone wheels, some of which reach the size of a mill-wheel. These wheels revolve in water at a rate of about three revolutions per second, and the stone is held firmly against the surface. This necessitates the workman lying in a horizontal position, and the occupation is consequently not a healthy one.' Like the policemen's lot, it seems— 'not an 'appy one'. However, there is nothing in the nature of things to prevent you staining your finds and shoving them into a tumbling drum in the homely British way.

As indicated on p. 136, the walls of the amygdale housing an agate or other concretion of mineralogical chalcedony are often coated with green delessite, which adheres to the agate for some time after its release from the parent rock. Potato-stones look like very grubby potatoes, but some specimens from the Mendips show green when scratched. This, though, is by no means an infallible test. I have agates, whose 'skin' is grey or brown, and in any case this is soon worn off as they are shuffled by the waves among the shingle of a beach, so that the harder silica is exposed. In this condition the porcellanous layers come to the surface and the stone may look like a rounded blob of fossil blancmange, pitted like a thimble; and, if not blancmange, it will be translucent jelly. The vulnerable protuberances become rubbed off, revealing the inner twirly-whirlies. The agates found in the potato-stones from the Mendips, the Bristol area and South Wales are mainly of the jasper type, composing designs in purple, red, white and yellow, rather like those in an old-fashioned Paisley shawl. The silica is somewhat sugary, which is a sign of substitution for limestone, and absorbent, the design in the raw not showing clearly unless wetted. Cornish agates incline to be flinty and the colouring is poor. The Scottish Old Red Sandstone lavas are as a rule quite soft, so that their agates can be chiselled out with comparative ease; sandstone in a conglomerate may be a tougher proposition; basalt and andesite are quite hard and tend to splinter.

15.5   OPAL

Opal is hydrated chalcedony of the formula $SiO_2.nH_2O$, where n is a variable integer, so that the two shade into each other almost imperceptibly. The usual proportions are about 90 per cent of silica and 10 per cent of water, but they vary, and so do the specific gravity from 1·9 to 2·3, hardness from 5 to $6\frac{1}{2}$, and refractive index from 1·44 to 1·46, all of them somewhat below those of chalcedony.[4] Like the latter, opal is amorphous, massive reniform or stalactitic, and may be of any colour bar violet, translucent to opaque, though some varieties are transparent. Most opals display a milky sheen, shading into an iridescent glimmer, which in *precious opal* becomes a brilliant display of rainbow colours, due to the interference of light waves reflected from inclusions of a different refractive index.

Precious opal may take the form of *harlequin opal*, where lights of different colours have a mosaic structure, or *flash opal*, with a single area of colour, changing with the angle of viewing. These come mainly from Australia, Hungary, Mexico and the U.S.A. But the humbler varieties of opal are not uncommon in the British Isles. The mode of occurrence is similar to that of chalcedony as an alteration product in volcanic rocks, such as basalts, andesites and trachytes, although opal may be found in sandstone, as it is in Queensland, New South Wales, and apparently in Sutherland, Scotland[76]; also as a replacement mineral in fossil wood.' Such *wood opal* may attain gem quality.

The commonest kind of opal is *common opal* and *semi-opal*, translucent to opaque in this order, which is also that of decreasing colour. They may be found at a number of Cornish and Dartmoor localities, as well as in Scotland and Northern Ireland. *Milk opal, wax, resin* and *ferruginous opals* are sub-varieties of common opal. These names are descriptive and give a good idea of the colouring, although various secondary tints may be present, especially in milk opal. *Cacholong* is an opaque, white or cream-coloured variety. *Hyalite* is vitreous, colourless and transparent. An interesting variety is *hydrophane*, which is more or less opaque when dry, but becomes transparent upon immersion in water. This property is related to that of iridescent opals whose colour play is conditional upon their being imbued with liquid; they are commonly sold permeated with oil, which, though tends to darken with time, ruining the effect.[67]

Fire opal, usually red or yellow with iridescence, may be transparent or translucent, shading over into *jasp opal*, such as is found in Skye (p. 49). It is known from several Cornish localities, including Botallack, Rosewarne, Wheal Gorland and St. Day.[8] Opals are usually cut *en cabochon* or in flat plates, but fire opal, when of sufficient transparency, may be facetted. *Girasol* is a variety with a blue sheen, though Mac-Callien's[37] 'girasol' from Kincardineshire is bluish with a golden sheen.

Obsidian is not a mineral, but a glassy acid lava of the same composition as granite, except that it has cooled too rapidly for crystallization. It is translucent, with a refractive index of about $1 \cdot 5$, fairly hard ($5-5\frac{1}{2}$), coloured bottle-green, or brown to black, and is used for ornamental objects, beads and the like. Some *porphyries* are also quite attractive for such purposes, especially when the felspar crystals are small, as, for instance, in the red porphyry dykes in the Kincardine Hills near Aviemore, in Inverness-shire, Scotland. The Charnwood Forest porphyry, mentioned on p. 24, is another case in point. A rock with large crystals is more suitable as a building stone. Finally, *quartz balls* in conglomerates baked by contact metamorphism may be of some interest, as they are translucent and variously shaded in pink, green, blue and purple, as can be seen to advantage near Sannox, in Arran.

16 Animal or vegetable

Organic gems are five in number: coral, ivory, pearl, amber and jet.

Our seas are too cold for the polyp *Corallium rubrum* or *nobile*, which lives in the offshore waters of the Mediterranean and whose calcareous skeleton, coloured rose-pink to ox-blood, though occasionally white or yellow, is used for beads and similar ornaments. True, the poles have shifted position over the geological time and the climates have changed in accord with these shifts. In the Carboniferous, the part of the Earth that is now Britain lay on the Equator, and even in the Tertiary crocodiles flourished in the Thames Valley. And there were corals. In fact, fossil coral of gem quality is known from Sutherland.[77]

16.1 FOSSIL IVORY

Ivory comes from the tusks of elephants and walruses, and once again they no longer live in the British Isles, so that it is no use trying to organize a safari without a time machine. With a time machine you might be able to bag a mammoth or two by dialling a suitable year in the Pleistocene or thereabouts. I do not suppose there would be a customs inspection on the way, but transporting the huge incurved tusks through the corridors of time could present its problems. Jokes apart, remains of mammoths have been found in Britain and Ireland, for instance, in Essex or in the caves of the counties Cork and Waterford, and, since tusks, being the hardest, are also the part of the skeleton best calculated to withstand the tooth of time, fossil ivory is theoretically available somewhere among the recent strata, more particularly in the south-east of England. In fact, I have once come upon a piece of stone that was definitely bone and looked like a fragment of a mammoth's tooth, though I would not vouch for the accuracy of this identification. To show that fossil ivory is not to be despised, I will quote from *Chambers's Encyclopaedia*: 'Tusks from Siberia are often of highest quality for commercial purposes. They regularly appear on the London market and are used for every purpose to which African and Indian ivory is put. Inferior tusks are employed in the manufacture of carbon pigments.' Thus, should you bring back an inferior tusk from your palaeontological safari, there is no need to despair—as one might put it, *nil carborandum*: you will know what to do. In all honesty, however, I do not think there is much future in this venture.

16.2   RIVER PEARLS

With pearls the position is rather different.

The river pearls of Britain were well known to the Romans, and were mentioned, for instance, by the geographer Pomponius Mela in A.D. 43.[6] Nor were they overlooked by Suetonius, Tacitus and Pliny, the last-named of whom, however, described them somewhat disparagingly as *parvos atque decolores* (small and devoid of colour). Still, pearls from the Irish rivers appear to have been highly esteemed in Europe in the Middle Ages. The mussel *Anodonta cygnea* is widely distributed throughout Ireland and it does produce pearls. Oddly enough, however, pearls do not figure in the legend and story of the Emerald Isle, nor even among its museum antiquities.[15]

Another pearl mussel, *Unio margaritifera*, occurs in the British streams. I have a vague notion that Queen Boudicca (Boadicea), who was somewhat unpopular with the Romans, possessed a river pearl of rare beauty, which is propably true, even if only a guess. In more recent times a Welsh pearl from the river Conway was presented by Sir Richard Wynne to another British queen, Catherine of Braganza, consort of Charles II, and is now in the Royal Crown.

The Honours, or Crown Jewels, of Scotland, which may be admired in Edinburgh Castle, also contain a fine river pearl (of Scottish origin), and M. Weinstein records[67] that 'some years ago' a pearl from a Perth-shire river was sold for £100. In fact, fishing for pearls has long been a favourite summer occupation among the Scottish and Irish tinkers.

The equipment is simplicity itself: waders, or at least rubber Welling-tons; a drum, an old bucket or a large tin can, with a glass fitted in at the bottom; a forked stick; and plenty of patience. The use of the first of these items calls for no comment beyond perhaps a reminder that water in a mountain river can be numbingly cold. The drum with a glass bottom, when half immersed, allows the river bed to be seen clearly on the same principle on which glass-bottomed boats are used for viewing the 'sea-gardens' in Bermuda and the Bahamas. The object of the forked stick is to dislodge the pebbles among which the mussels hide. If you wish, you may, of course, equip yourself with a frogman's outfit and explore deep pools—there are diverse ways of doing this.

The open season extends from June to August,[26] May being excluded, although it has no 'r' in its name: possibly the month is too cold and the mountain rivers too dangerous, being in spate from the melting snows.

In England nowadays most rivers are too polluted to harbour pearl mussels, but somewhere in the Pennines, the Lake District or in the Yorkshire Moors, possibly on Dartmoor, they can still be found. K. Blakemore and G. Andrews[3] record (p. 42) that 'An old Yorkshireman was interviewed on television recently, and he revealed that he had spent a lifetime fishing pearl mussels out of the rivers of his native county. He was, not unnaturally, secretive concerning the exact whereabouts of his fruitful mussel beds, however.' On the whole, though, pearl fishing does not rank high in the rat race, and there are quicker ways of coming into money and rheumatism.

When an irritating foreign body, such as a grain of sand, finds its way between the living mollusc and its shell the mollusc secretes layer upon layer of mother-or-pearl round the offender, and so a pearl is born. Cultured pearls are grown by inserting suitable foreign bodies, including tin Buddhas, into unsuspecting mussles, and this is quite an industry in Japan. So far, however, river pearls have happily remained untouched by culture.

A pearl cyst has a specific gravity of about 2·75. The play of colour is due to inner reflections as in opal. The material is 90 per cent carbonate of lime, the rest being organic matter and water. In imitations glass beads are coated with the so-called *essence d'orient*, which is a preparation made from fish scales. Alternatively, hollow spherules of opalescent glass are filled with wax and this fishy substance.[67]

16.3 AMBER

Amber is the resin of fossil conifers and similar trees, mainly from the lower Tertiary, found in rounded grains or lumps in strata of estuarine origin, in coal and lignite; and where these have become submerged by land movements amber is washed up, owing to its lightness, on the sea beaches. *A Guide to the Collection of Gemstones in the Geological Museum* states reassuringly: 'the small insects occasionally found entombed in it (amber) are eloquent proof of its terrestrial origin'[39] (evidently nothing to do with the UFOs!). The 'entombed insects' are, of course, those 'dragons' mentioned on p. 136.

Amber is resinous, transparent to translucent, though it may also be nearly opaque. It is amorphous or platy, very light (specific gravity $1 \cdot 0 - 1 \cdot 1$) and quite soft ($2 - 2\frac{1}{2}$), so that it can be readily fashioned into such objects as beads, cigarette holders, etc.; it is brittle and breaks with a conchoidal fracture. In addition to resin, it contains succinic acid and volatile oils, and conforms approximately to the formula $C_{40}H_6O_4$, which makes it combustible and fusible. The colour is typically a wax- or honey-yellow, but red, green and blue ambers are known. The Sicilian amber is of a darkish brown colour and sometimes exhibits a blue-green fluorescence.[26]

Amber is the Greek *elektron*, as its property of attracting on being rubbed chaff and other light particles has been known from antiquity; as such it has given name to electricity, the attraction being now known to be due to an electric charge.

Ambroid, or *pressed amber*, is made from small pieces of amber which have been heated and welded together under pressure. It shows a flow structure and elongated air bubbles, which are absent from the amber that has not been thus interfered with. *Kauri gum*, or *copal resin*, from New Zealand is a similar substance of recent origin and can be distinguished from true amber by being more readily fusible.[39] Still, you are not really likely to find any of it on a British or Irish beach. Plastic imitations are a different matter; they might infiltrate the flotsam and jetsam, but can be identified by their greater specific gravity.

The main source of amber in Europe is the east Baltic coast, especially East Prussia and the Island of Rügen, Galicia (Poland), Rumania and Sicily. Farther afield Mexico and Burma deserve mention. We have seen, however, that some amber is to be found on the Isle of Wight and in south-east England, on the shores of East Anglia and more sparsely northwards, well into Scotland as far as Fifeshire, if, alas!, no longer in the Kensington sand. Fossil resins have also been recorded in north English mines. The red *copal* (not to be confused with Kauri gum, which, though, may also be fossil), from the old Settling-stones lead mine in Northumberland, has already been referred to on p. 58. Greg and Lettsom,[31] however, also describe a variety, called *middletonite*, of specific gravity 1·6, reddish-brown in reflected and deep-red in transmitted light, which used to occur in coal seams at the Middleton Collieries near Leeds, in Yorkshire, as well as at Newcastle-upon-Tyne. This again resembles the material I have found on an Arran beach.

Yet even if we leave open the issue of the red amber from the Irish Sea (p. 58), some yellow amber has been found on the beaches near Dublin and elsewhere. It will also be recalled that, in any event about 100 years ago, amber was obtained from lignite at Craignashoke and from coal on Rathlin Island, in Ulster.[31]

In these circumstances the usual insistence that amber in the Bronze Age Irish ornaments must necessarily have come from the Baltic does not seem to be wholly warranted. Be this as it may, the Ulster Museum has a fine necklace of that date from Kurin, county Londonderry, while S. P. O'Riordain has described another necklace, found in a grave at Tara and consisting of one jet, four amber, eight tubular bronze and four faience beads.[19]

With regard to the ancient British amber articles C. E. N. Bromhead writes in *Practical Geology in Ancient Britain*[6] (p. 71):

> 'One of the finest early amber objects in the world is the Bronze Age cup found in a barrow at Hove and now in the Brighton Museum; the bowl is 3½ inches wide and 2½ inches high, and there is a handle, so that the original block must have been exceptionally large. A badly broken cup was found near Dor-

chester, some 50 beads and rings at Glastonbury, and Roman amber is known.   There is no reason to suppose that any foreign material was imported across the North Sea, at any rate until Saxon times.'

16.4 JET

The use of *jet* beads, rings, bracelets and other ornaments in Britain from Neolithic times onwards is very well documented, and numerous examples of these may be seen at the British Museum. Nowadays jet is not very popular, but it is still used for mourning jewellery.

The name *jet* appears to be a corruption of the Graeco-Roman *gagates*, and according to Pliny it used to be found near the river Gages. British jet has come mainly from the Jurassic shales of Yorkshire, and Whitby in particular (see p. 30), where it continues to support a minor industry, though most of the material is now imported from Spain.[67]

The distribution of jet ornaments in Scotland points to their origin in Bute and on Moray Firth.[37]   I have a piece of jet from the Sound of Bute.   There does not appear to be any native jet in Ireland, and the occasional beads of this material, such as in the Tara necklace, may have come from Bute or perhaps Yorkshire.   There is, however, some lignite in Northern Ireland, outcropping in the Interbasaltic Bed, mainly in Antrim, and ancient lignite ornaments are known.[19]

Indeed, jet is a compact variety of lignite, usually found in thin seams. Its specific gravity is about 1·3 and hardness between 3 and 4, so that it could be worked easily with primitive tools, but it does not soil the hands and will take a good polish.   Jet is readily combustible and burns with a bright flame, giving off a pungent smoke, thought at one time to have medicinal properties.   Like amber, jet becomes electrically charged when rubbed.

References

1. BALL, V. 1888–9. *J. geol. Soc. Dublin*, **7**, p. 163.
2. BARNETT, G. W. T. 3.9.1969. Private communication.
3. BLAKEMORE, K. and ANDREWS, G. 1966. *Collecting gems and decorative stones*. Foyle, London.
4. BÖRNER, R. (translated and edited by W. Mykura). 1967. *Minerals, rocks and gemstones*. Oliver & Boyd, Edinburgh.
5. BRISTOW, C. M. 17.9.1968. Private communication.
6. BROMHEAD, C. E. M. 1948. 'Practical geology in Ancient Britain', *Proc. geol. Ass.*, **59**, Part II, pp. 65–76.
7. CHARLESWORTH, J. K. 1966. *The geology of Ireland—an introduction*. Oliver & Boyd, Edinburgh.
8. COLLINS, J. H. 1871. *A handbook to the mineralogy of Cornwall and Devon*. Longmans, London.
9. CONSTABLE, Mrs E. 1969. Private communication.
10. CUNNINGHAM, M. A. 26.9.1969. Private communication.
11. DAVIDSON, W. F. 15.5.1969. Private communication.
12. DEWEY, H. and SMITH, B. 1922. Special reports on the mineral resources of Great Britain, **23**, Part II, North Wales. *Mem. geol. Surv. Great Britain*, London.
13. DINES, H. G. and PHEMISTER, J. 1965. The metalliferous mining region of south-west England. *Mem. geol. Surv. Great Britain*, London.
14. DOUGHTY, P. S. 26.6.1968. Private communication.
15. ——. 25.7.1968. Private communication.
16. ——. 26.8.1969. Private communication.
17. ——. 24.9.1969. Private communication.
18. ——. 28.1.1970. Private communication.
19. ——. 4.2.1970. Private communication.
20. DUNHAM, K. C. 1948. Geology of the northern Pennine orefield. *Mem. geol. Surv. Great Britain*, London.
21. —— *et al.* 1952. Fluorspar. 4th edn. *Mem. geol. Surv. Great Britain*, London.
22. EXLEY, C. S. 1958. 'Magmatic differentiation and alteration of the St. Austell granite', *Qtrly J. geol. Soc. Lond.*, **114**, pp. 197 ff.
23. FIRSOFF, V. A. 1951. *Arran with camera and sketchbook*. Hale, London.
24. ——. 1954. *In the hills of Breadalbane*. Hale, London.
25. FIRTH, J. N. M. 21.7.1968. Private communication.
26. FISHER, P. J. 1965. *Jewels*. Batsford, London.
27. FORD, T. D. and SARJEANT, W. A. S. 1963–65. 'The Peak District mineral index', *Bull. Peak Distr. Mines Hist. Soc.*, **2**, pp. 122 ff.

28. FRANCIS, J. G. 1861. *Beach rambles in search of seaside pebbles and crystals*. London.
29. FRONDEL, C. 1962. *The (Dana's) system of mineralogy*, Vol. 3, *Silica Minerals*. Wiley, New York.
30. GARRAD, L. S. 3.7.1968. Private communication.
31. GREG, R. P. and LETTSOM, W. G. 1858. *Manual of the mineralogy of Great Britain and Ireland*. John van Voorst, London.
32. HARRISON, R. K. 5.8.1969. Private communication.
33. HEDDLE, FORSTER M. (edited by J. G. Goodchild). 1901. *The Mineralogy of Scotland*. David Douglas, Edinburgh.
34. HINES, P. G. 16.7.1969. Private communication.
35. JACKSON, J. S. 4.7.1968. Private communication.
36. JONES, K. A. 3.9.1969. Private communication.
37. MacCALLIEN, W. J. 1967. *Scottish gem stones*. Quantum Reprints, London.
38. MacGREGOR, M. 1940. Synopsis of the mineral resources of Scotland. *Mem. geol. Surv. Great Britain*, London.
39. McLINTOCK, W. F. P. 1951. *A guide to the collection of gemstones in the Geological Museum*. H.M.S.O., London.
40. MACNAIR, P. 1908. *The geology and scenery of the Grampians*. Glasgow.
41. MACPHERSON, H. G. 26.1.1970. Private communication.
42. MORTON, G. H. 1868–69. 'The mineral veins of Shelve', *Proc. Liverpool geol. Soc.*, pp. 38 ff.
43. NORTH, F. J. 1917. *The minerals of Glamorgan*. Cardiff Naturalists' Society.
44. PEACH, B. N., and HORNE, J. 1930. *Chapters on the geology of Scotland*. Oxford Univ. Press.
45. PENHALLURICK, R. D. 11.7.1968. Private communication.
46. ——. 1968. Private communication.
47. PITCHER, W. S. and READ, H. H. 1958. 'The main Donegal granite', *Qtrly J. geol. Soc. Lond.*, **114**, pp. 259 ff.
48. POSTLETHWAITE, J. 1913. *Mines and mining in the Lake District*. W. H. Moss & Sons, Whitehaven.
49. PRINGLE, J. and GEORGE, N. T. 1948. *British regional geology, South Wales*. 2nd edn. H.M.S.O., London.
50. READ, H. H. 1948. *British regional geology, The Grampian Highlands*. H.M.S.O., Edinburgh.
51. ROBSON, D. A. *A guide to the geology of Northumberland and the Borders*. Nat. Hist. Soc. Northumberland, Durham and Newcastle upon Tyne, Newcastle upon Tyne.
52. ROGERS, C. 1968. *A collector's guide to minerals, rocks and gemstones in Cornwall and Devon*. Bradford Barton, Truro.
53. RUSHTON, D. 17.12.1969. Private communication.
54. RUSSELL, A. 1948. *Mineralog. Mag.*, **28** (September), p. 353.
55. SELWYN, A. 1948. *The retail jeweller's handbook*. Heywood, London.
56. SHACKLETON, E. H. 1966. *Lakeland geology*. Dalesman, Clapham, Yorks.

57. SMITH, BERNARD. 1922. Special Reports on the Mineral Resources of Great Britain, **23**, Part I, West Shropshire. *Mem. geol. Surv. Great Britain*, London.

58. SMITH, B. and GEORGE, N. T. 1961. *British regional geology, North Wales.* H.M.S.O., London.

59. SMITH, HERBERT G. F. 1952. *Gemstones.* Methuen, London.

60. STATHAM, Miss P. M. 29.9.1969. Private communication.

61. STRONG, M. W. 30.10.1968. Private communication.

62. THOMAS, T. N. 30.10.1969. Private communication.

63. ——2. 5.2.1970. Private communication.

64. TRUEMAN, A. E. 1938. *The Scenery of England and Wales.* Gollancz, London.

65. VARGAS, G. and M. 1969. *Faceting for amateurs.* Published by the authors. Desert Printers, Palm Desert, Calif., U.S.A.

66. WEBSTER, R. 1966. *Practical gemmology.* 4th edn. N.A.G. Press, London.

67. WEINSTEIN, M. 1946. *Precious and semi-precious stones.* Pitman, London.

Additional References

68. FIRSOFF, V. A. 1949. *The Cairngorms on foot and ski.* Hale, London.

69. ——. 1952. 'The gem stones of Arran', *Gemmologist*, June.

70. ——. 1965. *On foot in the Cairngorms.* Chambers, Edinburgh & London.

71. GEIKIE, Sir A. 1900. *Geology of Central and Western Fife and Kinross.* Geological Survey of Scotland.

72. GORDON, S. 1925. *The Cairngorm Hills of Scotland.* Cassell, London.

73. HOGG, T. 1825. *Manual of mining.* Polybank, Truro.

74. KIRKALDY, J. F. 1965. *Minerals and rocks in colour.* Blandford Press, London.

75. 'Synthetic crystals', *Fortune*, August 1950, p. 95.

76. FREIR, D. S. 1970. 'A letter from Sutherland', *Gems*, **2** (4), p. 9 ff.

77. ——. 16.4.1971. Private communication.

78. PEACH, B. N. *et al.* 1907. *The Geological Structure of the North-West Highlands of Scotland.* Geological Survey of Great Britain. Glasgow.

Index